Collin Langan
708/349/6828

quality RESEARCH papers

FOURTH EDITION

Your Guide to Writing

quality RESEARCH papers

For Students of Religion and Theology

NANCY JEAN VYHMEISTER
TERRY DWAIN ROBERTSON

ZONDERVAN ACADEMIC

Quality Research Papers

Requests for information should be addressed to:
Zondervan, *3900 Sparks Dr. SE, Grand Rapids, Michigan 49546*

ISBN 978-0-310-10666-1 (softcover)

ISBN 978-0-310-10668-5 (ebook)

Cover image: © Gaudilab / Shutterstock
Interior design: Kait Lamphere

Printed in the United States of America

HB 10.08.2020

CONTENTS

Part 2: Educational Settings for Theological Research

Part 3: Carrying Out the Research

Part 4:
Presenting the Research

LIST OF ILLUSTRATIONS

Tables

Figures

PREFACE

Books giving instructions for doing student research in biblical, theological, and pastoral areas tend to be somewhat one-sided, often concentrating on composition rather than sources and barely touching on format. Possibly the authors assume that students have already taken a course in research methods and know how to organize and format a paper. More often than not, this is not true. To fill that need, this handbook presents the main aspects of research writing—bibliography, search techniques, organization, and form—in a balanced perspective.

Born of a great need at the Seminario Adventista Latinoamericano de Teologia, the original text was written in Spanish in 1980 for South American graduate students. The first English version (1989) was designed to meet the needs of students working in English as a second language at the Adventist International Institute of Advanced Studies in the Philippines. The 2001 Zondervan edition incorporated my experience teaching research and dissertation writing to graduate students at the Seventh-day Adventist Theological Seminary at Andrews University in Berrien Springs, Michigan, through the 1990s. That second edition took into consideration teaching experience at the Adventist University of Africa. It also tried to catch up with important advances in internet technology since the first edition. The third edition intended to show students how things were done in 2013. This fourth edition is an update in both form and content.

The ideas and techniques in this book are not original. They have been collected from many authors, as the bibliography will show. Over the years, these instructions have been given, with slight variations, to students in the Americas, Asia, and Africa. The students' reactions and concerns have helped to shape this handbook. Therefore, this book is the result of the combined efforts of many people. To all who have in any way contributed, many thanks!

Different research formats exist. The first one used in this text is based on Kate Turabian's work, followed by the University of Chicago and commonly used for theology and religion. Matters of detail may be consulted in either Turabian's ninth edition or the *Chicago Manual of Style*.[1] Given the widespread use of APA, we have included information on that system.[2] The *SBL Handbook of Style* is also used widely.[3] We have attempted to show the main systems used.

This fourth edition banks heavily on the expertise of Terry Robertson, seminary librarian at Andrews University, who also teaches research at the Theological Seminary of Andrews University. His much younger eyes and mind do a good job handling today's technology. Thank you, Terry, for your many contributions, especially for the chapters on library and internet research. With this edition, he has become coauthor.

Others have added their wisdom to this work. Bonnie Proctor, dissertation secretary at Andrews University for many years, made available her vast experience in interpreting Turabian and APA. Linda Bauer, who has worked extensively with the Turabian in-text style, helped greatly. David Penno, of the Andrews University Seminary, has been helpful with DMin papers. My daughter-in-law, Shawna Vyhmeister, director of research at Middle East University, has also been a great help. To all of you, my heartfelt thanks!

Quality Research Papers has four purposes:

1. To stimulate and develop students' capacity for doing careful and fruitful research.
2. To help students improve their ability to express clearly the results of their research.
3. To assist theology students in meeting the requirements of their educational programs.
4. To allay students' fear of doing research by improving their skills and tools.

---

1. Kate Turabian was dissertation secretary at the University of Chicago from 1930 to 1958; her seminal work (1937) has been repeatedly revised and updated. The most recent version: Kate L. Turabian, *A Manual for Writers of Research Papers, Theses, and Dissertations: Chicago Style for Students and Researchers*, 9th ed., rev. Wayne C. Booth, Gregory G. Colomb, Joseph M. Williams, Joseph Bizup, William T. FitzGerald, and the University of Chicago Press Editorial Staff (Chicago, IL: University of Chicago Press, 2018). *The Chicago Manual of Style*, 17th ed. (Chicago, IL: University of Chicago Press, 2017) has more details and may be useful to advanced researchers and professors of research.

2. See *Publication Manual of the American Psychological Association*, 7th ed. (Washington, DC: American Psychological Association, 2020).

3. *The SBL Handbook of Style: For Biblical Studies and Related Disciplines*, 2nd ed. (Atlanta, GA: SBL Press, 2014).

By following the instructions in this book, your paper should be first-class in content and format. Because many people learn better when they are shown rather than when they are told, models are provided to show how different parts of a paper should look.

Chapters 2 through 8 describe types of research done by ministerial and seminary students: literary and historical, exegesis, description, program development, case study, action research, writing for publication, book reviews, theses, and dissertations. Chapters 9 through 17 show students the process of writing the paper, while chapter 18 discusses reference notes and bibliographical entries. Chapter 19 presents statistics, graphs, and tables as used in research. Chapter 20 deals with proper paper format. Chapter 21 shows how to do Turabian notes and bibliographies; chapter 22 deals with the Turabian in-text style, while chapter 23 provides models for APA in-text notes and reference lists. Together, these chapters give the basic guidelines for students in theological education who desire to achieve success in research.

May your research be fruitful, stimulating, and even enjoyable.

Nancy Jean Vyhmeister

AUTHORS' NOTE

We learn better when we see examples. For this reason, we have asked Zondervan to show slightly different ways of doing three things for those who have language or computer issues. For some of us the en-dash, often used in printed books between numbers, is difficult because of our poor computer skills or problem computers. Thus the hyphen is used throughout this book, just as students will use it in their papers: 9-10, 57-60, and so on. Also, there are different ways of abbreviating numbers. To show the readers one acceptable way, this book writes out all numbers in full: 155-159. Because people from the rest of the world are not familiar with cities in the United States, we are asking—both Zondervan and the students who will use this book—to consistently use the postal abbreviation for the states in the United States: NY, IL, FL, etc. We want things to be as consistent as possible, thus providing simplicity for the novice writers.

Thank you!

Nancy and Terry

chapter one

DEFINITION OF RESEARCH

The term *research* is used as a verb, a noun, and even as an adjective. Research as an action can be defined as a method of study that, through careful investigation of all evidence bearing on a definable problem, arrives at a solution. To research a topic is to collect, organize, evaluate, and present data. This process cannot take place without analysis and synthesis, for research is more than a compilation of information. The results of research must be presented in a clear and concise way so that anyone can follow the process, without having to repeat any of the steps, to see how you, the researcher, arrived at your conclusions. The end product is "research" as a noun. How many times have you heard the claim, "Research proves that . . ."? As an adjective, the term *research* modifies a larger category, as in the case of papers. Of all the different types of papers you may write throughout your education and career, the "research" paper has a special status. Hence the title of this book, *Quality Research Papers*.

Research as an action is a complex system of inquiry. You learn to ask good questions to find good answers. You seek knowledge about how to gather information, to understand, to find evidence. We will use the following definition of research as an action: Doing research is the grounded, intentional, and savvy analysis of an object in conversation with peers/experts for the purpose of creating knowledge. Each element of this definition deserves further explanation.

1. Grounded: Objective research begins with prior knowledge, both yours and the collective knowledge of the discipline. To this prior knowledge you will add facts, not suppositions or possibilities. Research is done with the head and not the heart. Research looks at facts, not conjectures or even possibilities, much less long-cherished pet ideas. Thus the first phase of research is connecting with what is already known. As Bryan

Gaensler, astronomer at the Dunlap Institute, University of Toronto, tweeted, "Research is spending 6 hours reading 35 papers, so you can write one sentence containing 2 references."[1]

2. Intentional: Research requires effort. It does not just happen. A researcher must develop and use a clear method and a logical system. Research is not easy; it requires time, energy, thought, and effort.
3. Savvy: Research does not look for someone's ideas about matters somehow related to the problem; it seeks precise answers to the specific question being asked. The information presented must be from authoritative sources, speak to the problem, and be duly documented. The challenge is that with the proliferation of sources, discerning veridical information from misinformation, disinformation, or incomplete information requires heightened alertness to all facets of information literacy.
4. Analysis of an object: The object may be a natural object, such as an archaeological artifact; it may be an idea, such as theodicy; or it may be a text, such as a parable of Jesus. It might even be a mission procedure or church activity. The nature of the object determines what methods will be needed. A research topic asks a question or solves a problem about the object. It is impractical to do adequate research on a large topic. The research paper is not an encyclopedia. A specific, clearly delineated problem is the only one that can be solved.
5. Conversation: All writing assumes a reader. An author is sharing thoughts using the medium of writing to communicate something to someone. Research writing assumes readers who are also competent on the topic. Connecting your interpretation of the findings with other related writings brings you into the conversation.
6. Create knowledge: The reward for doing research is the joy of discovery that enriches your life and ministry. Documenting that discovery so that readers can benefit with you should be exciting.

Research as an action may produce a ten-page paper on Nazareth in the time of Christ. Research is what the writer of an MA thesis does for weeks. Persistent research—over long months—goes into producing a dissertation. As used in this book, the term *research* applies to all scholarly studies at undergraduate, graduate, and postgraduate levels. Some teachers may call it a *research essay*; others may label it a *term paper*. When a student, starting with a research question, carefully

1. Bryan Gaensler (@SciBry) "Research is spending 6 hours reading 35 papers, so you can write one sentence containing 2 references," Twitter, April 26, 2018, 2:51 p.m., https://twitter.com/scibry/status/989623027393531905?lang=en.

examines the evidence and brings together a coherent argument, thus answering the question, and then creates a document, the result is research as a noun.

Research is the quest for truth, for reality—for God is the Creator of reality—whether it be scientific, historical, or religious. Growing in knowledge is a biblical requirement, as elaborated on by New Testament scholar Andreas Köstenberger.[2] This makes doing research a worshipful activity for believers. Yet, because God is the ultimate reality, and human beings are limited and finite, our journey toward truth and our discoveries along the way must not be considered as having arrived. We are unable to see the whole picture. What we may perceive as "truth" today may be corrected tomorrow by a new discovery. For this reason, even a careful researcher must be humble. The attitude must be one of learning it all, not knowing it all.[3]

After interviewing many researchers, Angela Brew was able to categorize the responses into four variations on how research is experienced.[4]

1. The *domino variation*: finding the answer to each distinct research question inspires, points to, or helps with a new research question. One solution always leads to a new question.
2. The *trading variation*: research is creating a product for others to use. It assumes being a part of community that learns from one another.
3. The *layer variation*: research is looking beneath the surface, ever digging deeper.
4. The *journey variation*: research is transformative, leading to growth in knowledge and understanding.

After reflecting on how you experience research, one or more of these variations may appeal to you. It is also possible that as you write papers for different courses, you may feel each project fits one or another of the metaphors better.

What Ellen White wrote in 1892 is true today: "Truth is eternal. . . . We must study the truth for ourselves. No living man should be relied upon to think for us."[5]

---

2. Andreas J. Köstenberger, *Excellence: The Character of God and the Pursuit of Scholarly Virtue* (Wheaton, IL: Crossway, 2011), 63. "We need not be embarrassed by our faith, nor should our faith commitments be considered a necessary obstacle to our academic work. Instead our faith should motivate us to pursue academic excellence, attaining the highest scholarly standards on the basis of publicly available evidence."

3. Satya Nadella, Hit Refresh: The Quest to Rediscover Microsoft's Soul and Imaging a Better Future for Everyone (New York, NY: Harper Business, 2017), 97.

4. Angela Brew, *The Nature of Research: Inquiry in Academic Contexts* (New York, NY: Routledge Falmer, 2001), 24-25.

5. Ellen White, "The Bible Our Guide," *The Bible Echo*, October 15, 1892.

The Research Process

Although the research process will be studied carefully in the following chapters, at this point a brief synthesis of this endeavor is useful. In addition, we will consider some of the hindrances to the successful completion of research.

In its simplest form, the research process involves identification, collection, evaluation, and presentation. Once you have selected a topic, you must identify the problem or issue to be tackled. The issue must be specific, often expressed as a research question, not something vague and general. Once you know exactly what the problem to be solved is, you can begin collecting data. Gather information carefully from many sources. Organize your data in a way that is clear and logical to you and others. After you have gathered all the information, you will need to analyze and evaluate it. Not all sources are equally valuable; not all opinions are of the same weight. Finally, after you have gathered the evidence, you must draw conclusions regarding the solution of the problem. You will then write a research report that gives a clear view of the problem, of the information gathered, and of the solution reached.

Some of the most dangerous pitfalls for researchers are those related to a previous mindset. Throughout history, thoughtful humans have attempted to make sense out of the world in which they live. People see what is happening around them and draw conclusions as to the causes and effects. These conclusions find expression in language, and because of the limitations of language, it is often necessary to express the realities beyond full comprehension using imagery and metaphors. Since birth, all researchers have been immersed in a social context and have shared in the sense-making experience of their families and communities. This provides them a unique personal mindset for making sense of the world. Expressions of this mindset are often known as presuppositions.

The danger for researchers is that they assume their readers share their worldview. But when the reader disagrees with or misunderstands the worldview, the reader perceives the research as "biased." When the reader shares the values, the writing is considered "objective." When the reader disagrees with the values as expressed, the ideas are labeled as "prejudice." When sources are rejected or not taken seriously for reasons other than the content or argument, the omission is labeled "epistemic injustice." Thus researchers benefit from being transparent about their interpretive framework and making a good-faith effort to minimize the potential for misunderstanding. One must, then, recognize what these presuppositions are and state them in the introduction to the research. For example, if you accept the Genesis 1:26 statement that human beings have been made in the image of God, whatever conclusions you reach on the treatment of psychological issues in children will reflect that basic understanding.

Other research errors are those of hurriedness, inaccuracy, and carelessness. It is easy to come to premature conclusions without having finished the research because of lack of time or an insufficiently broad bibliography. It is also easy to miss an important detail or to write down an erroneous fact. Researchers do not mean to make this kind of mistake. But these errors do happen, especially to students who are scrambling to survive the term. Research demands extreme caution and care—and much time.

Kinds of Academic Writing

Many different types of papers are written as part of theological education. Here is a list of eleven different ones. Your school may have additional types of papers. Pay attention to your professor's instructions.

1. Essay: a short paper (1-10 pages) that explores a topic from a personal point of view, without the rigor of a research paper. The opinions of the writer may be prominent, but referenced footnotes are required for all quotations, citations, and allusions.
2. Report: a short paper (1-10 pages) that summarizes findings on an assigned topic. All quotations must be referenced.
3. Sermon: a paper written as the basis for a later oral presentation. While research may be needed, it is not reported in the same way as in other papers. However, quotations should be referenced in the written version turned in to the professor.
4. Term paper or research paper: a major paper (15-30 pages) that investigates a specific issue. Such a paper needs a clear introduction as well as a summary and conclusions. All quotations, citations, and allusions are referenced.
5. Book review: a short (1-4 pages) paper that describes and evaluates a book or article. The professor sets the parameters for this paper.
6. Project: a paper, either for a class or a degree, that emphasizes planning, doing extensive reading and writing, and executing a project on the basis of that careful reading. Projects are common in applied theology, from undergraduate through graduate courses, but especially in the Doctor of Ministry program.

7. Pastoral theology paper: a paper (20-30 pages) that applies the findings of research to a pastoral situation (see chapter 8).
8. Case study: a paper (20-30 pages) that presents a case, analyzes factors affecting it, interprets what has happened theologically, and proposes pastoral action to explain or resolve the situation. The case study is used in practical theology (see chapter 5).
9. Thesis: a major paper required for the completion of a master's degree. Its length is usually around 100-120 pages. A written proposal must be approved before the task is undertaken. Theses may have to be defended before an examination committee (see chapter 7).
10. DMin dissertation: a paper that completes the Doctor of Ministry program. It tends to be practical, as is the degree. Its length is at least 150 pages and may be longer (see chapter 8).
11. PhD/ThD dissertation: a major study, similar to a thesis, but longer and more complex, often 250-300 pages long. It must be written on an issue not previously researched (see chapter 7).

While all of these papers are different and are measured and evaluated by different criteria, professors still expect to find the following general attributes in any one of them:

1. Correct English, including spelling, grammar, syntax, and paragraph construction
2. Clarity of expression
3. Logical organization
4. Appropriate introduction and summary
5. Conclusions naturally derived from evidence
6. Correct format, as chosen by the individual institution for a specific program

What Research Is Not

Perhaps giving some ideas on what research is not will help to clarify what it is.

Research is not simply a compilation of quotations. True, quotations are used to document and clarify findings. But research is not the result of an afternoon spent with scissors, glue, and photocopies. A good research paper shows that its author has assimilated and synthesized—digested, if you like—the material and drawn logical conclusions.

Research is not simply rewriting other people's words and ideas into a neat description. In secondary or high school, we wrote papers by summarizing what we found in the textbook and the encyclopedia. The paper we proudly handed in gave a nice description of Outer Mongolia or the migration of Canada geese. It might have qualified as research at that level; however, that no longer counts. At the college level, students need to analyze—break ideas and facts into small parts—and then organize those ideas and facts into the appropriate thought "boxes." Only then can they write the research report or essay.

Research is not a defense of or apology for one's own convictions. This type of writing too often ignores unfavorable evidence and tends to look at one's position through rose-colored glasses. Research seeks truth; it does not hide for any reason—what may disagree with esteemed ideas. If the position being maintained is tenable, research can defend it; if the position is not based on truth, it is defended in vain. We cannot allow ourselves to use unsound arguments, even for a good cause.

Likewise, research is not polemical. Its objective is to clearly present truth, not to fight others' positions, even if those may be erroneous. In good research, truth is presented in such a logical and convincing way that there is no need for harsh language.

Research is not merely the presentation of one's own opinions. Research demands facts, data, information. Naturally, the conclusions we reach are modified by our personal opinions, but whoever reads the research report must be able to follow the logic and the evidence to see how we reached our conclusions.

Finally, especially for theology students, research is not a sermon. It is different in content, style, and language. Some research may be involved in the preparation of a sermon, but the main purpose of a sermon is to reach the heart and help change people's lives. The language and the message are appropriate to this goal. Research, by contrast, seeks to inform and convince the mind. Research vocabulary is neutral, free of superlatives and emotional language. A sermon becomes effective through the delivery, whereas in research writing, there is no dramatic rendition from the pulpit. What appears on paper must stand, just as it is written, without any further embellishment.

The Value of Research

No one doubts the importance of the research that advances the treatment of cancer. Nor do most people wonder why some erudites sit at their desks and read, study, and write day after day. But some students question the importance of doing research papers since they are not researchers and do not plan to become researchers. They should realize that going through the discipline of research is valuable beyond the information obtained in the course of preparing the paper.

Learning to do research teaches you how to recognize a problem and how to go about solving it. Even educated people will not know all the answers; they should, however, know where to find answers. Doing a research paper helps you learn how to find answers—on the internet, in a library, or even through surveys and interviews. Then, of course, you will have to interpret the answers and draw conclusions regarding their meaning.

Writing a research paper can teach you far more than a teacher could. On the topic of a research paper, you become an expert, sometimes knowing more about it than the professor who assigned the paper. Besides, when you learn by doing, you learn better.

Preparing a quality research paper teaches skills of observation, analysis, synthesis, and judgment. You will learn to think differently when you think research. The ability to think critically—and that does not mean criticizing others or their ideas, but weighing carefully all the evidence—is enhanced by learning the research process.

In addition, writing a research paper helps develop character. When the going is hard and the task becomes drudgery, sticking with the work is a discipline that enhances the worth of any student.

Finally, the preparation of a research paper gives opportunity for the development of good writing skills. Learning to write well takes hours of writing and rewriting. (Just think how glad you can be to do all this on a computer.) In the end, being able to write clearly is a worthy achievement, which will prove useful to you as a student now and later as a professional.

Aside from these considerations, we should mention the satisfaction of a job accomplished and the joy of discovery as important outcomes of writing research papers. Most students agree that research done well is worth the time and effort it takes.

With this chapter as a general basis, the following chapters will describe different kinds of papers you may be asked to produce. Once you recognize the different kinds of papers, you will be ready to make decisions on your own masterpiece.

Part One

Kinds of Theological Education Research

A student faces various kinds of research in theological studies, whether undergraduate or graduate. We will make note of the different kinds of theses and dissertations.

The purpose here is to present to students the different possibilities available in theological research. Each type of paper has its own rules, its own ways of being done. Looking at all of them will help you to be sure what the character of the paper requested really is. When students and professors are aware of the different kinds of theological research, they can decide together which is the best research for the desired learning outcomes for the student.

This section of the book may first be read rapidly. Once you find the kind of research that intrigues you, talk to your professor. Once the two of you have decided which kind of research you will be doing, go back and study that chapter carefully. Then you will be able to write a good paper—to everyone's satisfaction and to the glory of God.

chapter two

BIBLICAL EXEGESIS AND INTERPRETATION

Biblical exegesis is a structured research method used in theological education. With reference to the definition of research provided in chapter 1, the "object" you will be analyzing in this case is a text, a documented communication created by an author. This chapter focuses on the biblical text and involves a systematic process using standard reference tools. In principle, the same general mindset applies to any research in any field of study that focuses on a text, though the reference tools may differ. The exegesis paper you will do for your university or seminary professor does require that you think carefully, develop a bibliography, read pertinent sources, take notes, organize the topic, and write the paper.

In this chapter you will read about a research-oriented exegetical process at an intermediate level. This chapter also lists commonly used sources and describes an acceptable final form for the exegetical paper.

Today many of the resources and tools used in the exegetical process have also been published online and can be accessed through the internet. These include the Bible, both in the original languages and in translation, lexicons, grammars, encyclopedias, maps, and background information, as well as the full text of books in the public domain. Several commercial software programs include excellent libraries of resources and tools for doing exegesis. These include Logos Bible Software and Accordance.

Many current publishers of reference works and commentaries advertise their books on Google Books by providing a "limited preview," and what you need might be included. Google Scholar covers journal articles and other scholarly papers; much is open access. Other items you will be able to access through your library. Chapter 14 will show you how to access and use internet resources.

An important part of biblical research is your attitude. You need to begin by asking yourself: Am I seeking to grow in my knowledge of God? Am I working for a grade? Do I accept the Bible as God's Word in human language? Or do I understand the Bible as spiritual stories or advice written by human beings and perhaps modified over time? The purpose of this chapter is to show you how to write as "one who correctly exegetes the word of truth" (my paraphrase of 2 Timothy 2:15).

Steps in the Exegetical Process

Many different schemes of exegesis exist. You want to be sure to use one that keeps Scripture uppermost. To broaden what this chapter says about exegesis, you could look at the following:

Brown, William P. *A Handbook to Old Testament Exegesis*. Louisville, KY: Westminster John Knox, 2017.

Duvall, J. Scott, and J. Daniel Hays. *Grasping God's Word*. 3rd ed. Grand Rapids, MI: Zondervan, 2012.

Fee, Gordon D. *New Testament Exegesis: A Handbook for Students and Pastors*. 3rd ed. Louisville, KY: Westminster John Knox, 2002.

Fee, Gordon D., and Douglas Stuart. *How to Read the Bible for All Its Worth*. 4th ed. Grand Rapids, MI: Zondervan, 2014.

VanGemeren, Willem A. *A Guide to Old Testament Theology and Exegesis*. Grand Rapids, MI: Zondervan, 1999.

The system described here starts with the biblical text in its canonical context.[1] This method assumes the authority and unity of Scripture and seeks to ascertain the meaning of the Bible, both for its original readers or hearers and for readers today.

Step 1: Determine the Canonical Context

Read in its canonical setting the passage you want to study. Find out what it is a part of and how it functions within that setting. Look for the markers that indicate its beginning and end, as well as its relation to what precedes and what follows. Outline your passage, taking into consideration the genre (discourse,

1. See Grant R. Osborne, *The Hermeneutical Spiral* (Downers Grove, IL: InterVarsity Press, 1993), 19-40; Lee Gugliotto also begins with the context; see his massive *Handbook for Bible Study* (Hagerstown, MD: Review and Herald, 1996). For doctoral students I recommend Stanislaw Bazylinski, *A Guide to Biblical Research: Introductory Notes*, 3rd ed. (Rome: Gregorian and Biblical Press, 2016).

poetry, story, etc.) and structure of the passage, especially as it fits within the particular book of the Bible you are working with.

After you have studied your Bible passage and its context, you may want to compare what you have determined about the organization of the content and argument in both the larger and immediate contexts with what other authors have written. This can be a safeguard to you.

This information is part of what is given in an Old Testament or New Testament introduction (used in the technical sense for a work that tells about various Bible books) or in the opening section of a Bible commentary on the passage. However, because perspectives vary and authors' presuppositions may cause them to see things in a particular light, begin by trusting your own conclusions and be slow to adopt another's views unless you find compelling evidence. This "dialogue" can help you clarify any issues that might be ambiguous in your evaluation of the canonical context. Read with care and thought. At this point, do not read interpretations (such as in commentaries) of your passage—only gather facts and evidence on the canonical context.

The following introductions may be helpful:

Arnold, Bill T., and Bryan E. Beyer. *Encountering the Old Testament*. 3rd ed. Grand Rapids, MI: Baker Academic, 2015.

Carson, D. A., and Douglas Moo. *Introduction to the New Testament*. 2nd ed. Grand Rapids, MI: Zondervan, 2009.

Elwell, Walter, and Robert W. Yarbrough. *Encountering the New Testament*. 3rd ed. Grand Rapids, MI: Baker, 2013.

Goldingay, John. *An Introduction to the Old Testament: Exploring Text, Approaches and Issues*. Downers Grove, IL: IVP Academic, 2015.

Gundry, Robert H. *A Survey of the New Testament*. 5th ed. Grand Rapids, MI: Zondervan, 2012.

Hess, Richard S. *The Old Testament: A Historical, Theological, and Critical Introduction*. Grand Rapids, MI: Baker Academic, 2016.

Hill, Andrew E., and John H. Walton. *A Survey of the Old Testament*. Grand Rapids, MI: Zondervan, 2017.

Köstenberger, Andreas J., L. Scott Kellum, and Charles L. Quarles. *The Cradle, the Cross, and the Crown: An Introduction to the New Testament*. Nashville, KY: Broadman & Holman Academic, 2016.

Longman, Tremper, III, and Raymond B. Dillard. *An Introduction to the Old Testament*. 2nd ed. Grand Rapids, MI: Zondervan, 2009.

McKenzie, Steven L., and John Kaltner. *The Old Testament: Its Background, Growth, and Content*. Nashville, TN: Abingdon, 2007. Reprint, Eugene, OR: Wipf & Stock, 2014

Powell, Mark Allan. *Introducing the New Testament: A Historical, Literary, and Theological Survey*. 2nd ed. Grand Rapids, MI: Baker Academic, 2018.

Sweeney, Marvin A. *Tanak: A Theological and Critical Introduction to the Jewish Bible*. Minneapolis, MN: Fortress, 2012.

Step 2: Establish the Text

After demarcating the passage to be studied (that is, determining its beginning and its end), establish the text. This means determining as accurately as possible, by means of textual criticism, the reading closest to the original. No variant reading in the whole of Scripture contradicts the basic biblical message. However, there are textual variants of significance, and a good exegesis paper will identify and discuss these, both in terms of manuscript support and how they influence the interpretation of the text. These will be identified in an apparatus that is found in the original language Hebrew and Greek texts listed below. An important example of these is the *Comma Johanneum* (1 John 5:7-8), used for generations as a New Testament proof of the doctrine of the Trinity. This phrase has now been shown to be a late addition (eleventh century) to the Bible text. There is no point in doing exegesis on a doubtful variant. A research paper on when and how this variant came to be included in certain manuscripts would be more properly classified as church history or historical theology, but no longer exegesis.

Biblical exegesis at this level expects the use of the original languages, Hebrew and Greek. Here is where you will find programs such as Logos Bible Software or Accordance very helpful.

For the Old Testament, the following original language texts are reliable:

Biblia Hebraica Stuttgartensia, 5th ed. Stuttgart: Deutsche Bibelstiftung, 2014. (Other editions of this are also fine.)

Rahlfs, Alfred, and Robert Hanhart, eds. *Septuaginta*. Stuttgart: Deutsche Bibelstiftung, 2014. (Other editions are also fine.)

To help your not-so-perfect knowledge of Septuagint Greek:

Pietersma, Albert, and Benjamin G. Wright, eds. *A New English Translation of the Septuagint*. New York, NY: Oxford University Press, 2007.

Two editions of the Greek New Testament are recommended. The first is easy to read and use, but its restricted textual apparatus only includes problems that could affect Bible translation. The second has an exhaustive, much more challenging-to-use textual apparatus:

Greek New Testament. 5th rev. ed. Stuttgart: Deutsche Bibelgesellschaft, 2014. (Often labeled UBS5.)

Nestle, Eberhard, Erwin Nestle, Barbara Aland, and Kurt Aland, eds. *Novum Testamentum Graece*. 28th ed. Stuttgart: Württembergische Bibelanstalt, 2012. (Often labeled NA28.)

A companion to the United Bible Societies' Greek New Testament, *A Textual Commentary*, clarifies the decisions on textual criticism made by the Bible Societies' Committee of New Testament Scholars. The certainty attributed to the authenticity of a phrase or word is designated by the letters A, B, C, and D. Reasons for the choice are given for each passage. The volume is a useful tool for determining New Testament text:

Metzger, Bruce M. *A Textual Commentary on the Greek New Testament*. 2nd ed. New York, NY: United Bible Society, 2002.

See also:

Omanson, Roger L. *The Textual Guide to the Greek New Testament*. Stuttgart: Deutsche Bibelgesellschaft, 2006.

For those whose biblical languages are poor, an interlinear Bible may help:

Kohlenberger, John R., III. *The Interlinear NIV Hebrew-English Old Testament*. Grand Rapids, MI: Zondervan, 1987.

Mounce, Robert, and William D. Mounce. *The Zondervan Greek and English Interlinear* (NASB/NIV). 2nd ed. Grand Rapids, MI: Zondervan, 2011.

Or get serious about learning biblical languages. Try the two books *Greek for the Rest of Us* and *Hebrew for the Rest of Us* before you sign up for a Greek or Hebrew class.[2]

Another possibility for helping you understand a text is to compare different Bible versions. This comparison—together with a study of notes to the text—will provide additional evidence for determining the most authentic text. If determining the most authentic text were unambiguous and straightforward, this step would be unnecessary. It is the ambiguities and uncertainties

2. William D. Mounce, *Greek for the Rest of Us*, 2nd ed. (Grand Rapids, MI: Zondervan, 2014); Lee M. Fields, *Hebrew for the Rest of Us: Using Hebrew Tools without Mastering Biblical Hebrew* (Grand Rapids, MI: Zondervan, 2008).

in the manuscript tradition that validate this exercise. The exegete does need to come to a decision and then make the case for that decision. Naturally, serious Bible translations, rather than popular ones, should be used for this comparative study. Modern versions constitute an improvement over the King James Version (prepared in 1611) because they use manuscripts not available at that time. While you may enjoy reading paraphrases, such as the older *Living Bible*, scholarly translations such as the following are preferred.

Common English Bible. Published in 2011, the CEB combines a commitment to both accuracy and readability.

English Standard Version. Published in 2001, the ESV attempts a literal yet up-to-date translation. It is available in several digital forms.

New American Standard Bible. Published in 1971, revised in 1996, the NASB uses formal but clear English. There are abundant notes and references.

New International Version. A revision of this popular version was completed in 2011. Done by an international team of scholars, it follows the translation principles of dynamic equivalence.

New Revised Standard Version. This revision of the RSV by a committee of scholars was completed in 1989. It incorporates discoveries and research not included in the RSV and uses inclusive language.

If your native language is one other than English, look for a Bible translation that attempts to be faithful to the original languages rather than one prepared for popular reading. The further you are from the original languages, the more possibilities you will have of adding to or subtracting from the intended meaning.

Step 3: Establish the Translation

Now you ask: What is the meaning of the original text? To begin to establish the translation, take into account vocabulary and grammar.

Some reliable dictionaries and lexicons are the following:

Bauer, Walter. *A Greek-English Lexicon of the New Testament and Other Early Christian Literature*. 3rd ed. Revised and edited by Frederick W. Danker. Chicago, IL: University of Chicago Press, 2000.

Brown, Francis, S. R. Driver, and C. A. Briggs. *The Brown-Driver-Briggs Hebrew and English Lexicon*. Peabody, MA: Hendrickson, 1996.

Holladay, William L. *A Concise Hebrew and Aramaic Lexicon of the Old Testament*. Grand Rapids, MI: Eerdmans, 1971.

Koehler, L., and W. Baumgartner. *Hebrew and Aramaic Lexicon of the Old Testament.* 2nd ed. Leiden: Brill, 1994.

Liddell, Henry George, and Robert Scott. *A Greek-English Lexicon*. 9th ed. with rev. supplement. Oxford: Clarendon, 1996.

Some helpful grammars are:

Blass, Friedrich, and Albert Debrunner. Trans. and ed. Robert W. Funk. *A Greek Grammar of the New Testament and Other Early Christian Literature*. Chicago, IL: University of Chicago Press, 1961.

Gesenius, W., and E. Kautsch. *Gesenius' Hebrew Grammar*. 2nd English ed. Revised by A. E. Cowley. Oxford: Clarendon, 1970.

Joüon, Paul. *A Grammar of Biblical Hebrew*. 2nd ed. Translated and revised by T. Muraoka. 2 vols. SubsidiaBiblica. Rome: Biblical Institute Press, 2006.

Moulton, James Hope, Wilbert Howard, and Nigel Turner. *Moulton's Grammar of New Testament Greek*. New ed. 4 vols. Edinburgh: T&T Clark, 2019.

Porter, Stanley E., Jeffrey T. Reed, and Matthew Brook O'Donnell. *Fundamentals of New Testament Greek*. Grand Rapids, MI: Eerdmans, 2010.

Van der Merwe, Christo H. J., Jacobus A. Naudé, and Jan H. Kroeze. *A Biblical Hebrew Reference Grammar*. 2nd ed. London: Bloomsbury, 2017.

The Greek and Hebrew grammars you have used in class can also help you. You may also use electronic tools, such as Logos Bible Software and Accordance.

Step 4: Establish the Meaning

Establishing the meaning goes beyond the simple translation of the text. Now the question is asked: What does the passage mean? In order to determine the meaning of a text, study the syntax of the sentences. In addition, investigate the meaning of important words.

Syntax

While grammar and general word definitions are helpful, making sense is often more complex and involves understanding not only the parts but also how they work together and influence each other. This is what we mean by syntax. In studying the syntax of a passage, look at the structure of the sentence and the function of the words. Look for idiomatic phrases and hard-to-translate prepositions. In Hebrew, look for constructs showing possession or other relations. In short, look for any element that might modify the first, direct, and obvious translation of the passage. For step 4, the following books are useful:

Arnold, Bill T., and John H. Choi. *A Guide to Biblical Hebrew Syntax*. 2nd ed. New York, NY: Cambridge University Press, 2018.
Brooks, James A., and Carlton L. Winberry. *Syntax of New Testament Greek*. Washington, DC: University Press of America, 1988.
Caragounis, Chrys C. *The Development of Greek and the New Testament: Morphology, Syntax, Phonology, and Textual Transmission*. Grand Rapids, MI: Baker Academic, 2006.
Köstenberger, Andreas J., Benjamin L. Merkle, and Robert L. Plummer. *Going Deeper with New Testament Greek: An Intermediate Study of the Grammar and Syntax of the New Testament*. Nashville, TN: B&H Academic, 2016.
Mathewson, David, and Elodie Ballentine Emig. *Intermediate Greek Grammar: Syntax for Students of the New Testament*. Grand Rapids, MI: Baker Academic, 2016.
Moule, C. F. D. *An Idiom Book of the New Testament Greek*. 2nd ed. Cambridge, UK: Cambridge University Press, 1978.
Wallace, Daniel B. *Greek Grammar beyond the Basics: An Exegetical Syntax of the New Testament*. Grand Rapids, MI: Zondervan, 1996.
Waltke, Bruce K., and M. O'Connor. *An Introduction to Biblical Hebrew Syntax*. Winona Lake, IN: Eisenbrauns, 1990.

Word Study

Words often have a range of meanings that might help explain their use in a specific context. For this reason, it might be helpful to look up important nouns and verbs in a concordance to see how they are used in other passages. Start with other occurrences of these words in the same book, then in other passages by the same author, and then in other authors of the same period. Afterward, study these same words in theological dictionaries.

Concordances

Using a concordance in English is not as effective as using one in Hebrew or Greek. English concordances list the words that appear in a given English version; Young and Strong work from the King James Version. *Young's Concordance* does show for each English word what the original language word is, but a given Greek or Hebrew word is not always translated in the same way. To find all the uses of a certain word, you need to use a Greek or Hebrew concordance, either in book form or in one of the Bible software programs.

Hatch, Edwin, and Henry Redpath. *A Concordance to the Septuagint and Other Greek Versions of the Old Testament*. 2nd ed. Grand Rapids, MI: Baker, 1998.

Kohlenberger, John R., III, Edward W. Goodrick, and James A. Swanson. *The Greek-English Concordance to the New Testament.* Grand Rapids, MI: Zondervan 1997.

Kohlenberger, John R., III, and James A. Swanson. *Hebrew-English Concordance to the Old Testament.* Grand Rapids, MI: Zondervan, 1998.

Moulton, W. F. *A Concordance to the Greek Testament.* 6th ed. London: T&T Clark, 2002.

Wigram, George. *The Englishman's Greek Concordance of the New Testament.* Peabody, MA: Hendrickson, 1996.

Wigram, George. *The Englishman's Hebrew Concordance of the Old Testament.* Peabody, MA: Hendrickson, 1996.

The source of the information is secondary; whatever works, paper or electronic, is fine. What counts is that the information is reliable.

Theological dictionaries

Theological dictionaries and books containing word studies are useful to the process of exegesis. However, these take the process of word analysis to the next level: interpretation and synthesis. When consulting them, it becomes critical to distinguish between fact and opinion, and that is not always easy. The facts will be helpful, but the opinions will need to be filtered through what you have already discovered.

For the Old Testament:

Botterweck, G. J., and H. Ringren. *Theological Dictionary of the Old Testament* (*TDOT*). 15 vols. Grand Rapids, MI: Eerdmans, 1974-2006.

Harris, R. Laird, Gleason L. Archer, and Bruce K. Waltke. *Theological Wordbook of the Old Testament* (*TWOT*). 2 vols. Chicago, IL: Moody Press, 1981.

Jenni, Ernst, and Klaus Westermann. *Theological Lexicon of the Old Testament.* 3 vols. Peabody, MA: Hendrickson, 1997.

VanGemeren, Willem A., ed. *New International Dictionary of Old Testament Theology and Exegesis* (*NIDOTTE*). 5 vols. Grand Rapids, MI: Zondervan, 1997.

TDOT was finally completed in 2006, but without an index. *TWOT* is a condensation and adaptation of the German on which *TDOT* is based. It keys the words to Strong's concordance numbers, thus permitting someone who knows little or no Hebrew to benefit from its contents. *NIDOTTE* has a Scripture index and an English topical index that allow those who may not be strong in Hebrew to take advantage of a wealth of information. Jenni and Westermann's

Theological Lexicon of the Old Testament was written in German in the 1970s and may be somewhat dated, as are most of the original language works.

For the New Testament:

Balz, Horst, and Gerhard Schneider. *Exegetical Dictionary of the New Testament* (*EDNT*). 3 vols. Grand Rapids, MI: Eerdmans, 1990.

Brown, Colin, ed. *The New International Dictionary of New Testament Theology* (*NIDNTT*). 4 vols. Grand Rapids, MI: Zondervan, 1978-1986.

Kittel, G., and G. Friedrich, eds. *Theological Dictionary of the New Testament* (*TDNT*). 10 vols. Grand Rapids, MI: Eerdmans, 1964-1976.

Silva, Moisés, ed. *New International Dictionary of New Testament Theology and Exegesis (NIDNTTE)*. Grand Rapids, MI: Zondervan, 2014 (new edition of *NIDNTT*).

Verbrugge, Verlyn D., ed. *New International Dictionary of New Testament Theology: Abridged Edition*. Grand Rapids, MI: Zondervan, 2003 (abridgment and reorganization of *NIDNTT*).

TDNT is a classic, indispensable to biblical scholars. The single most important book of the set, volume 10, contains indexes by Greek, Hebrew, and English words and also by texts commented. *TDNT* comments on families of words and on words of theological importance. *NIDNTTE* is to *TDNT* what *NIDOTTE* is to *TDOT* (see above): less complicated, more conservative, and easier to handle. It also contains much less information.

At the end of this step, you should have a clear, accurate, and smooth translation of the passage—the cumulative result of the first four steps. On the basis of this translation, which should be arrived at independent of any existing Bible translation, the next three steps should be undertaken.

Step 5: Establish the Historical and Geographical Context

This step of exegesis considers the historical and geographical context of the passage. It asks: What was happening at the time this passage was written that might help explain the text?

Historical information is needed to clarify the text and suggest explanations for what was said or what happened or why it was stated that way. Knowledge of the sociopolitical and economic situation of the time is important to understanding the passage. Also, knowledge of the geography and climate of the region, as well as of the customs of the people, helps bring the biblical text to life.

Ben Witherington III points out that the "tendency to overspiritualize the Bible and ignore its social, religious, or political contexts is a mistake," leading to "errors in judgment when reading the Bible." He continues, "The contextual study of the Bible is an absolute must."[3]

For historical and geographical information, the following sources are useful:

Aharoni, Yohanan. *The Carta Bible Atlas*. 5th ed. Jerusalem: Carta, 2011.

Bromiley, Geoffrey, ed. *International Standard Bible Encyclopedia*. 4 vols. Rev. ed. Grand Rapids, MI: Eerdmans, 1979-1988.

Freedman, David Noel, ed. *Anchor Bible Dictionary*. 6 vols. New York, NY: Doubleday, 1992.

Rainey, Anson F., and R. Steven Notley. *The Sacred Bridge: Carta's Atlas of the Biblical World*. 2nd ed. Jerusalem: Carta, 2014.

Rasmussen, Carl. *Zondervan Atlas of the Bible*. 2nd ed. Grand Rapids, MI: Zondervan, 2010.

Sakenfeld, Katharine Doob, ed. *The New Interpreter's Dictionary of the Bible*. 5 vols. Nashville, TN: Abingdon, 2006-2009.

Silva, Moisés. *Zondervan Encyclopedia of the Bible*. Grand Rapids, MI: Zondervan, 2009.

See also the two *Encountering* books from step 1.

A related type of information is obtained from biblical archaeology. The excavations and their interpretation provide interesting data on the way people lived. Information concerning ancient languages has also come from archaeological discoveries. Some material on biblical archaeology is found in the dictionaries listed on the previous page. Many books have been written on the topic; these four are among the most useful. Your professor may have additional suggestions.

Baker Encyclopedia of Bible Places: Towns and Cities, Countries and States, Archaeology and Topography. Grand Rapids, MI: Baker, 1995.

Blaiklock, Edward M., and R. K. Harrison, eds. *The New International Dictionary of Biblical Archaeology*. Grand Rapids, MI: Zondervan, 1983.

Kaiser, Walter C., ed. *NIV Archaeological Bible: An Illustrated Walk through Biblical History and Culture*. Grand Rapids, MI: Zondervan, 2005.

Stern, Ephraim, ed. *The New Encyclopedia of Archaeological Excavations in the Holy Land*. 4 vols. New York, NY: Simon & Schuster, 1993.

3. Ben Witherington III, *Is There a Doctor in the House?* (Grand Rapids, MI: Zondervan, 2011), 55.

Step 6: Establish the Original Theological Meaning

In this step of exegesis the question is: What did the passage mean to those who first heard or read it? On the basis of the previous steps and informed by your own biblical and theological understanding, bring out the author's intended meaning.

Once you have established for yourself a clear understanding of the theological meaning of the passage, you can validate your conclusions by reading what competent commentators have written. Now you should be ready to read other writers' opinions without danger of being carried away by the postures of scholars. To read commentaries before making your own interpretation could shortcut the discovery process and let you settle for secondhand knowledge. Reading them now gives the opportunity of corroborating what you already know, of broadening your knowledge, or even of defending your position against that of other authors who do not see things as you do.

Step 7: Establish the Application for Today

Once the meaning for the people who received the message or sang the psalm or heard the prophecy has been determined, we can be confident that we understand the text. The last step of exegesis applies theological meaning to life as it is experienced today, either to you personally or to the larger community of faith. This application forms the basis of preaching and teaching.

This step is difficult but necessary if Scripture is to speak to our times. This step of exegesis may not be required in a theoretical paper, but it is an integral part of biblical interpretation, especially for preaching.

By carefully following these seven steps of exegesis, you can be reasonably sure of coming to a correct interpretation of Scripture. Naturally, biases and presuppositions can lead us astray. However, careful and prayerful study of the Bible, starting from the text itself, allows the Bible to speak for itself, to tell us what it wants to say (exegesis), without having us read into it (eisegesis) what we would like it to say.

Presentation of Exegesis

Not all of the search and study undertaken in these seven steps of exegesis is reported. Much of what you do is important to your research but irrelevant to the reader. The written report will not contain the parsing of the verbs or a list of all 56 occurrences of *dechomai* in the New Testament.

In any exegetical study, there must be sufficient detail to make clear to the reader how you came to certain conclusions. To ask the reader to accept by faith that you know what you are saying falls short of the rigor demanded of research. If the tense of the verb is important to the interpretation of the verse, the study must point that out and give a clear explanation of why it is important. If knowing Jewish marriage customs clarifies the passage, you must describe and document those customs. If an aspect of the climate explains something in the text, you must note it.

The written presentation could be made in seven parts: one for each of the steps. However, there may be little to say about some of these steps. Another possibility is to do a phrase-by-phrase commentary. It is easier to work in small units than to deal with a whole passage. A weakness of this method, however, is that it tends to blur the unity of the passage; a strength of this system is that it gives equal importance to all details in the passage being exegeted.

A better solution might be to divide the study into three sections. The first is the introduction, stating the purpose of the research and giving the context of the text studied. The next section provides a translation of the passage, with notes explaining how you arrived at that translation. The third interprets the text, giving the theological meaning of the passage and its present application. There you must present evidence of having addressed all seven questions. The following outline, given as a model to intermediate Greek students, illustrates this approach. The titles in caps may be applied to sections or to chapters. Check with your professor.

- I. INTRODUCTION
    - A. Passage selected
    - B. Reasons for choosing this passage
    - C. Setting of the passage
    - D. Author
    - E. Date
    - F. Audience
    - G. Literary interrelations
    - H. Historical/geographical/socioeconomic context
- II. THE TEXT
    - A. Translation of the passage
    - B. Information on
        1. Textual problems
        2. Grammar and syntax
        3. Important words

III. INTERPRETATION
   A. Meaning for original readers
   B. Application for today's Christians
IV. BIBLIOGRAPHY

In presenting exegetical papers, we often need to quote Greek or Hebrew words. These may be transliterated (see a reasonable transliteration scheme in appendix A) or typed in the original language. WordPerfect™ and Microsoft Word™ have Greek and Hebrew fonts. You may also use the fonts that come with Bible software or download fonts from the internet.

As was noted at the beginning of the chapter, exegesis as a form of research may be frowned on by some who think of research in terms of surveys, experiments, or archival searching. Nevertheless, an exegesis paper following the seven steps outlined in this chapter allows the exegete to show excellent research techniques and style. It also contributes to the fund of biblical knowledge. And if that is not research, what is?

chapter three

LITERARY RESEARCH

By "literary research" we refer to research done using documents as the primary source of evidence. These may be printed or online. You are attempting to answer a question whose answer is found in what people thought or said in "writing." This is different from exegesis because the "object" you are analyzing is not a text but an idea, an event, a context, or all three interwoven around a theme. In this kind of research, you will investigate a topic, answer a question, fill in the blanks. In short, you will solve a problem.

In theological education, the three main areas in which you will do literary research are theology, history, and pastoral theology. Obviously, you will come at your question with a biblical frame of reference.

Primary and Secondary Sources

Before considering the different types of literary research, we need to review two important kinds of sources: primary and secondary. Research depends on both of them.

Primary Sources

These sources are those beyond (or behind) which there is nothing more. To use a legal metaphor, primary sources are the documentary evidence upon which you build your case. These, by definition, are the original documents of a story, of any information. A primary source could be a letter. It could be the text of a speech. It could be a tweet. It could be an archaeological report. It is never a report about what someone else wrote. It has to be what an author, a person, wrote down on computer, parchment, paper, stone, or clay. And every document has a story, a history.

For biologists, primary sources report on the original findings of the researcher. For social scientists, primary sources are the documented interviews and surveys they conduct. For historians, primary resources are those documents closest in time and place to the event in question. In theology, primary sources are defined by the research method.

When working with historical resources, I may be able to find published primary sources online: a translation of Homer's *Iliad*, for example. That is helpful. Finding primary sources of unpublished letters and documents may be much harder.

In the strictest sense, only the original manuscript of the Gospel of John penned by John himself or Paul's Epistle to the Romans as it left his hand would count as a primary source. In practical reality, however, a critical edition of the Greek New Testament functions as a primary source. Its translations may not be primary sources as such, but may be considered as such when necessary.

In historical research, the closer to our time the topic of our research, the more primary resources we may expect to find. The Baptist Church in Montevideo (mentioned below) probably has documentation from its early days. Unless we have access to archives, we probably will not find primary materials from the nineteenth century.

Rule of thumb: serious historical research involves finding as much primary source material as possible. For example, if you were writing about Augustine, you would use *De Trinitate* or Augustine's *Confessions*.

By contrast, theological research takes a theme or concept and applies a method. For example, the theme might be the Trinity. The chosen method might be to compare and contrast two authors on the relationship of the Father, Son, and Holy Spirit. These authors may be from the early church, such as Origen and Irenaeus, or from later Catholic traditions, such as Augustine and Aquinas; or it may be twentieth-century authors, such as Karl Barth and Robert W. Jensen. In this case, the method defines the primary sources as those texts that are to be analyzed.

Another method might be to apply Trinitarian theology to the care of the environment. In this case the primary texts would be the key propositions you are analyzing, such as the various positions on the intersection of the Trinity and creation/environment. In many works on themes such as this and using methods that reason through research questions, each reference could function as both primary and secondary. The author's assertions and conclusions could serve as a primary source, while in the same work the literature review and the commentary on prior authors' positions function like a secondary source.

Secondary Sources

A secondary source is what someone wrote about a primary source. Secondary sources explain primary sources, but they are one step removed from the original. To continue the legal metaphor, secondary sources are the testimonies witnesses give related to the evidence.

For some research questions, we may not have access to primary sources. We must use secondary sources: secondhand information about the original letter or tablet or document. Sometimes we use what someone else wrote about a source even if we did not see the source. Just as in a courtroom, conclusive evidence may not exist, and we must infer a verdict based on testimony that is secondhand. Such a secondary source in research must be documented in the footnotes: this is what I found and here is where I found it.

In theological research, secondary sources, as defined by the method, include commentary and discussions of the theme in the works of the selected primary sources. For example, when working on the Trinitarian position of Augustine, Matthew Levering's *The Theology of Augustine* would be a pertinent secondary source.[1]

Theology

The objective of theological research is to document an orderly and coherent account of theistic beliefs. Theological research papers work toward this goal using one of several different methods. You might write a biblical theology—for example, the theology of returning tithe. You might also study someone's theological position on some specific topic. You could compare the theological positions of two persons on one specific topic.

With reference to our definition of research, the "object" of theological research can be classified as an ideal object, or topic—for example, inspiration and revelation, justification and sanctification, eschatology, pneumatology. In theological topics, there exists an ongoing conversation. Research involves listening in on these conversations and then joining the conversation with your own contribution.

Biblical Theology

Those who accept the Bible's authority will start with a "thus says the Lord" perspective. In other words, the primary evidence for their account derives from

1. Matthew Levering, *The Theology of Augustine: An Introductory Guide to His Most Important Works* (Grand Rapids, MI: Baker Academic, 2013). The index is particularly helpful.

Scripture. While biblical exegesis seeks to understand one passage, biblical theology seeks to understand the full canonical scope of the topic. Micro-exegesis of pertinent Scriptures becomes the evidence for a macro-exegesis of a theme in Scriptures. Because of time, space, and scope constraints, the goal may be very specific. As examples, here are the titles of some biblical theology theses:

> "The Doctrine of Forgiveness as Based on the Greek Word *aphiēmi*"
> "An Examination of the Hebrew *šabbāt* in the Old Testament"
> "Walking as a Metaphor: A Study of the Interrelation of Justification and Sanctification"
> "The Divinity and Preexistence of Christ in Isaiah"

Because you are entering a conversation, a literature review on the topic is expected. An excellent place to begin is by consulting standard theological dictionaries such as:

Dyrness, William A., and Veli-Matti Kärkkäinen, eds. *Global Dictionary of Theology: A Resource for the Worldwide Church*. Downers Grove, IL: IVP Academic, 2008.

Fahlbusch, Erwin, et al., eds. *The Encyclopedia of Christianity*. 5 vols. Grand Rapids, MI: Eerdmans, 2008.

Gonzalez, Justo L., ed. *The Westminster Dictionary of Theologians*. Louisville, KY: Westminster John Knox, 2006.

Kurian, George Thomas, ed. *The Encyclopedia of Christian Civilization*. 4 vols. Malden, MA: Blackwell, 2011.

Lacoste, Jean-Yves, ed. *Encyclopedia of Christian Theology*. New York, NY: Routledge, 2005.

Livingstone, E. A. *The Oxford Dictionary of the Christian Church*. 3rd ed. Oxford: Oxford University Press, 2005.

Markham, Ian S., ed. *The Student's Companion to the Theologians*. Oxford: Wiley-Blackwell, 2013.

Treier, Daniel J., and Walter A. Elwell, eds. *Evangelical Dictionary of Theology*, 3rd ed. Grand Rapids, MI: Baker Academic, 2017.

Analysis of an Author's Writings on a Biblical Issue

Frequently students are asked to write about what a certain author had to say on a biblical topic. Many doctoral dissertations do this kind of research. Here are a few examples:

> "The Seventh-day Sabbath in the Writings of Andreas Bodenstein"
> "Inerrancy and Sovereignty in the Writings of Carl F. H. Henry"

"*Sobornost* [cooperation, unity] in the Writings of Aleksei Stepanovich Khomiakov"

To write this kind of paper, you must read everything an author has written or spoken on the topic. You will then organize your findings in a logical way and give a summary for the benefit of your readers. They will then understand from a few pages what this author wrote in hundreds of pages.

So that the reader can check your quotations, you must provide references. Where you are studying will determine what the style of these references must be, but you must provide careful information for your reader.

You may wish to consider the following items:

1. How did your author change his or her opinion on the topic over time?
2. How did your author's ideas fit into what was being said or written at that time?
3. How did your author's ideas fit into the biblical scheme of things?
4. How do your author's ideas fit into today's thinking?

Comparison of Two (or More) Theologians

First, let it be said that under normal circumstances, two theologians are probably enough. You don't want to finish your dissertation just before you retire!

In comparing the ideas of two theologians, you must first analyze the positions of each of them. You probably will want to take a small portion of the thinking: one item. Here is a title of a real dissertation using the comparison method: "A Comparison of the Positions on Predestination Espoused by Zwingli and Calvin."

After the introduction of the paper, you will analyze Author A's point of view. Then you will analyze Author B's point of view. Then you will compare the two points of view. To complete the paper, you will need a summary and conclusion.

Quotations are important because they present the evidence of the author's positions. Even more important is the need to respect the original context of the quotations so that the author's original meaning is not distorted. Naturally, every quotation or allusion will have its reference. Your reader must be able to verify what you say the author quoted really did say.

For more detailed resources on theological method, see the following:

Kibbe, Michael. *From Topic to Thesis: A Guide to Theological Research*. Downers Grove, IL: IVP Academic, 2016.

Pazmiño, Robert W. *Doing Theological Research: An Introductory Guide for Survival in Theological Education*. Eugene, OR: Wipf & Stock, 2009.

Peckham, John. *Canonical Theology: The Biblical Canon, Sola Scriptura, and Theological Method*. Grand Rapids, MI: Eerdmans, 2016.

Stone, Howard V. *How to Think Theologically*. Minneapolis, MN: Fortress, 2006.

Veeneman, Mary M. *Introducing Theological Method: A Survey of Contemporary Theologians and Approaches*. Grand Rapids, MI: Baker Academic, 2017.

Walsh, Carey, and Mark W. Elliot, eds. *Biblical Theology: Past, Present, and Future*. Eugene, OR: Cascade, 2016.

Yaghjian, Lucretia B. *Writing Theology Well: A Rhetoric for Theological and Biblical Writers*. 2nd ed. London: T&T Clark, 2017.

Historiography

Richard T. Vann defines historiography as "the writing of history, especially the writing of history based on the critical examination of sources, the selection of particular details from the authentic materials in those sources, and the synthesis of those details into a narrative that stands the test of critical examination."[2] Christian historiography covers the story or narrative of the Christian church from its beginnings in the first century down to the present.

Three kinds of historical papers are common to theology students: historical events, historical theology, and historical people.

Historical Events

It is difficult to cover a long period of time in a student historical paper. Even a dissertation cannot usually cover more than a brief period. Therefore, choose a historical incident rather than a period.

For example, Kenneth Scott Latourette dedicated 1,552 pages to tracing the history of Christianity from the Reformation to the present.[3] D. E. Mungello took 248 pages to tell the story of Christians in Hangzhou, China, during approximately one hundred years (seventeenth to eighteenth centuries).[4] Be modest in your attempts.

---

2. Richard T. Vann, "Historiography," *Encyclopædia Britannica*, https://www.britannica.com/topic/historiography.

3. Kenneth Scott Latourette, *A History of Christianity*, vol. 2, *From the Reformation to the Present*, rev. ed. (San Francisco, CA: Harper San Francisco, 1975).

4. D. E. Mungello, *The Forgotten Christians of Hangzhou* (Honolulu, HI: University of Hawaii Press, 1994).

Here are some suggestions for doable topics:

"SIL Bible Translation in Mali, 2000-2010"
"The Redwood Church, 1985-2010"
"The First Ten Years of Baptist Mission in Montevideo, Uruguay"

Take note of what was said above about primary and secondary sources. I could reconstruct the history of the Baptist Church in Montevideo from what was written years after the fact. Primary sources would be letters written by the first missionary or church documents from the early years. Secondary sources would be what others have written about those years before I ever came on the scene. I will need both primary and secondary sources to do a credible job.

Historical research can often be problematic because the primary sources are not readily available. For example, Mungello had to obtain special permission to work in the Hangzhou library, where papers and books were kept. He also had to be able to read Chinese. Historical research on events since the beginning of the nineteenth century tend to have way too much information available, and it is necessary to delimit resources because of lack of time and space. For example, between HathiTrust, digital periodical collections, and digital archives such as the Digital Public Library of America, the volume of published and unpublished sources is vast. Those are just some of the difficulties in original research.

Historical research tends to be presented in chronological order. However, there may be times when a topical arrangement of the material is better. Your choice is usually informed by your professor's idea of which way is best.

Historical Theology

Sometimes it is difficult to decide whether historical theology belongs under theology or under history. It contains elements of both. This is the type of study that analyzes changes in a belief or doctrine over time. The longer the period you study, the more pages you will need to present the history.

When we study historical theology, we will often discuss a person involved. For example, it would be hard to study predestination in the Reformation era without dealing with Calvin. Therefore, some biography may be involved. In a historical theology paper, we start with a doctrine or belief at the beginning of our period and then trace its evolution through the period we agreed to study. As changes in doctrine are noted, we need to pay attention to people and institutions involved.

Some sample topics are the following:

"The Theology of Ordination during the Reformation"
"The Development of Roman Catholic Futurism"
"Righteousness by Faith in the Seventh-day Adventist Church, 1900 to 1920"
"The Pretribulation Rapture in the Thinking of the Plymouth Brethren"

Historical People

As time goes on, people who were outstanding in the history and life of their church pass on. With them, we lose a treasury of information. Their biographies, carefully written and documented, can be of encouragement to future generations.

The life story of anyone who has impacted others can be a good research topic. The individual need not even be a learned professor; the life of common people can provide encouragement to those who read about them.

Biographies depend on primary and secondary sources. Letters—a legacy of times gone by—can provide primary materials for the biography. Diaries are a rich source of information. Interviews with people who knew the individual are also useful. If the person has been long gone, you can still prepare a biography, but you would have a hard time doing more than summarizing what has been written about someone like David Livingstone.

In your research biography, there will be footnotes referring to letters, documents, certificates, church books, interviews, and so on. Your written work needs to convince your readers (of whom the most important is your professor) that you are doing serious research and not just reminiscing.

For a detailed and thorough discussion of historical methods, see:

Bradley, James E., and Richard A. Muller. *Church History: An Introduction to Research Methods and Resources*. 2nd ed. Grand Rapids, MI: Eerdmans, 2016.

Green, Jay D. *Christian Historiography: Five Rival Versions*. Waco, TX: Baylor University Press, 2015.

A short list of specialized reference sources includes:

Barrett, David B., George T. Kurian, and Todd M. Johnson. *World Christian Encyclopedia: A Comparative Survey of Churches and Religions in the Modern World*. 2nd ed. 2 vols. Oxford: Oxford University Press, 2001.

Benedetto, Robert, ed. *The New Westminster Dictionary of Church History*. Louisville, KY: Westminster John Knox Press, 2008.

Di Berardino, Angelo, ed. *Encyclopedia of Ancient Christianity*. 3 vols. Downers Grove, IL: IVP Academic, 2014.

Gaustad, Edwin Scott, and Philip R. Barlow, eds. *New Historical Atlas of Religion in America*. New York, NY: Oxford University Press, 2001.
Hillerbrand, Hans J. *The Oxford Encyclopedia of the Reformation*. 4 vols. New York, NY: Oxford University Press, 1996.
Kurian, George T., and Mark A. Lamport, eds, *Encyclopedia of Christianity in the United States*. 5 vols. Lanham, MD: Rowman & Littlefield, 2016.
Littell, Franklin H. *Historical Atlas of Christianity*. 2nd ed. New York, NY: Continuum, 2002.

Pastoral Theology

How do small groups work? Which evangelistic method is the best for a given time and location? How does a pastor deal with conflict in the church? These are questions that can be answered theoretically by a research paper.

Since there is (should be?) a biblical basis for what pastors do, what the Bible says cannot be omitted. The largest part of the paper, however, will describe, analyze, and summarize what others have written about the issue.

It is difficult to prescribe the organization of the topic, as each research paper will be different. One caveat is that all information about one aspect of the topic must be in one place. The paper will end with a summary of findings and the author's conclusions.

Here are a couple of titles:

"Small Groups as a Basis for Evangelism"
"Youth Leadership in ABC Church"

Most pastoral theology papers emulate the first part of a project that has practical applications. We will come back to these in chapter 5.

chapter four

HUMAN SUBJECT RESEARCH, PART 1

Descriptive Methods

Another category of research has as its "object" for analysis the responses to specific questions in specific contexts by people, "human subjects." The essential methodological foundation for collecting the data used in this category is labeled "descriptive research." After alerting the student to the Institutional Review Board, chapter 4 describes three different methods of descriptive research: quantitative, qualitative, and mixed methods. Chapter 5 describes three specific types of human subject research: program development, case study, and action research.

The Institutional Review Board

Know that every university has an Institutional Review Board, sometimes called the Human Subject Research Board. To protect the student researcher and the population surveyed or interviewed, as well as the school's reputation, most universities require that all papers or theses or dissertations in which information is solicited from live people—no matter how it is obtained—must be reviewed by a special board.

This board will study the proposal, together with the instruments or questionnaires or interview schedules, and decide how these questions will affect the respondents. The idea is to protect people from those who ask too many questions or questions that impinge on people's privacy.

If you are getting information from people, be sure to study the rules of your institution on the matter of getting and reporting that information. If you follow those rules, you will save yourself a lot of trouble.

Descriptive Research

Descriptive research does exactly what its name says: it describes, usually one or more characteristics of a group of people, technically called a population. This is not a literary or poetical description, but a concrete and concise depiction of reality. Sometimes the information gathered is strictly quantitative, with numbers and percentages; other times it is qualitative, including the "why" along with the "how many." Most pastoral and theological human subject research benefits from both quantitative and qualitative methods, and when the two intentionally blend, the resulting method is labeled as a "mixed method." This chapter first presents the steps of descriptive research, as well as techniques for conducting surveys and interviews, followed by practical applications of its use.

Within the pastoral setting, descriptive research could portray a congregation: how many members there are, what age groups they belong to, what their professions and occupations are, whether they live in apartments or houses, how often they attend church, whether they tithe, and so on. Descriptive research could also be employed to study the population of an area where a church is to be planted[1] or the way pastors perceive the usefulness of their seminary training. In pastoral/theological research, descriptive research is often a segment of the paper or project, used as the basis for program development.

The purpose of descriptive research is to make reality known. On the basis of the description, conclusions may be reached and decisions made. During the Roman Empire, the census was not merely intended to let Rome know how many citizens the empire had. On the basis of a census, taxes were levied and armies were organized. Today, descriptive research is used to find out how many people watch a certain television program in order to decide what the best airing time is. A marketing company of a particular soap product surveys a large group of teenagers not only to discover how many are washing their face with their product but also to determine the best way to get more of them to use this particular soap. Descriptive research on the preschool children in a certain town

1. Edgar Elliston's *Introduction to Missiological Research Design* takes students through the steps needed to complete research in mission at the master's or doctoral level. Elliston says this kind of descriptive research "provides one important way of discerning what God has done and is doing. It may also help one to discern how to cooperate with Him." Edgar Elliston, *Introduction to Missiological Research Design* (Pasadena, CA: William Carey, 2011), xxi.

may be useful in deciding whether the school needs to add another classroom in the next three years.

Descriptive research may have first been used to document need for change by John Howard, who began to fret in 1773 over the inhumane conditions of the prisons in Bedford, England. To prove what he was saying, he traveled all over England, visiting jails and noting the exact number of prisoners, what crimes they had committed, the conditions under which they were held, and other matters concerning the prison system. After completing his descriptive study, he stood before the House of Commons and gave a detailed and precise report that became the basis for important prison reforms. Howard later compared English prisons with jails in other European countries. His book *The State of Prisons* (1777) was one of the first comparative-descriptive studies. After studying the prisons of the land, he went on to investigate the conditions in hospitals. In one of these places he contracted an illness and died, a martyr for research.

This interesting story aside, it is evident that the report Howard prepared did not resolve any problem. It provided only the information necessary to set change in motion. This is the usefulness of descriptive research. It is what journalists do in newspapers and magazines.

According to Stephen Isaac and William B. Michael, the purposes of descriptive research are:

1. To collect detailed factual information that describes existing phenomena.
2. To identify problems or justify conditions and practices.
3. To make comparisons and evaluations.
4. To determine what others are doing with similar problems or situations and benefit from their experience in making future plans and decisions.[2]

Obtaining precise data is not always easy. A little boy, asked if he loves his mother, will normally answer "Yes!" Human beings want to please the people who ask them questions. Personal observations may not provide accurate data either; what you see may be tainted by personal bias. If neither respondent nor observer is trustworthy, how can you be sure you are really seeing all there is to see? Use as many different methods as possible to get information. To describe a congregation, get information from the church membership records, the church

2. Stephen Isaac and William B. Michael, *Handbook in Research and Evaluation*, 2nd ed. (San Diego, CA: EdITS, 1981), 46.

treasurer's records, the Sabbath or Sunday school attendance records, the lay ministries records, and any other records that may be appropriate. In addition, survey the members, getting specific information from them. Interview former pastors or other persons who might have important information. Finally, add personal observations. The secret for obtaining a complete and accurate description lies in using several approaches, tapping into different sources.

Descriptive research usually studies a situation at a given moment in time. A specialized type of descriptive research studies a person, case, or situation over time. A study of the growth of a church over ten years would be an example. Some descriptions over time may prove difficult or impossible for theology students, except as dissertations. See chapter 8 on DMin projects.

Steps in Descriptive Research

The descriptive research process may be divided into four steps: defining the objectives, designing the approach, collecting the data, and writing the results. Usually the first two steps take most of the time.

Defining the Objectives

Within the framework of the purpose of the study, what is the information to be obtained? And from whom can it be obtained? What facts and characteristics are to be uncovered? These questions must be answered in order to accomplish the first step.

In research on the function of deacons in a church, the objective of the survey might be to discover who the deacons are—how old they are, where they live, where they work, how long they have been church members. One might also wish to find out what they do in the church—visit members, take care of the church property, keep order during services—and how they consider their responsibilities—whether they feel needed, adequately prepared, or satisfied. Knowing exactly what you need to find out is the foundation of good descriptive research.

Designing the Approach

Once you have determined what you need to find out, the second step is to decide on the best way to obtain the different kinds of information. Personal interviews may be appropriate to gather some data. Other information is best obtained by using a questionnaire. Still more data can be obtained from records. Personal observation is valid as well.

For each of these approaches, a strategy must be developed. Will all the deacons (past and present) be interviewed? If not, how will you choose who will be interviewed? When and where will you do the interviews? Will the survey of church members' impressions of the deacons' work be anonymous? How can you get the greatest number of members to reply to your survey? Techniques for surveying, sampling, and interviewing are important enough to be considered under separate headings.

Before designing your own instruments, strategies, and procedures, you must read widely, both on the topic or situation to be studied and on possible methodologies to use. For example, if you are planning to survey the personal devotional habits of young people, you should read everything written about the devotional habits of young Christians. The Association of Religious Data Archives (ARDA) and the Atla Religion Database are excellent places to look for this information.

After extensive reading on the theory, the methodology, and the situation to be studied, consultation with the professor guiding the study is in order. Since some of the techniques of descriptive research are foreign to theological education, students might well look for professors in education, sociology, or psychology who may be willing to assist in the process.

If at all possible, find instruments (collective name for surveys, questionnaires, interview outlines, etc.) that have already been prepared by a credible researcher. Finding them may take time, but preparing good ones will probably take longer. DMin projects, reported online in Research in Ministry,[3] should provide some examples.

Once the instruments have been designed, some form of validation is appropriate. A pilot study, using a small number of respondents, may be used to find out if the questions are well worded, clearly understandable, and easy to answer. A panel of experts might also be used to study the instruments and advise on their appropriateness. Even better, both methods can be employed.

Collecting the Data

Collecting the data is the exciting part of the research. After all the hard work of preparing the forms, it is fun to send out questionnaires and get them back. It is interesting to go through the interview process. It is satisfying to finally be nearing the goal.

This elation, however, brings with it a major danger. You may trust your memory and not write down the findings precisely and accurately. It then becomes impossible to reconstruct the information obtained. The only antidote to this problem is to set up the easiest possible way to record every piece of data in an organized and orderly fashion. The importance of clear notes or recordings cannot be overemphasized.

3. "Research in Ministry," American Theological Library Association. https://rim.atla.com/.

Writing the Results

As in all research papers, there must be an introduction. This gives the background, the definition of the problem, the purpose, the limitations and delimitations, and the definition of terms.

Following the introduction, a descriptive research paper or thesis needs to have what is termed a "review of literature." This section or chapter reports on the preparatory reading, both on the topic—the population investigated (youth, deacons, women administrators, etc.), the methodology used (surveys, scales, ranking, etc.)—and on the theoretical framework, if appropriate. See more on the review of literature in chapter 7.

The review of literature is followed by a section or chapter on the research method employed: how the questionnaire was developed, tested, and applied; how the sampling was done; how the interview was designed and carried out. This description of the method explains how the research was accomplished. It helps the reader judge the quality of the study and may assist in future research design.

Then comes the description of the results. What was discovered? The topics are organized in some logical way and described in turn. Often the questions of the survey are taken one after the other or, if the questionnaire is long, by related groups of questions.

Finally, the whole process is summarized. On the basis of this summary, conclusions are drawn. Pastoral research usually ends with recommendations for action. Recommendations for further study may also be added.

The language of the report must be clear and precise. Generalities have no place. The following examples give precise data: how many, what percent. They also use language that only affirms what the subjects said—not what they are assumed to have done or believed. Here are two examples from an old dissertation:

> Nearly half of the 140 pastors surveyed (48.5 percent) said they had completed a four-year theology course, while 42 (30 percent) responded that they had taken a three-year course. Seventeen individuals (12 percent) reported completing a two-year course, while 13 of those surveyed (9.5 percent) stated that they had no college training before entering the ministry.[4]
>
> The ministers surveyed were asked to express their desire for further study at the future Adventist Latin American Seminary. Only 2.6

4. Nancy Vyhmeister, "Implications of Selected Curricular Determinants for Seventh-day Adventist Graduate Theological Education in the South American Division," (EdD dissertation, Andrews University, 1978), 204-205.

percent indicated that they did not wish to study further, whereas 41.4 percent indicated that they would study if part of their expenses were paid, and 27.5 percent stated that they would like to study even if none of their expenses were paid by their employers.[5]

Sampling

When Gallup polls want to know which candidate the citizens are going to elect, they do not ask each registered voter. They sample the population. That is, they poll a representative group. Regardless of the kind of instrument used to get information—survey, interview, checklist—sampling is a way to get a lot of information from not so many people.

When a seamstress wants to buy thread for a sewing project, she takes to the store a small piece of the cloth she will sew, not the entire piece of cloth needed for the final project. That sample may be too small to show the full pattern or the design, but it does provide the color, and that is enough to choose the correct color of thread. In human subject research, since it isn't practical to examine the entire population, a sampling of the population is used. The sample must be small enough to be manageable. At the same time the sample must be large enough to represent the population, and it must contain the same types of people in the same proportion in which they appear in the total population. Large or small, the sample needs to be sufficient to reliably answer your question.

There are rules for determining the size of your sample. Rather than calculating it yourself, I suggest using a sample size calculator such as the one at Creative Research Systems, where you will be asked the size of your population, the confidence level you wish your sample to have, and the margin of error you can tolerate.[6] You can be happy with a 95 percent confidence level and a 5 percent margin of error. Put in your total population, and you will have the information. If you are still not sure, ask a statistician. Better yet, if your population is small, get information from all of them.

Random, representative, and cluster sampling are ways to get the information you need. We describe these three next.

Random Sampling

Random sampling is a technique used to ensure—as far as possible—an unbiased representation of a population. Here "random" does not mean "chance."

5. Ibid., 229.
6. See "Sample Size Calculator," Creative Research Systems, https://www.surveysystem.com/sscalc.htm.

The researcher designs ways to achieve a fair representation by polling every tenth name on the list or interviewing every fourth candidate. However, before random sampling is applied, the population must be studied to ascertain that the method used guarantees, as nearly as possible, a representative sampling.

Random sampling can be applied to the total population. For example, every sixth member of the church—regardless of age, sex, or other factors—receives a questionnaire. Random sampling avoids the possibility of choosing only one's friends (or enemies) to answer the questions. It can be a safeguard for the research and the researcher.

Representative Sampling

To represent the population, the sample must include all the different kinds of people in the group, and it must include them in the proportion in which they are found. Thus a representative sample (often called stratified sample) will include men and women, old and young, rich and poor, Asians and Latinos, black and white, and whatever other kinds of people are in the group. If there are more women than men in the church, the sample must contain more women. If there are more old women than young women, the sample must also represent this characteristic of the total group.

Stratified sampling can be added to random sampling. Perhaps every sixth man between 20 and 40, every sixth woman between 41 and 60, and every sixth unmarried female receives a questionnaire. The benefits of using both kinds of sampling are compounded.

Cluster Sampling

Cluster sampling selects sample clusters or groups out of the population and studies all members of those groups. For example, Betty wants to study third-grade children in her city. She finds that there are 56 third-grade classes, of which 40 are in public schools, 10 in church-related schools, and 6 in private schools. She also notes that 25 have between 20 and 30 children, 15 have fewer than 15 children, 10 have between 31 and 40 children, and 6 have more than 40 third graders. Once the classrooms are divided into categories, she can randomly choose one room from each category. Betty will then study all the third graders in the clusters (classrooms) chosen.

This approach to sampling could be appropriate for studying churches, Bible classes, or youth groups. Proximity of the subjects makes the study easy to conduct. The dynamics of group interaction, the sharing in the study, may also enrich the study.

Surveys

Surveys or polls have become increasingly popular in recent years, especially with regards to politics. Some of these surveys are done orally—usually on the phone when you are busy with something else. Vendors survey customers. As a librarian, I receive invitations to participate in publisher surveys. What do I think about their new ebook package or new database interface? Some promise to enter me in a drawing for a nice gift card. (I have yet to win.) My doctor's office emails a survey invitation after every office visit. All share the same intention: to obtain information. While information obtained from a questionnaire is extensive, it tends to be shallow. Many people are polled, but not at great depth. This type of research is called quantitative and depends to a great extent on numbers.

A well-prepared questionnaire can obtain data that describes reality. A poorly prepared one may be useless or, even worse, give distorted information. Preparing questionnaires that will elicit the information needed is difficult and takes time and expertise. The tips given below can help you, but if you are serious about your research, please get help from a professional.

Tips for Preparing a Questionnaire

1. Know exactly what information you want to obtain. Know also what you are going to do with the information you get.
2. Make the questionnaire as short as possible. No one wants to take any more time than is absolutely necessary to answer questions. The chances that a questionnaire may be thrown in the wastebasket increase in direct proportion to its length and complexity.
3. Ask only for information not available elsewhere. For example, do not ask members to give their address or date of baptism if the church clerk has that information. Ask only for what you need.
4. Be sure the topic of the survey is important enough to justify the respondents' time and effort to complete it. A survey on the local church school will be more important to a mother of small children than a questionnaire about retirement homes.
5. Ask questions that elicit precise, factual data rather than impressions or opinions. A question such as "How many hours do you spend each week reading?" will get better information on reading habits than "Do you like to read?"
6. Formulate the questions in a clear, straightforward manner, with little possibility for misunderstanding. This will mean writing the questions, trying them out on people of similar background to those who will be

surveyed, and rewriting them until they are clear. Use language familiar to those who will be surveyed.

7. Put the items in a logical order. Make one thing naturally follow another. People asked to answer a survey get frustrated when the questionnaire does not make sense to them. Frustrated people may throw the paper away or answer carelessly, rendering the results useless.
8. Make the format simple and convenient to answer. Doing this enhances the chances that respondents will complete the questionnaire accurately and promptly. Consideration for the respondent translates into better data for the researcher.
9. Give clear instructions for filling out the form. Start out the page with instructions on how to answer correctly. An example may be helpful to the respondents.
10. Leave demographic questions, those about the respondent's age, gender, education, and so on, until the end of the questionnaire.

Survey Questions

Many kinds of questions appear in questionnaires. However, they can all be classified as closed or open.

Closed questions

In a closed question, several possible answers are given, from which the respondent must choose. These questions are easy to answer and easy to correct, but the answers may not include all possibilities. The respondent may not be able to give a correct response or may skip the question. An example of a closed question:

> On average, how much time do you spend each day in personal, private Bible study and reading? Do not count time spent in family worship or studying the children's Bible lesson.
>
> ( ) More than one hour a day
> ( ) From 45 minutes to one hour a day
> ( ) From 30 to 45 minutes a day
> ( ) From 15 to 30 minutes a day
> ( ) Less than 15 minutes a day

This question is worded in such a way that it is impossible to discover how many church members are not studying the Bible at all. To find that out—embarrassing as it may be to the members—one needs to add another category:

( ) No study at all.

Another form of closed question is the scale, which reduces the answer to a numerical value. For example, a question seeking to evaluate a certain aspect of a training program could offer these three options:

1 = Very valuable
2 = Of some value
3 = Of little value

Respondents may be asked to agree or disagree with a statement. To the assertion "Deacons should give a good example by paying a faithful tithe," the options could be: (1) Disagree; (2) Not Sure; (3) Agree.

Asked about how members consider the preparation of elders to lead the congregation, the options might be: (1) Not prepared; (2) Little prepared; (3) Acceptably prepared; (4) Well prepared; (5) Very well prepared.

Usually these scales are prepared with an uneven number of options. The gradation must be clear and the continuum obvious.

Open questions

An open question allows respondents to answer however they wish without prompting. Because answers vary so greatly, the tabulating of open answers is long and involved. However, if the survey is attempting to discover the favorite hymns of a congregation or the lay training most needed by the elders, the question has to be open in order to allow real freedom.

For example, in a survey on theological education, respondents were asked, "What course or courses, which you did not study as part of your ministerial training, do you now wish you could have taken?" The responses were tabulated and ranked to provide the overall answer to the question.[7] Of the 322 respondents, 103 did not suggest any additions. Of those who suggested additions, 49 wanted more course work on church administration and organization. So far, we are dealing with numbers. If the questions had included why? or how? we would have qualitative research, briefly described below.

Survey Returns

The ideal would be to have a 100 percent return—that is, to have every questionnaire completed and returned in time for the tabulation. This rarely

7. This question was part of my doctoral dissertation. Fortunately, my early-teen children came through for me and did the tabulation (by hand, before computers). I did have to increase their allowance that month.

happens. Letters get lost, respondents fail to return papers, and questionnaires are incorrectly filled out. The survey results give information on only a portion of the population.

A researcher must plan well and work hard to get maximum cooperation. If the questionnaire is prepared according to the tips given above, if anonymity is guaranteed, if there is some type of follow-up, the possibility of reaching a fairly high level of response is good.

In most areas of the world, anonymity is an important factor in obtaining responses. People want their opinions to be known, but do not want others to know what they think. In one survey on a sensitive issue, respondents mailed their returns from other cities so that not even the postmark could give them away. Even in a small survey, it is wise to make provision for anonymity, which provides respondents an opportunity to speak up without having to sign their name.

Student researchers may have difficulty getting responses to their surveys and questionnaires. For this reason, a cover letter written by their faculty sponsor—especially if the sponsor is well known—can be helpful. This letter points out the importance of the study and urges people to participate. It can definitely raise the percentage of return.

Making it easy to return the survey is important. A sheet of paper given out to the congregation during the church service should be picked up as soon as it is filled out. If the people are merely asked to leave the papers on a table on the way out of church, they may forget. Pencils or pens should be provided. If the questionnaire is mailed, a stamped, self-addressed envelope encourages respondents to answer and mail the survey. (This, of course, functions only within the same country.)

Follow-up is not easy; getting responses takes time and (sometimes) money. Insistence may be the only way to get a complete picture of reality. It is well known that the first ones to answer are those who are totally for or against something. Those who are moderate in their views may need to be prodded to divulge their opinions. Without a fair representation, the results would be skewed.

A second request for answers to a questionnaire may be general: "To all those church members who did not turn in the form last week." But this system is not accurate. Some may have forgotten what they did and turn in a second form. To be more precise, you need to know to whom the questionnaires were given and who did not respond. Using a code number on the form sent out will permit resending the survey to those who did not answer without compromising anonymity. Consult with a statistician on how to accomplish this.

Using the best techniques should assure a good return — perhaps not 100 percent, but certainly well above 60 percent. Make an effort to achieve as high a percentage as possible. A student's adviser or thesis committee often determines the minimum percentage acceptable.

Interviews and Focus Groups

We now go from numbers to ideas. When you report an interview, you indicate what the person thought and felt. That is qualitative research. Ideas are far more important than numbers. Feelings come into play, which makes the reporting more difficult. If you are doing much qualitative research, you may want to spend some time on the internet or in a qualitative research class—usually a part of education or psychology programs.

An interview allows the researcher to find out what people think and feel, one person at a time. A focus group not only gives the researcher an idea of what the people think and say, but it allows for interaction among the participants. Let's look at how each of these works.

Interviews

Interviews permit a deeper and fuller understanding of the attitudes of a respondent. Whereas the survey may have room only for "agree" and "disagree" answers, an interview can tell the researcher why the person disagrees or agrees. Interviewing takes time but provides information not available through a survey.

For an interview to afford the best information possible, the interviewer should record the conversation. However, an audio recording can only be made with the express permission of the person interviewed. It might help for the interviewer to say that the interview is being recorded to diminish the risk of distortion. Usually, after this explanation, the person interviewed will be happy to have the conversation recorded.

The interviewer should explain clearly what information is needed and why. Ethical behavior demands that the interviewer obtain permission to use materials from the interview in the research report. If the name of the interviewed person is given in the thesis (even in a footnote), the person has the right to see and approve these portions before they are published. If the person interviewed is unhappy, far better to modify a quotation or remove it from the paper than to anger someone who has cooperated in the study.

Go to the interview with a written outline of the questions to be asked. The conversation may depart from this outline, but at least you will have a framework for your interview. If you are interviewing several people on the same topic, fill out the outline for each one. Then you can copy and paste the interview responses into a table, which will help to organize the information obtained.

Interviews with a purpose, an outline, and a recording system will result in good information. They should be interesting as well. For in-depth information on opinions and attitudes, interviews are superior to surveys. Because of the depth and volume of information obtained in an interview, the number of persons interviewed is much smaller than the number of those surveyed. Remember, qualitative research does not deal with numbers, but with ideas and people. Students who wish to do purely qualitative research would do well to consult the following books:

Cresswell, John W. *Qualitative Inquiry and Research Design*. 4th ed. Thousand Oaks, CA: Sage, 2017.

Denzin, Norman, and Yvonna Lincoln. *The SAGE Handbook of Qualitative Research*. 5th ed. Thousand Oaks, CA: SAGE, 2017.

Silverman, David. *Doing Qualitative Research: A Practical Handbook*. 4th ed. London: SAGE, 2013.

Researching and recording the history of a congregation could be an excellent topic. Little information will come from church papers. Instead, most of it will come from the recollections of members. This kind of descriptive research is called oral history. On this topic, please see:

Deblasio, Donna M., Charles F. Ganzert, David H. Mould, Stephen H. Paschen, and Howard L. Sacks. *Catching Stories: A Practical Guide to Oral History*. Athens, OH: Ohio University Press, 2009.

Ritchie, Donald A. *Doing Oral History: A Practical Guide*. 3rd ed. Oxford: Oxford University Press, 2015.

Sommer, Barbara W., and Mary Kay Quinlan. *The Oral History Manual*. 3rd ed. New York, NY: Rowman and Littlefield, 2018.

Focus Groups

Some people refer to focus groups as "group interviews." You not only get the individuals' answers but note their interaction—which could be useful to you. Obviously, this is going to give you qualitative data. Use a focus group to get people's ideas and opinions. For example, you can use the information to develop items to include in a survey, to establish the needs for a program, or to help evaluate what has already been done.

The procedure is to invite eight to twelve people to a meeting to discuss a designated topic. (One good way to get people to come is to promise refreshments.) Bring your list of questions, much like those you would ask in an interview of a single person. The meeting should last between one and two hours. Since you will be busy directing the discussion, get someone to help you with seating and food. Your most important helper will be someone who takes notes or manages the recorders (which must be unobtrusive—people talk much better when they don't feel tied to a machine).

Once you have welcomed people, you will state the purpose of the meeting and let people know how you plan to use the information obtained. Then you may start with introductory questions. Ask general questions before specific ones. Make positive statements before negative ones. When participants give information, ask questions such as: "Would you explain further?" "Can you give an example?" Don't be afraid to say, "Tell us more." Give people time to respond.

Remember that you will need to get a signed statement of permission from each participant in order to use information provided in your written paper. When you are finished, thank people for their participation. If you had someone writing things down, go over the record as soon as possible, before you forget. The next step is to organize the ideas and statements.

Descriptive methods are often used in pastoral research. Knowing how to obtain and report information is vital to the process. Tables and graphs can enhance your report. See chapter 19 for information on how to create and use them.

Description of a Location

In preparation for developing a program, especially for anything that affects the community, such as outreach, evangelism, or a new church school, a description of the location is indispensable.

Find out how many people live in the area, how they earn their livelihood, what the educational level is, and what the social and health needs of the inhabitants are. Discover what other churches function in the area and what programs they run. Find out what kinds of schools, parks, and ballparks exist, if that information will help your planning. You may even need to study the transportation system to find the best location for the program you plan to run.

For many studies you will need to describe your own church. Number of members? Church attendance? Church activities? Financial support? Youth activities? Church school? On and on.

Be creative! Think of all the different factors that could affect the program you want to plan. Ask questions and more questions, but do so cautiously, carefully. Record all the information you obtain. Perhaps not all of it will go in your paper, but you will still have it.

chapter five

HUMAN SUBJECT RESEARCH, PART 2

Applications

Now we turn to three specific research applications that rely on descriptive methods: program development, case studies, and action research. All three relate to human subjects but from differing perspectives. In program development, the researcher creates a program, engages human subjects with the program, and then evaluates the effectiveness of the program in terms of desired outcomes pertaining to the human subjects. The case studies method begins with a human subject and draws conclusions from the experience of that human subject without necessarily anticipating any outcomes involving measurable change. Action research begins with a desired outcome, and the researcher and human subjects collaborate on achieving that outcome.

Program Development as Research

Program development, also called product or curriculum development, is another specialized form of research that is based on the responses of people and incorporates descriptive research. This section explains the application of this type of research in the pastoral setting. In program development research, the researcher determines the need for a program or intervention, establishes its theoretical basis, sets its objectives, designs it, implements it, and evaluates the results.

In an educational setting, program development often has to do with curriculum and classes. In church life, the program is whatever steps you deem necessary to solve a problem, whether it be a low percentage of tithe paying or deaconesses who do not know how to be deaconesses. Classes or seminars may be involved, but the "program" might just as well be a mentoring plan or one-on-one training.

For example, Pastor Bill arrives at Valley Church, which belongs to a conservative, mission-minded worldwide fellowship of churches. He soon observes that most of the 300 members are spectators, and the pastor is expected to do all the work. In conversation with the elders, he asks what members understand about the doctrine of spiritual gifts. The answer is quick: "Pastor, this is not a tongues-speaking church!" Pastor Bill realizes he has a problem. He needs to design and implement a program to change the situation. He can also use this opportunity to meet a course requirement in his seminary program.

Steps in Program Development

For the development of a program or intervention to be considered as research, specific steps must be followed. The steps presented here are designed especially for pastors.

1. Define the Problem

Decide what is wrong or needs fixing. Start with your own observation. Then ask questions of others. Pastor Bill's problem can be stated in this way: "At Valley Church, only 70 of 300 members take any part in the church's ministries, internal or external. Responses to questions indicate that the topic of spiritual gifts has not been considered in recent years."

2. Describe the "Population"

The "population" is a technical word for the group that needs help, for whom you are preparing the program. Descriptive research is used here.

Pastor Bill first needs to describe the church: membership, finances, ministries, participation. He needs to find out about the members: age, education, income, length of time as church members, place of residence. He must pay special attention to those who hold church positions. To document these needs and describe his church (steps 1 and 2), he will use descriptive research, as described in chapter 4.

If a program is to fit the needs of a whole church, the place to begin could be a church assessment. Christian Schwarz and associates offer a Natural Church Development survey to be used to determine where a church stands on eight different markers.[1]

1. See Jack Stephenson and David Wetzler, "The Five Steps of Natural Church Development," https://

3. State Goals and Objectives

The first two steps describe reality. This third step describes the ideal. What do we want to happen? What will things look like when the problem is solved? Goals (the final destination) and objectives (smaller goals along the way) point the way, keeping a researcher on track. They also serve as a norm against which to measure performance.

To be useful, goals and objectives must be expressed as outcomes. Pastor Bill's objective is not to teach the members about spiritual gifts, but to get them to recognize their giftedness and apply the gifts to useful ministry. They may acquire understanding, skills, attitudes, or appreciation. The question is: What will the church members know, feel, and do because of having gone through Pastor Bill's program? How will they show the knowledge, understanding, skills, and attitudes they have acquired?

To set goals and objectives, Pastor Bill and his elders—who are already part of the team—will first brainstorm, writing down all the possible desirable outcomes, regardless of importance. Once this brainstorming is done, the objectives can be prioritized, that is, ranked according to perceived importance. Here the focus group instructions are useful.

Although they do express positive outcomes, objectives such as the following are general and do not help to measure achievement:

- Valley Church members will understand the importance of spiritual gifts.
- Valley Church members will participate in the life of the church.

Questions arise: How will I know that the members understand? How will I know they are participating? How will this be visible? More measurable objectives would read somewhat as follows:

- Valley Church members who attend the workshop will evidence knowledge of the doctrine of spiritual gifts by explaining it to those who did not attend.
- Valley Church members will evidence participation in the life of the church by taking part in at least one church ministry or activity every month.

---

www.iaumc.org/files/websitepagefiles/NCD--5_Step_Workbook_LHTQXJX5.pdf, 13. Schwarz's landmark works on Natural Church Development are showcased at www.churchsmart.com. You can also download important materials about the program at this site.

Once set by the group, the objectives should be validated by the pastor (researcher) and other experts, such as experienced pastors from another church or seminary professors. Objectives considered acceptable by four of the five consulted would be retained.

4. Review the Literature

In this step the researcher must establish an acceptable literary basis for the project. The review of literature should generally include two aspects: (a) a theoretical basis for the program and (b) a review of similar programs.

The information gathered in these two areas usually will become one chapter or a major section of the research, depending on the length of the paper.

Theoretical basis

For Christians, the basis of bases is the Bible. What do the Scriptures say about the thrust and/or content of the program or intervention? What have other scholars and/or pastors written about the topic—in this case, the doctrine of spiritual gifts together with its implications for church life? What is the tradition of the particular church body on this topic?

Pastor Bill reads widely. He finds this theoretical review useful. He now feels he can defend his work by referring to what others have written.

Similar programs

Books do not yield as much information on the development and implementation of programs as does the periodical literature. Examine the Atla Religion Database, Research in Ministry, and ERIC (Education Resources Information Center) for sources. Look also in denominational literature; you may find what others in local churches are doing about common Christian problems. If the program being developed is entirely new, there may be little information on what others have already tried. Although little may be found, the search must be made and documented.

Pastor Bill finds several spiritual gift inventories and reports on how other churches have implemented gift discovery and application to ministry. He summarizes this information as part of his "review of literature" (see chapter 7 for more information on the review of literature).

5. Design the Program

Once the contents of the program have been determined—on the basis of the objectives chosen, the theoretical literature studied, and a clear understanding of the people for whom the intervention is intended—the program can be designed. The nature of the learners, the material to be presented, and the setting in which the learning experience will take place must be taken into consideration in the design. Since program development is being done as research, all of these aspects must be documented.

The design of the program includes deciding on the length and frequency of the meetings, the specific topics to be covered, the audiovisuals, the handouts, and the speakers or presenters. The program designer determines the steps to be taken in preparation for the meetings—such as obtaining permission from the church board, advertising, and making physical arrangements for the meetings. Even the evaluation, which will take place after the program is completed, must be designed at this time. Nothing is left to chance. Everything is planned, organized, and written down. Here the focus group may again be used profitably.

Pastor Bill has important decisions to make: What will be the formal aspects of his program? Whose help will he get? What will be the informal aspects of the intervention? He finally decides to have a series of sermons on discipleship, followed by a weekend workshop on spiritual gifts. At the same time, he will train counselors and mentors within the church to help those who attend the workshop and take the test to find a place to minister and develop their gift in ministry.

6. Prepare Materials and Resources

Write out lectures or talks, even if you are used to preaching with only a brief outline before you. Written materials become part of the research; together with copies of visual aids and handouts, they will go into the appendix of the paper. A good rule to follow is to include in the written paper everything that someone else would need to replicate the program.

Make all necessary arrangements for additional resources, human and material.

Get a second opinion from a trusted mentor. This could be your academic adviser or an experienced pastor.

Pastor Bill writes his sermons, prepares his PowerPoint presentations, gets the needed copies of the gifts-assessment questionnaires, invites his professor, and makes physical arrangements for every aspect of the program. He also prepares a test on spiritual gifts to use before and after the workshop to see what people learn.

7. Implement the Program

After going through all the preparatory steps—preparation of the workshop, permission from the church board, presentation to the church members, advertising, and so on—present the program according to your plan. It may be wise to make a first presentation of your program on a reduced scale in a small church or with a small group. Once you have learned how to do it, you can involve a large group.

Keep a journal, complete with dates, times, and names, as well as impressions—yours and those of the participants. Take note of everything that happens during the sessions. This information will be useful in evaluating the program and in presenting the written report.

8. Evaluate the Program

The evaluation must be multifaceted; several kinds of evaluation should be made by different people. For example, the church members involved in the program could be surveyed to find out how they felt about the program. A test on the doctrine of spiritual gifts, given before and after the program, could give objective information on acquisition of knowledge. The church officers can be interviewed. The participation of members in ministry can be monitored to see if the program has made any difference. A focus group may be called to help in the evaluation. Finally, Pastor Bill is entitled to make a subjective evaluation of what has happened.

Successful evaluation must be planned early and with care. Questions must be asked thoughtfully. If people think the pastor wants to hear that the program was successful, they may say exactly that, regardless of how they perceive what happened. Design evaluation questions that minimize this danger. For example, instead of asking whether they liked the program, ask what the participants liked most and least, or what should be added or deleted the next time the program is presented.

Program development demands weeks and months of reading, planning, preparation, presentation, and evaluation. It is, therefore, difficult to do for a class paper unless you, like Pastor Bill, are in a hands-on educational program. Program development is more appropriate for a thesis or major project, planned to take a longer period and under the direct supervision of a thesis or dissertation adviser.

9. Write the Paper

After the program has been produced, presented, and evaluated, it must be written up in a formal report. The next section deals with the writing and organization of the project or dissertation.

Pastor Bill starts his thinking in March, has the workshop in September, and completes his paper in January of the following year.

Organizing and Writing the Report

The organization of the paper will closely parallel the steps of the research. A conventional report of program development research has five chapters.

The first chapter—the introduction—should contain the same elements as any other introduction: the background, the statement of the problem, the purpose of the paper, an overview of the contents of the paper, and items such as the definition of terms and delimitations. The need and the objectives, as expressed in steps 1 and 2, must also be included. (In a short paper, this section may be called "Introduction" and not have the status of a chapter.)

Chapter 2 (or 1 if the first section is titled "Introduction") is the review of literature that includes the materials in step 4. If the program has an extensive biblical or theological basis, this may need to be written up in a separate chapter. If, however, the biblical and/or theological basis is evident in the talks or sermons of the program itself, and if footnoting is done there, the supervising professor may consider its exposition in that part of the paper to be sufficient.

Chapter 3 describes the group for whom the program was designed. If the information is relevant, this chapter may also describe the location and its inhabitants.

Chapter 4 presents the development of the program. This includes a report of everything from setting the goals, through obtaining the church board's permission, to the presentation of the program. Actual dates and places are reported. People participating usually are not mentioned by name but by position. The outline of events for the program is presented. The evaluation occupies a prominent place. In this chapter, refer to items that appear in the appendixes. This section is a complete history of the entire program and could easily be divided into three parts: preparation, presentation, and evaluation.

Chapter 5 contains the summary and conclusions. It may also provide suggestions for future implementation of such a program or further research. Should the introduction not be given chapter status, the summary and conclusions would not have a chapter number either.

The appendixes present a variety of materials, each in its own section. For example, there will be correspondence, invitations and publicity, the content of the presentations, illustrations (including PowerPoints and overheads), handouts, and evaluation questionnaires. Because the materials in the appendixes are vital to replicating the project, they must be complete, well organized, and carefully labeled.

The bibliography is the last item in the paper. However, last is not least; the bibliography may be the first thing a reader peruses.

Program development can be useful in pastoral work for preparing workshops, special weeks, weekend programs, lesson series, or training programs for church officers. Naturally, in the church setting, they may not be followed as precisely as these steps for a research project. However, following the suggestions given here will enhance the pastor's presentation of special programs in the church.

The Case Study as Research

Another method of research, often used in law and the social sciences, is the case study. This kind of research study is also prominent in advanced levels of pastoral studies, especially in pastoral care and counseling classes. This section contains a brief description of the social science case-study method and a detailed explanation of the pastoral-theological case study.

The Case Study in the Social Sciences

A case study in social science research involves an intensive study of the background, current status, and environmental interaction of a given social unit: an individual, a group, an institution, or a community. An example of this kind of study would be a school counselor's in-depth research on a pupil with a learning disability or the study of a family unit undergoing counseling.

The in-depth investigation of the case study results in a complete, well-organized picture of the person or group studied. The scope of the investigation may be limited in time, or it may follow the development of the person or group studied for weeks or even years. It may concentrate on specific factors, or it may cover all elements and events. In comparison with the survey (see chapter 4), which usually examines a small number of variables in a large group of people, the case study examines a large number of variables in one person or one small group.

Case studies are useful as background information in planning for further investigation. They bring to light variables that need further study. Case studies often provide hypotheses that guide additional research. They also provide useful anecdotes to illustrate generalized statistical findings. However, as case studies deal with individuals or small groups, they may not be representative of the total population. They do not lend themselves to generalization. In addition, case studies are often vulnerable to subjectivity. This happens because the cases chosen may be dramatic or highly emotional, or the researcher may become personally involved with the subject or subjects being described and thus fails to view the whole process in an objective manner.[2]

---

2. See Stephen Isaac and William Michael, *Handbook in Research and Evaluation* (San Diego, CA:

The Case Study in Pastoral Research

In pastoral research, the case study is similar to what was described above. It studies one situation, the activities of one group, or one incident. Naturally, a pastor's case study looks at an event or person or situation related to ministry. It must analyze the background of the incident, all of the factors that contributed to the interplay and interaction, and what actually happened.

A pastoral case study is different from one in social studies in that it brings into the study a biblical-theological point of view. Such a case study begins with a narration and ends in a theological understanding of how such an event should be handled. It is a tool for reflection. Since the case is usually taken from the pastoral researcher's own ministry, it leads to self-analysis and assists in establishing theological guidelines for handling future episodes of the same nature.

The case-study method for pastoral-theological reflection described in this chapter is used extensively in doctoral programs in ministry. The version described here owes much to the Doctor of Pastoral Studies program (DPS) of the South East Asia Graduate School of Theology (SEAGST).[3]

The case-study method is used in pastoral education to enable pastors to enhance their critical and creative ability for doing theology. Being able to do theology in ministry helps answer the nagging question "Why?" Why do I direct worship in this particular way? Why do I handle a broken relationship in the congregation in the way I do? Why do I preach in a certain way? It also helps answer the question "How?" How should I do this better? How can I help the teenagers understand and fulfill their place in God's service?

The case-study method helps pastors (and student pastors) learn from a situation, usually one in which they are involved. It is a tool to enhance awareness of the individuals involved, of the situation, of the message of Scripture, and of the pastor's own religious tradition. Doing a case study is doing theology—applying God's Word to everyday life.

This way of doing theology is not simply a tool. It is an experience. However, it is a disciplined experience. Reliving and rethinking a case brings theology out of experience. The result is a theologically sound, contextually viable pastoral action.

Knapp, 1971), 48; Robert K. Yin, *Case Study Research: Design and Method*, 6th ed. (Los Angeles, CA: SAGE, 2017); another excellent recent book on the topic is Dawson R. Hancock and Bob Algozzine, *Doing Case Study Research: A Practical Guide for Beginning Researchers*, 3rd ed. (New York, NY: Teachers College Press, 2016).

3. Special thanks to Tjaard Hommes, former director of the DPS program for SEAGST. The case-study method was for years the only one accepted by SEAGST for the DPS dissertation (*Handbook* [Manila: Association for Theological Education in South East Asia, 2000], 123).

Parts of a Case Study

The case study for pastoral theology is divided into four major areas: observation, analysis, interpretation, and action. In a case study, these areas will be chapters; in a dissertation, they will be parts, divided into chapters.

Observation

The first activity involved in developing a case study is careful observation of the case. This demands effort to listen, to see, to hear, and even to experience. Everything that is said and done in relation to the incident or case must be noted. Close observation is the basis for understanding.

Once a case has been observed, it should be written down. Use simple sentences that clearly tell the story. The words, activities, and gestures of the people involved are written into the case. What a person said should be recorded, not how the researcher thinks the person felt. Body language—a raised eyebrow, a frown—is also recorded for later analysis and interpretation. Observable facts and activities are written into the case; they form the basis of the study.

Details are important insofar as they relate to the incident. If a detail does not appear in the case, the feelings it suggests cannot be analyzed, and the theology it calls for cannot be interpreted. Irrelevant items, however, cloud the picture. For example, a woman wearing a red dress may not be essential—unless the case deals with the elder's reactions to a woman who wears a red dress the day she has the Scripture reading in church. The rule is to include all details necessary to the case and exclude all those that do not explain what people do or think.

To protect the privacy of the individuals involved in the case, personal names usually are changed. No one should be hurt or embarrassed by the contents of a case study. The precise town where the case took place may not be mentioned, but the general location must be given because of the importance of sociocultural factors involved in the case.

An introductory section containing important background information often precedes the written case. Of special interest is the writer's relation to the case. Other matters, such as location and time, may also be included.

In a paper or thesis, the case is presented in double-spaced format, with numbered lines.

The following example comes from Mindanao, in the southern Philippines.[4]

---

4. Reuel Almocera, "Christianity Encounters Filipino Spirit-world Beliefs: A Case Study" (DPS dissertation, SEAGST, 1990). This dissertation is available at the library of the Adventist International Institute of Advanced Studies, Silang, Cavite, Philippines, or from the James White Library, Andrews University, Berrien Springs, Michigan.

FRUCTUOSO

Fructuoso did not receive much of an education. His parents were poor and his home barrio was far from a town where a government high school operated. But he could read and write. He used to say that this was almost enough to satisfy his hunger for knowledge and truth.

When the Second World War broke out, Fructuoso joined the guerrilla resistance movement. Since most of the guerrillas had only bolo-knives for weapons, many of them, Fructuoso included, relied heavily on anting-anting[5] for protection, defense, and survival. Fructuoso testified that these amulets, claimed to have originated from the spirits, were powerful and effective. He insisted that he survived the war largely because of their power. He often expressed his belief in these supernatural beings.

After the war Fructuoso became an evangelical Christian. The American pastor who instructed him in preparation for baptism told Fructuoso that although the Bible speaks of devils and demons, the spirits he feared were mostly a product of human imagination and animistic influences. So when Fructuoso decided to be baptized, he abandoned his amulets by throwing them into the sea. He ended his allegiance to his abyan[6] and devoted his loyalty to Jesus Christ.

Fructuoso's economic life flourished after his baptism. He transformed a choice piece of land into a coconut plantation, and by a moderate standard, he was rich. He became influential in the community and in the church. In fact, he was a church elder for twenty years.

At sixty years of age, Fructuoso contracted a strange disease. He went to the best hospitals and secured the services of notable physicians. He submitted himself to modern diagnostic tests. He was declared normal and healthy. Fructuoso knew, however, that something was wrong. More than once his stomach bloated when the tide was high. Besides, his stool looked like mud, smelled like rotten fish, and yielded unidentifiable creeping creatures.

Unsatisfied with the physicians' diagnosis, Fructuoso consulted a mananambal,[7] who explained that an unidentified sorcerer had cast a spell on Fructuoso, causing his disease. The mananambal suggested that the spirits must be appeased or Fructuoso would die. He prescribed a ritual that included the sacrifice of three pigs.

5. Anting-anting is a talisman, usually a piece of paper soaked in "holy oil" inside a small bottle. This is tied to the user's body and is carried by the individual most of the time. For a more extensive treatment of the subject, see Ben E. Garcia, *Diwata ng Anting-Anting* (Cebu City: Sto. Rosario Parish, 1982).

6. An abyan is believed to be the patron spirit or the supernatural being that gives magical powers to the anting-anting.

7. A mananambal is a practitioner of the spirit world for healing and casting out spirits. He is believed to be able to heal because of his own powerful contact with the spirit world.

Fructuoso solicited some counsel from his fellow church members regarding the prescription of the mananambal. Some encouraged him not to submit to such a ritual. But some of the older church members urged him to go ahead; however, they counseled him to first resign from his eldership.

Finally, Fructuoso went through the ritual. Soon after, he got well. After attending church services in other places far from his home for some months, he resumed regular church attendance despite the accusing looks of some members.

Analysis: The Horizontal Dimension

Once the case has been written out, the next step is to carefully analyze the events, interactions, and reactions of the person or persons involved in the case. Of special importance are the views expressed by these people. Obviously, the work done at this stage presupposes a well-written case that includes all the elements on which to base an analysis.

The task of analysis is to understand, not to make judgments regarding the rightness or wrongness of anyone's actions. What makes people do what they do? Key questions to be asked in the analysis of the case are:

- What kind of dynamics affect the way people think and feel about themselves, about others, about life?
- What kind of views, feelings, relationships, interactions, reactions, expectations, and priorities seem to motivate the persons involved?
- What kind of power plays, external influences, likes or dislikes, self-understandings or misunderstandings seem to color the case?
- What kind of psychological, social, cultural, political, economic, spiritual, and theological factors seem to play a role in the case?

The analysis is a description of the factors that make people think and act the way they do. The analysis must be done critically, yet with imagination. It must look behind the words used to the feelings expressed. The analysis must be aided by disciplines such as sociology and psychology. The analysis takes into account those local cultural values that shape life and give it structure. It also values the theological understanding of the people involved in the case.

The research for the analysis of the case is done in the selected areas of local history, sociology, psychology, religion, values, and more. Some of the information may be obtained from one's own experience as well as the experience of others who know the situation where the case took place. However, a great deal of research must be done in the library. One must investigate what others have thought and written about the dynamics seen in the case. Choose the three most important areas.

In Fructuoso's case, the most obvious societal factors had to do with beliefs regarding the spirit world, illness, and healing. Also important was the American pastor's worldview that clashed with the local understanding.

Interpretation: The Vertical Dimension

The third activity, called interpretation, has a vertical dimension—it involves interpreting the case in the light of theology. The key question is: What do the Bible, theology, and the church's tradition and doctrine say about the case? Of prime importance in the interpretation is the theology of the case: What is biblically and theologically right or wrong about the issue?

The interpretation must be based on Scripture and informed by the study of the Christian faith and tradition. The writings of theologians, the church's teachings, and the church's practice must be taken into account. In addition, the insight of pastoral counselors, the research of psychologists or sociologists of religion, and the comments of students of relationships between church and culture should be explored as sources of materials contributing to the interpretation.

In Fructuoso's case the theological issue was evil spirits. Do they exist? What or who are they? How powerful are they? What does the Bible say about them? How do Christians relate to the evil powers?

Some cases are complex and bring up many theological issues. To deal with all of them may force the writer to be superficial. To choose the most important and focus on it is the better part of valor and intelligence. The questions asked in narrowing and delimiting a research topic may well be applied here.

Action: What Needs to Be Done

The fourth activity is that of action planning. Here one evaluates any action already taken and outlines appropriate future pastoral strategies for responding to the case.

The strategy should include not only what one proposes to do but also the rationale for choosing that strategy. The strategy planned must be realistic, contextual, and appropriate to the local situation. Furthermore, it must be correct in light of the principles derived from the research from the interpretation section.

The key questions to ask are: Which action is most appropriate and creative in the light of the Scriptures, Christian faith and tradition, and the local situation? Why is this course of action best? These questions must be answered with great pastoral creativity based on theologically sound principles.

In a real-life situation involving a complex case, more than one action plan might be possible—or even desirable. However, a case-study writer should resist the temptation to deal with all likely action strategies. In the normal case study, a student should pursue only one action plan in response to the key issue or problem of the case. Alternative suggestions could be mentioned, but need not be developed. If the case describes pastoral action already accomplished, what has been done might be discussed and evaluated.

The Fructuoso case concluded with a plan for giving biblically sound teaching on the spirit world, with emphasis on its reality and Christ's power over it. The action proposed a Christian exorcism ceremony, in which lay leaders and pastors would participate to show Christ's triumph over evil spirits.

Writing the Case Study

Writing a case study is much the same as writing a research paper. The normal methodology for research is used. The format for research papers, as described in this book, is employed. While following academic rigor, the case study provides some room for creativity and imagination.

The four activities described above form the outline for the written case study. Class papers and doctoral theses do, however, have differences between them.

Case-Study Papers

The written case—the product of observation—together with the introduction (purpose, background, etc.) becomes the first chapter in the case study. The case probably will be no more than two pages (double spaced). Each line is numbered to facilitate reference to it in later parts of the paper. Names of places and people must be disguised to preserve the confidentiality of those involved.

The analysis, a study of the horizontal dimensions of the case—sociocultural, psychological, economic, and political factors involved—constitutes the second chapter of the case study. It is written as a research paper, with subheadings as needed to organize the material. Footnotes are also used to document information brought in from sources other than the case itself or the imagination of the researcher. For example, the case from the Philippines might require an explanation of a Filipino value. Information on that way of thinking might be gleaned from the journal *Philippine Values Digest* and would need to be footnoted.

The format of the interpretation, which is chapter 3, is similar to that of the second chapter. Its content is different in that it looks at the vertical dimensions—the theological, biblical, and church-related aspect of the question. Again, footnoting should be used to reference biblical, theological, or church polity sources.

The final section of the case study is the action. It is prefaced by a synthesis/summary of the analysis and interpretation, which serves as the basis for the action. This summary brings into focus the factors affecting the case and establishes the appropriate theological response. It is also useful for those who only read introduction, summary, and conclusions of research work. The action plan uses an essay format and describes pastoral action already accomplished and yet to be done. An outline format (see chapter 12) may be used if a procedure is outlined.

The bibliography presents a list of materials consulted, whether quotations or citations from the items were used or not. The purpose of this list is not only to impress the professors and free one's self from charges of plagiarism but also to provide future researchers with a starting point for their endeavors.

Case-Study Dissertations

When a case study is developed into a dissertation for a professional doctorate in theology, the parts can be outlined as follows.

1. Presentation

Chapter 1 includes introductory remarks and the written case—the product of observation. The case will probably be no more than two pages (double spaced). Each line is numbered, to facilitate reference to it in later parts of the paper.

Chapter 2 contains the introduction, that is, the pastoral and theological issues, methodology, delimitations, significance, definition of terms (if needed), and overview of the dissertation.

2. Analysis

The analysis, a study of the sociocultural, psychological, economic, and political factors involved in the case, may have as many chapters as needed to discuss the different problems. "Fructuoso" had two chapters: sociocultural and psychosocial dynamics, and the dynamics of Filipino folk religion as expressed in the case.

3. Interpretation

The interpretation studies the theological, biblical, and church-related aspects of the case study. The number of chapters depends on the number of issues investigated. No more than three chapters are normally allowed. "Fructuoso" had a chapter on spirits and demons in the Bible and a chapter on healing rituals.

4. Action

The action section of the study is prefaced by a synthesis/summary of the analysis and interpretation, which serves as the rationale for the action. This summary brings into focus the factors affecting the case and establishes the appropriate theological response. This section usually has two chapters. Bibliography and appendixes (as needed) close the study.

To summarize, the case-study method requires observation of a situation, analysis of what is happening, interpretation of the dynamics of the case in light of the Bible and Christian faith-tradition, and a plan for action dealing with the key issue or problem. When all of these parts are put together carefully, this practical way of doing theology becomes a method of research.

Action Research

Bradbury, Lewis, and Embury give the following definition of action research: "We find it useful to conceive of action research as placing equal emphasis on three elements: creating genuine relationships, bringing in useful concepts to the dialogue from which those involved can extend together into collaborative experiments, and developing experiments that are used to enrich a next cycle of inquiry for action."[8]

Hillary Bradbury notes that "action research is a democratic and participative orientation to knowledge creation. It brings together action and reflection, theory and practice, in the pursuit of practical solutions to issues of pressing concern. Action research is a pragmatic co-creation of knowing *with*, not *about*, people."[9]

David Coghlan applies "action research" to organizations. One of the important aspects of this kind of research is "collaborative democratic partnership."[10]

Action research had its origin in the educational setting. It was the natural outgrowth of the way peers get together to solve problems. A group of teachers, usually with a leader who was one of them, assembled to solve a problem.

---

8. Hillary Bradbury, Rolla Lewis, and Dusty Columbia Embury, "Education Action Research: With and for the Next Generation," in *The Wiley Handbook of Action Research in Education*, ed. Craig A. Mertler (Hoboken, NJ: John Wiley & Sons, 2019), sect. 1.4.

9. Hillary Bradbury, "Introduction: How to Situate and Define Action Research," in *The SAGE Handbook of Action Research*, ed. Hillary Bradbury, 3rd ed. (Los Angeles, CA: SAGE, 2015), 1.

10. David Coghlan, *Doing Action Research in Your Own Organization*, 5th ed. (Los Angeles, CA: SAGE, 2019), 5.

Together they decided what pieces of information were needed and designated different individuals to find the needed information. They then met again, shared the information gathered, considered how their findings answered their questions, and decided what further information was needed. This process repeated itself until the group felt they had found a solution to their problem and were ready to implement it.

People usually do something, check how it works, make modifications, and then continue their process. Herein lies the basis of action research, which is simply doing and reflecting at the same time. The deciders and the doers are the same people. Participation in the research generates commitment. Hult and Lennung note:

> Action research simultaneously assists in practical problem-solving and expands scientific knowledge, as well as enhances the competencies of the respective actors, being performed collaboratively in an immediate situation using data feedback in a cyclical process aiming at an increased understanding of a given social situation, primarily applicable for the understanding of change processes in social systems and undertaken within a mutually acceptable ethical framework.[11]

Action research has become an important part of the Doctor of Ministry program, especially in some universities. Here we will present action research as carried out by students doing pastoral research, usually for a DMin project.

Stages of the Study

The research begins with the definition of the problem. Once the researcher has a problem statement, the researcher convenes a group who will go through the research as co-researchers. These people, chosen for their abilities, perhaps among church officers, will help to modify the statement of the problem.

Once there is agreement on what the problem is and how it might be resolved, the members of the group take on different aspects of the work. When they meet again, they report on what they have done and can determine what more needs to be done and how it can be done.

The research design will be modified as it progresses. The cyclic process should improve the design over time.

---

11. Margareta Hult and Sven-Åke Lennung, "Towards a Definition of Action Research: A Note and Bibliography," *Journal of Management Studies* 17, no. 2 (1980), abstract, https://doi.org/10.1111/j.1467-6486.1980.tb00087.x.

Information needed for decision making will be gathered first from the literature. Further information will come from use of the descriptive methods, both quantitative and qualitative. In true action research, all of those involved in the process will have a part in the research. When action research is done by a pastor/student, the assistants have little part in the research, but much say in the group work.

When there is sufficient information—of all kinds—the researcher is ready to implement a plan. Usually the participants will help in the implementation.

Finally, when the implementation has been completed and evaluated, the student/pastor/researcher gets the privilege of writing up the results. Otherwise, the degree would belong to the assistants.

Difficulties with Action Research

A pastor or researcher may have trouble finding appropriate companions in research. In many places the perceived distance between church members and their pastor makes cooperation difficult. Not only may the pastor not find many appropriate co-researchers, but competition may arise among those who are chosen or not chosen.

The need for confidentiality could become troublesome. To keep a group of lay leaders from speaking out of turn may be hard. While the pastor is not attempting to maintain secrecy, anything members of the committee might say outside the committee could be troublesome.

The time factor could be problematic. A pastor often has to work under time constraints to complete a research project. Working with a group may tend to slow down the process of gathering information and making decisions. Furthermore, the fact that the pastor is getting something out of the process (a degree) while they get only a thank-you may complicate relationships.

In spite of these difficulties, the use of action research in planning and organizing pastoral research is worth considering. To a certain extent the group interview or focus group described in chapter 4 is a useful modification of action research.

Development of the Paper

The parts of the paper will be similar to those described in the early part of this chapter, in the section "Steps in Program Development," or in chapter 8 for a DMin project/dissertation.

The process of research, writing, presentation, and defense will follow the normal process of each institution.

Further Reading on Human Subject Research

Ammerman, Nancy T., Jackson W. Carroll, Carl S. Dudley, and William McKinney, eds. *Studying Congregations: A New Handbook*. Nashville, TN: Abingdon, 1998.

Association of Religion Data Archives. http://www.thearda.com.

Cameron, Helen, Philip Richter, Douglas Davies, and Frances Ward, eds. *Studying Local Churches: A Handbook*. London: SCM, 2005.

Duce, Cameron, and Catherine Duce. *Researching Practice in Ministry and Mission: A Companion*. London: SCM, 2013.

Elliston, Edgar J., et al. *Introduction to Missiological Research Design*. Pasadena, CA: William Carey, 2011.

Moschella, Mary Clark. *Ethnography as a Pastoral Practice: Introduction*. Cleveland, OH: Pilgrim, 2008.

Sensing, Tim. *Qualitative Research: A Multi-Methods Approach to Projects for Doctor of Ministry Theses*. Eugene, OR: Wipf & Stock, 2011.

Strausberg, Michael, and Steven Engler, eds. *The Routledge Handbook of Research Methods in the Study of Religion*. Routledge Handbooks. London: Routledge, 2011.

Woods, C. Jeff. *Designing Religious Research Studies*. Eugene, OR: Wipf & Stock, 2016.

Part Two

Educational Settings for Theological Research

This second section of the book describes various educational settings or programs in which students engage in theological research, be they undergraduate or graduate. We will take note of different levels of research writing.

The purpose here is to present the different settings in which students will engage in theological research. Each setting has its own expectations and its own pedagogical purposes. Looking at all of them will help you understand the desired outcomes of the writing assignment.

Like the first, this section of the book may first be scanned. Once you determine the setting of research in which you find yourself, go back and study that chapter carefully. Then you will be able to write a good paper and maximize your learning experience.

chapter six

CLASS RESEARCH PAPERS

This chapter will share a few thoughts and suggestions for the research paper that is assigned in a particular class and must be completed within the term. While much of what you do for these assignments corresponds to expectations common to all academic writing, there are a few significant distinctions. Being aware of these distinctions and engaging certain intentional strategies has the potential to transform these assignments from frustrating busy work to a delightful opportunity for knowledge discovery and creation.

Why Research Papers?

One reason may be tradition. "I was required to do it, so that's the way it must be. End of discussion." When I was in graduate school, almost every class had a twenty-plus page formal research paper requirement. After reviewing syllabi in the current professional degree curriculum here in my university, I am noticing that many alternative writing assignments are used:

- reflection papers, to encourage reflective thinking and the application of the topic to life and ministry
- sermons, focusing on explaining a topic to a general audience in a typical church setting
- reading reports, analyzing and synthesizing significant readings
- group presentations, sharing what is learned on a topic with the class

And so forth. So while there is a long tradition associated with the standard research paper, professors have begun exploring alternative document-based learning opportunities.

I appreciate that many students welcome the variety of assignments. But it means fewer opportunities to hone a skill that brings its own rewards. Just as learning to play a musical instrument is mastered through much practice, so too engaging in research skills requires practice to achieve expertise.

Better reasons for giving this type of assignment are founded on the professors' enthusiasm for empowering students on their journey from novice to expert. This transformation can only be achieved through intentional and guided mentoring. Assigning the research paper becomes an invitation, an opportunity for students to grow in knowledge and take important strides on that journey. The professor has been to the mountaintop and has found the view to be magnificent. Make the most of the invitation to follow her.

The research assignment journey assumes making progress along several dimensions. The first is the knowledge of the field of study; a second is to meet colleagues who through their writings share expertise in the field of study; a third involves the analytical skills needed to engage in the conversations in the field of study; the fourth is to find your voice in effectively communicating your discoveries in the field of study. At the end of the day, your professor will delight in your progress.

For these reasons and more, the formal research paper assignment continues to be a time-tested method of introducing you to the field of study represented by the course.

Thinking about the Assignment?

The Association of College and Research Libraries (ACRL) recently published a "Framework for Information Literacy." While their six core ideas are focused on using information, the framework concept can help make sense of research assignments, namely, that successful research involves not only knowledge but also skills and disposition.

Students engage the knowledge needed to complete the assignment from their professor and disciplinary community. Most of this book addresses the skills useful to you as you write the paper. But your disposition transforms this chore into a delight. A disposition is an informed attitude based on values, expectations, and inclinations. Having an attitude that anticipates with delight the learning to be achieved from the assignment is foundational to success.

Professors lecture and students engage in their wisdom. Required readings open the doors wider to include learning from trustworthy colleagues. Examinations allow you to synthesize the learning you have gleaned as represented by correct answers. But research papers set you free to explore in depth what really interests you. The intrinsic rewards that come from this path to knowledge creation warrant gratitude.

Key Differences between Term Papers and Theses/Dissertations

Term papers, theses, and dissertations share the same expectations with regard to academic writing, methods of research, use of resources, etc. That should be clear after reading the rest of this book. The two principle differences that distinguish term papers and theses from dissertations are time and expertise.

One term is not much time, especially when you are taking several classes, and each one anticipates your full-time attention. A thesis may be completed in one term, but usually when it is the only academic work in hand. Dissertations can take years. But the term paper must be done quickly in just a few weeks. That old saying is right on target, "Time flies when you are having fun." You must plan well, keep on task, and avoid distractions. You will never do your best work crunching out a paper just before it is due.

The other difference is expertise. By the time students begin working on a thesis or dissertation, they are already experts on the topic. They know the disciplinary authorities and understand the scholarly community. They have spent countless hours reading in the field and understand the jargon. But the student taking course work may be studying a new topic, a new field of inquiry, for the first time. In a church history survey course, you gained some understanding of the time and impact of Martin Luther. But that first research assignment provided you the challenge to deeply focus on a single issue in Luther's writings. In an introduction to the Gospels, you learned much about the social backgrounds, literary genres, and themes of the Scriptures. But that first exegesis paper applies all that general information to understanding one pericope or saying. In the journey toward expertise, everyone has to start sometime.

The Uncertainty Principle

In the information science profession, we do research. And one object of the research is how you, the student, experience research. Carol Kuhlthau, professor emerita in library and information science at Rutgers University, introduced a model of the Information Search Process (ISP). She was the first to include the affective domain in trying to understand how students go about doing research, and this is illustrated through her "uncertainty principle."

> Uncertainty is a cognitive state that commonly causes symptoms of anxiety and lack of confidence. Uncertainty and anxiety can be expected in the early stages of the information searching process. Uncertainty, confusion, and frustration are associated with vague, unclear thoughts about a topic or problem.
>
> As knowledge states shift to more clearly focused thoughts, a parallel shift occurs in feelings of increased confidence. Uncertainty due to a lack of understanding, a gap in meaning, or a limited construct initiates the process of information seeking.[1]

Her observations are most applicable to novice researchers and should be considered as descriptive, not prescriptive. The point is that if you identify with what she describes, embrace the hope embedded in the norm, and press on toward the finish. No matter how uncertain and anxious you may feel early on, at some point you will figure out the answer and gain clarity and confidence.

> The model of the ISP is articulated in a holistic view of information seeking from the user's perspective in six stages:
>
> - *Initiation*, when a person first becomes aware of a lack of knowledge or understanding, and feelings of uncertainty and apprehension are common.
> - *Selection*, when a general area, topic, or problem is identified and initial uncertainty often gives way to a brief sense of optimism and a readiness to begin the search.
> - *Exploration*, when inconsistent, incompatible information is encountered and uncertainty, confusion, and doubt frequently increase and people find themselves "in the dip" of confidence.
> - *Formulation*, when a focused perspective is formed and uncertainty diminishes as confidence begins to increase.

1. Carol Collier Kuhlthau, *Seeking Meaning: A Process Approach to Library and Information Services* (Norwood, NJ: Ablex, 1993), 111.

- *Collection*, when information pertinent to the focused perspective is gathered and uncertainty subsides as interest and involvement deepens.
- *Presentation*, when the search is completed with a new understanding enabling the person to explain his or her learning to others or in someway [*sic*] put the learning to use.[2]

The affective thread in this model moves from uncertainty to confidence. The cognitive thread moves from vague to focus to increased interest. And the activity moves from exploring to documenting. The defining moment when these transitions occur is when a focus formulation is achieved, when it all comes together for you. When this happens can vary from project to project based on prior knowledge, mentoring support, clarity of expectations, and so forth. By the time you are ready to tackle a thesis or dissertation, the uncertainty is largely mitigated, and you are ready for the joy of the journey.

Practical Strategies

- Start the information search process as early in the term as possible, the first week is ideal. During the exploring phase, be sure to take just enough notes so you can find the sources again. Then take the comprehensive notes described in chapter 15 during the documenting phase.
- Plan a minimum of three hours per page, including a commitment to working a balanced proportion of the time per week. Taking the time early in the term allows your thinking to mature before the due date.
- Plan plenty of time to revise and rewrite. Steven Pinker, a Harvard professor who writes about writing, states: "I rework every sentence a few times before going on to the next, and revise the whole chapter two or three times before I show it to anyone. Then, with feedback in hand, I revise each chapter twice more before circling back and giving the entire book two complete passes of polishing."[3] If that is what the most expert authority on writing practices, then doing likewise is evidence of following best practice.

---

2. Carol Collier Kuhlthau, "Information Search Process," Rutgers School of Communication and Information, 2018, https://wp.comminfo.rutgers.edu/ckuhlthau/information-search-process/.

3. Steven Pinker, *The Sense of Style: The Thinking Person's Guide to Writing in the 21st Century* (New York, NY: Viking, 2015), 76.

- Use the writing centers at your institution. Your tuition and fees cover that support. Get your money's worth. Even if you have had a positive writing experience and feel confident about your writing ability, the extra readers can provide helpful suggestions.
- Be patient with the professors. It is quite likely they have forgotten what it felt like to write that first paper. Don't be shy about asking questions. You probably will get more quality time from the professor early in the term rather than close to the end of the term.

Research Paper Assessment

Many professors use a rubric to grade the paper, and this rubric is included in the syllabus. Study the rubric. Make sure you understand all the categories and make every effort to meet the expectations.

I used the following rubric in my research methods course. If your professor doesn't provide a rubric, this one may provide some guidance for you as you prepare your project for submission.

ELEMENTS	A RANGE (4)	B RANGE (3)	C RANGE (2)	D RANGE (1)	F – FAIL (0)
Document Formatting: Title page Table of Contents General document settings Headings Page numbers Block quotes	The appearance and word processing of the document is of a high professional standard. Follows assigned formatting, requiring four or less detailed corrections.	The appearance and word processing of the document is of professional standard. Follows assigned formatting, but requires detailed corrections in five to ten instances.	The appearance and word processing of the document is adequately presented, but lacks a consistent application of assigned formatting. Requires detailed corrections in ten or more instances.	The appearance and word processing in the document is poor. Some evidence of following assigned formatting, but requires some corrections on most pages.	No evidence to indicate effort to follow assigned formatting
Document Formatting: Abbreviations Footnotes Bibliography	Uses correct abbreviations. Follows correctly an accepted style. Formatted correctly. Requires four or fewer detailed corrections.	Uses correct abbreviations. Follows correctly an accepted style. Formatted correctly, but requires detailed corrections in five to ten instances.	Correct abbreviations not used consistently. Standard references correctly entered in footnotes and bibliography. Nonstandard references incorrect.	Correct abbreviations not used consistently. Required bibliographic elements of the footnotes and bibliography present, but does not follow accepted style.	Does not use standard abbreviations. Does not follow any accepted style.
Sources: Selection	Employs effectively reliable and reputable primary, secondary, and tertiary literatures. Uses the most current academic publications available on the topic. Includes recognized disciplinary experts with diverse interpretations or points of view.	Employs effectively reliable and reputable primary, secondary, and tertiary literatures. Uses some current academic publications available on the topic. Sources do not illustrate the diversity of opinion on a topic.	Employs two classes out of the primary, secondary, and tertiary literatures. Uses old or out-of-date sources when current resources are available. Does not use sources with different perspectives.	Poor selection of sources. Uses primarily nonscholarly sources or old, out-of-date sources.	Uses only nonscholarly sources.

(cont.)

ELEMENTS	A RANGE (4)	B RANGE (3)	C RANGE (2)	D RANGE (1)	F – FAIL (0)
Sources: Use and integration	Supports key points with examples from a wide range of academic literature. Quoted material is expertly integrated into the body of the work. The analysis suggests new ways to perceive the material or identifies gaps or shortcomings in the literature.	Supports key points with examples from a wide range of academic literature. Quoted material is competently integrated into the body of work.	Does not support every key point with examples from academic literature. Quoted material is sometimes irrelevant or poorly integrated into the body of work.	Points are not supported by academic literature. Quoted material is often irrelevant or poorly integrated into the body of work.	Does not support any point with examples from academic literature. Quoted material is often irrelevant or poorly integrated into the body of work.
Communication and Language	Meets all expectations for theological plain style in an academic voice. Uses language appropriately and articulately. No more than 1 spelling, grammatical, or style mistake per page.	Meets standard expectations for theological plain style in an academic voice. Uses language appropriately and articulately. No more than 2 spelling, grammatical, or style mistakes per page.	Paper is generally well written, but sometimes lacks purpose or relevance to the topic. Averages 1 to 4 spelling, grammatical, or style mistakes per page.	Paper is generally well written, but often lacks purpose or relevance to the topic. Reader is easily distracted. Averages 5 to 10 spelling, grammatical, and style mistakes per page.	Paper is poorly written, lacks purpose or relevance to the topic. Has multiple spelling, grammatical, and style mistakes on every page.

(cont.)

ELEMENTS	A RANGE (4)	B RANGE (3)	C RANGE (2)	D RANGE (1)	F – FAIL (0)
Method	Follows creatively a specific disciplinary method, addressing all elements called for by the method. The methodology is clear to the reader.	Follows a specific disciplinary method, addressing some but not all elements called for by the method. The methodology is clear to the reader.	Follows a specific disciplinary method, addressing some elements called for by the method, but the methodology is not clear to the reader.	Follows somewhat a specific disciplinary method, addressing only one or two elements called for by the method. The methodology is not clear to the reader.	Does not follow a recognizable method.
Argumentation	States claims clearly and reliably based on strong grounds and warrants, and incorporates qualifiers and rebuttals.	States claims clearly based on reliable grounds and warrants. Limited use of qualifiers and rebuttals.	States claims that may be based on grounds and warrants, but the argument is not clear.	States claims that may be based on some grounds and warrants, but the argument is not clear and is questionable on more than one point.	Uses fallacious arguments.
Conclusion	The conclusion is succinct and persuasive. It is strongly evidence based, and inferences are sound. It correlates with the introduction.	The conclusion is persuasive. It is evidence based, and inferences are sound. It correlates with the introduction.	The conclusion may have some merit, but some of the evidence is weak or inferences are questionable. It doesn't correlate with the introduction.	The conclusion is not persuasive. The evidence is weak, and the inferences are questionable.	The conclusion is not persuasive at all. The evidence is scant or nonexistent. Inferences are highly questionable.

chapter seven

ACADEMIC THESES AND DISSERTATIONS

A first theological degree is usually earned by passing courses and examinations. The second one culminates with major research, often called a thesis, at the master's level. At the doctoral level, the same kind of work—but longer and more complex—is known as a doctoral thesis or dissertation. Theses and dissertations have many common elements. One of these is the review of literature, which is important enough to deserve a separate section of the chapter. Then in the discussion of theses and dissertations that follows, the writing process from proposal to defense will be covered.

Review of Literature

A review of literature, which usually appears right after the introduction (this review would be chapter 2 if the introduction is called chapter 1) and sometimes in the proposal, reports on the books and journal articles that have already been written about the topic under research. It provides the background for the painting, so to speak. In large strokes, the review of literature paints a backdrop against which the research will be done. One professor described the review of related literature as a salute to the past: recognition of the research and study already done on one's topic. After a gentlemanly tip of the hat, one goes on to further research of the topic. Another description of a review of literature puts it this way: before inventing a new electronic device, an inventor or designer looks at all existing ones—computers, cell phones, tablets, electronic readers, iPads, and so on. This survey becomes a starting point for the inventing process.

A review of literature shows your adviser or committee that you have made a thorough investigation of the topic and have read the main works already written on it. It guarantees that there will be no going over the same ground others have covered, no "reinventing the wheel." A thorough review of the literature shows you know of what you speak.

If the proposal has a review of literature, it will reflect extensive reading; however, it certainly will not embody the total reading for the thesis or dissertation. More items that belong in the review of literature will appear in the course of your reading. They may be added later. Conversely, you may decide to remove some item from the final version of the review of related literature.

This summary of the status of research is not a series of book reviews or critiques (see chapter 9). It synthesizes information from many sources about the issue and its background and previous attempts to resolve the problem. Not only does the review of literature consider information on your problem, it also looks at studies that have used a similar methodology to solve a different problem.

The style of writing is descriptive. Synthesis is key: putting ideas together to present a big picture. Normally, the review of literature does not include interaction or discussion with the authors reviewed. Evaluation is at a minimum. For example, imagine part of a review of literature on the theological significance (tongue-in-cheek, of course) of the durian, that Asian fruit that has only lovers and haters:

> Professor Adriel Sandoval, in agreement with Yeng Ka Seng and Komarno, states that durian will be the fruit of the tree of life. (References for all three.) Sandoval goes so far as to suggest that only the durian could have been tempting enough to Adam and Eve to cause them to disobey God's instructions. (Reference.) In clear opposition to his position is that of Vasinee Suvonapong, who claims that durian came into being only after the fall, once decay and decomposition had set in. (Reference.)

Students often ask how long the review of literature should be and how many items it should contain. There is no precise answer. While it should not take up too much space, the full picture should be given. As many items as are needed to show familiarity with the topic of the research should be blended into the review of literature. This aspect of the thesis or dissertation is assessed both qualitatively and quantitatively. Usually professors tend to be more impressed by quality than by quantity. However, the omission of an item considered important by an examiner at the thesis defense may be embarrassing and require rewriting.

The amount of research already done on the topic will, to a certain extent, determine the scope and breadth of the review. If there is little research on a topic, every item available needs to be included. If much has been written on the topic, the reviewer may take a selective approach.

When a review of literature is selective rather than comprehensive, a clear rationale for the selection and omission of materials must be given. In a 1990 thesis on preaching, an MTh student chose a time limitation; he reviewed "textbooks written on preaching since 1970." The rationale followed: "This time limitation was chosen because it is unlikely that books written and copyrighted before that date would still be in print and available for use as textbooks." One might also choose to limit the authors by nationality, gender, or approach. At times the literature on a specific aspect of the problem is reviewed. An MTh student in Asia, writing on "Christian Freedom in Colossians 2:6-23," did a comprehensive review of literature (all available commentaries on Colossians and Galatians) but focused only on the question: "From what did Christ's death on the cross free Christians?"

A review of literature needs to be organized. If there are few studies, one might follow a chronological or alphabetical order for the presentation. This is unusual, however. Most reviews of literature should be organized by topic, with headings and even subheadings. As the MTh student writing on Christian freedom read, he noticed that the answers given by Protestant, Catholic, and Seventh-day Adventist scholars differed significantly, so he divided the review into three parts. The first of these sections was then divided according to what the authors said. Forty-seven items were reviewed under the following organization:

- I. Protestant Authors
  - A. Authors Who Perceive Christian Freedom as Freedom from Law
    - 1. Freedom from the Moral Law
    - 2. Freedom from the Ceremonial Law
  - B. Authors Who Understand Christian Freedom as Freedom from Condemnation
- II. Roman Catholic Authors
- III. Seventh-day Adventist Authors

A review of literature may be exhaustive or representative. In the first case, every item is described; in the second, only specific items are described. These items are chosen as representative of a larger group, all of which are carefully referenced in the footnotes. When a representative review is written, the student must be sure that the item described does, in fact, accurately represent the others.

You are responsible not only for writing the review of literature but also for designing the rationale for excluding some materials and including others and for organizing the review. Yet your thesis or dissertation committee normally has the final word. Work closely with your adviser or committee to avoid surprises.

In different types of theses or dissertations, the review of literature includes different materials. For example, in descriptive research, the review of literature includes information on other research done on the same topic, on studies using the same procedure or methodology, and on the theory that undergirds the research. In program development research, the review of literature includes literature on the undergirding theoretical basis, the group for whom the program is to be developed, and on similar programs already developed. In a dissertation on one aspect of *Heilsgeschichte*, the review of literature might contain a history of the concept and evaluations of *Heilsgeschichte*.

At times, a thesis adviser or committee may allow alternatives to the review of literature. Two options are the annotated bibliography and the bibliographical essay. The annotated bibliography briefly describes each item, thus showing that the researcher has examined it already. The bibliographical essay synthesizes what has already been written on the topic and evaluates the usefulness of the sources listed. Some thesis or dissertation committees may prefer to have you put into footnotes a vast amount of information regarding previous studies and opinions on the topic instead of writing a separate review. The thesis or dissertation produced by this method may have as much space dedicated to footnotes as to text. Make sure you know what your adviser and committee want from you before you spend weeks doing what you think is appropriate.

Theses

The Master of Arts in Religion degree often requires a thesis; the Master of Theology degree always does. What is a thesis? A thesis is generally a long and complex research paper. Instructions given on research methodology throughout this book apply also to the thesis. In fact, the research method must be even more strictly applied to a thesis than to a class paper.

The MA thesis is expected to be about 75 to 80 pages in length. For an MA in Religion, the thesis usually is a bibliographical research paper. The student's thesis adviser or committee may give permission for the student to do a major exegetical paper. Professional master's degree programs may allow descriptive research, program development, or a church-growth study as a thesis. Other possibilities are the case study and the theological issue in ministry.

The MTh (or ThM) thesis will normally be from 100 to 125 pages long.

The choice of topic will depend on the student's area of concentration. This thesis is a half-step between the MA and the PhD or ThD.

A thesis—either MA or MTh—is expected to contribute something new to the fund of general knowledge. It cannot be a mere rehash of old materials. Since the thesis allows more space in which to develop the research, the topic will naturally be more complex than the topic for a term paper. However, you should select a problem that is amenable to treatment within the available time and resources, and within the allotted pages.

Thesis writing is directed by an adviser or supervisor, often with others who form the thesis committee. You must work closely with your adviser in choosing the topic and in writing the thesis proposal, which is then approved by a committee. Each school has its own way of doing theses. Please follow instructions carefully!

The thesis process may be divided into three main segments: proposal, writing, and defense. These three aspects are described in turn.

Proposal

A thesis proposal should contain the same elements as a paper proposal. However, each part must be developed in greater detail. Whereas two pages might be sufficient for a paper proposal, an MA or MTh thesis proposal may be eight to ten pages long.

Writing a proposal is not a waste of time. What goes into the proposal eventually goes into the thesis. By the time your proposal is presented and accepted, you will have completed a large part of the reading and research.

A proposal has a title page and a table of contents. It begins much as would any normal research paper; however, the similarities with a regular paper end quickly. The whole of the proposal is an explanation of what the thesis will contain—a prophetic description, perhaps.

Your MA or MTh proposal should begin with a background for the study and the statement of the problem. You should also present the purpose and objectives of the research as well as its significance. Any delimitations should be explained. (In a thesis, limitations such as lack of time or knowledge are not acceptable; they are considered excuses for poor work and their presence may suggest you need a different topic.) Define any terms that may not be clear to your readers. State your presuppositions if appropriate. Explain the method you are using. If the study is historical or bibliographical, a description of the methodology is fairly short, yet each step of the procedure must be carefully delineated. Describe the kinds of sources you will use, how you will go about your search for information, and how one part of the research will relate to another. If the thesis follows another form of research, an appropriate description of its steps must be included.

The proposal of descriptive research demands additional information. The "instrument"—that is, the questionnaire or interview schedule—forms part of the proposal, and the way in which it will be applied is fully described. Information on the population to be surveyed, sampling techniques, data to be obtained, and the statistical treatment of the data must be provided. In some cases, this section will be sufficiently long to merit an independent chapter. The adviser usually makes this decision.

Proposals for other kinds of research have their own characteristics. A proposal for an exegetical thesis will state the problem in the text; it will also take into account how others have tried to solve the problem. It will clearly delineate the method to be used. In a case-study proposal, the introduction will give the case, together with its background, and the topics that will be examined to explain the dynamics of the case, both sociological/psychological/cultural and theological. In a program development thesis, the steps to be taken must accompany the statement of the problem and the other basics noted in the first paragraphs of this section.

Following the methodology or procedure section, a detailed tentative outline is presented. This may be done in either format indicated in chapter 12 or in the format of a table of contents (chapter 20). The outline is prepared in close cooperation with the adviser, who usually makes sure the whole committee (if there is one) agrees on the proposed organization of the thesis. The tentative outline forms part of the proposal.

The last part of the proposal is a working bibliography that lists all items already considered. It will not include all the materials you will eventually use, for it is tentative and subject to change. However, the committee expects to see a promising list that includes all the best and recognized sources for the research.

A search for sources for a thesis must go beyond the library of the school where you are enrolled. You will get some materials through interlibrary loan; other items you must find at other libraries. (WorldCat, at www.worldcat.org, can help you find which libraries near you have an item.) Then there is the internet. Learn to use the latest technology. Plan on becoming a library addict before you finish your work.

Your adviser or thesis committee will meet with you to finalize the proposal. You will present your views, and the professors will stipulate their requirements. The proposal is either accepted as it is, accepted subject to certain changes, or rejected. A final copy of the thesis proposal is usually filed with the program director not only to certify that you have fulfilled this requirement but also to serve as a model for students who will follow you.

The proposal serves you and your adviser or committee as a guide to your writing. It is something of a contract made between the two sides. Departing from the path laid out in the proposal could be dangerous: "There is a way that seems right to a person, but its end is the way to death" (Prov 14:12).

Once the proposal has been approved, thesis research and writing begin in earnest. From now until you finish it, the thesis will dominate your life. Some suggestions for the writing and research of a thesis are given in the following section.

Thesis Writing

After your proposal has been accepted, you will continue reading, researching, and taking notes. The greatest part of the time needed to prepare a thesis is dedicated to these activities. Only when you complete this process should you begin to write. There is no point in writing a chapter without having all the information.

Perhaps the most important advice for a thesis writer is to work closely with the thesis adviser and/or committee. Be sure the adviser agrees with any deviation from the original plan. If the work is guided by a committee, make sure you have a committee decision on what you are to do, rather than one member's opinion. If your professor is one who writes out the comments on your work (or uses "Track Changes"), you are indeed blessed. Never mind the red! It is acceptable for you to nudge your adviser to give comments in writing. Suggest that you need to be sure you are doing the right thing. You need not mention that you are trying to make sure the professor does not have a change of heart and mind and ask you to do something different.

Plan enough time for the adviser and committee members to read all the parts of your thesis. Remember that professors are usually too busy to read your chapter overnight, simply because you have handed it in and are in a hurry to graduate. It is imperative to develop—and follow—a timeline that allows time for reading and corrections. This goes for both you and the adviser.

Thesis typing is a major enterprise. Finding a thesis typist may be almost as hard as writing the paper. In addition, you are still held responsible for typing and format errors. With today's technology, students usually do their own typing—on the computer. If you don't already do it easily, learning to touch-type and to use a word-processing program are highly recommended.

The quality of English required for a thesis demands special attention to editing. You are responsible for getting the necessary editorial help to polish the English. The adviser or committee chair may improve the language and style of writing with his or her corrections, but the adviser's main task is to direct in matters of content. The institutional thesis editor will indicate format corrections necessary, but does not have time to rewrite problematic English.

Generally, the thesis must be given to the examiners at least one week—or as much as four weeks—before the defense date. While the examiners read your thesis, you will have time to check for any mistakes in the paper and to prepare the abstract, vita, and any acknowledgments you wish to include.

The preliminary parts of a thesis include an abstract of the thesis and the approval sheet, prepared according to the school's obligatory format. A model of this approval sheet, as used in several schools, appears in chapter 20. The abstract is a brief summary of the problem studied, the findings of the research, and the conclusions reached. Its normal length is from 150 to 350 words, depending on the degree and the school.

The acknowledgments are a personal note of gratitude to whomever thanks are due. Some theses are dedicated to a special person, but this is not necessary. In any case, wisdom suggests moderation and reserve in the expressions of thanks.

The order of the preliminary pages is fixed by each school. However, the following is considered normal: blank page, abstract title page, abstract, thesis title page, blank page, approval sheet, dedication, table of contents, list of illustrations (including figures and tables), list of abbreviations, acknowledgments.

The vita, which gives the student's personal information as well as academic and professional history, follows the bibliography. This is the last item in the thesis. Check the format customary for your school and degree.

Oral Defense

When all the chapters of the thesis have been written, the conclusions have been drawn, and the bibliography is ready, the thesis adviser sets a date for the defense, if there is one. The student must make complete copies of the thesis for all the members of the committee, including the external examiner, if there is one. Each school has specific guidelines regarding the distribution of copies needed.

The oral examination or defense normally deals with the thesis and matters related to it. Usually you are given the chance to make a brief presentation of your research. Use visuals to impress the examiners. PowerPoint computer graphics add luster to the presentation.

When you come to the oral defense knowing that your thesis is well written, you need not fear. Professors are glad to "show off" a good student. Again, the need for working closely with the adviser and the committee cannot be overemphasized.

Even as late as the oral defense, changes in the thesis may be requested. Once these are completed and certified by the adviser, you are responsible for turning in the original to the dean or program coordinator. From this, as many copies as the school requires are made, always at your expense. These are bound, again at your expense, and kept as a permanent record of your intellectual achievement.

Dissertations

Most of what has been said about theses applies also to dissertations. The main difference is in the scope and length of the required work. A doctoral-quality dissertation takes time, effort, and finances. A student must plan on sufficient time for completing the dissertation—usually years!

A Doctor of Theology or Doctor of Philosophy dissertation is a major research project. It investigates a complex or difficult problem in the area of the candidate's major emphasis. This dissertation will be at least 250 pages long and may be as long as 500 pages.

The writing of a ThD/PhD dissertation takes for granted that the candidate has the language tools needed to do exhaustive research in the chosen area. A knowledge of biblical languages is presupposed. Normally, the candidate must pass examinations in French and/or German. Other languages may be needed, depending on the topic. For example, a study on early church fathers would demand knowledge of Latin.

As with the thesis, the main stages of a dissertation are three: proposal, research and writing, and defense.

Proposal

Divergent philosophies guide the proposal process in various schools. Fortunately, most schools require students to take a class in which they receive specific instructions on preparing the proposal and writing the dissertation. Be thankful if your school is one of these.

Some schools prefer to have a proposal that contains as many as three chapters of the dissertation. These schools usually have a previous step, which may be called "topic approval" or some such thing. Only after the short, unofficial proposal has been accepted can a student get down to business on the long proposal.

The long proposal usually includes three chapters: introduction, review of literature, and methodology. A bibliography is also required. All of this work is done in close association with the adviser and the dissertation committee.

Other schools want a short and succinct presentation of no more than ten to twelve pages, not counting the bibliography. This short proposal shows, in a few pages, that you know exactly what you are going to do and how you are going to do it. The review of literature is built into the research proposal, especially in the background, justification, viability, and methodology sections. All the essential ideas listed must be present but may not need their own separate headings. This proposal has three main parts: research proposal, outline, and bibliography. The outline includes chapter titles and two levels of subheadings. Here is a tentative outline for one:

I. RESEARCH PROPOSAL
   A. Background of the Problem (as needed)
   B. Statement of the Problem
   C. Purpose of the Research
   D. Justification for the Research
   E. Viability of the Research
   F. Scope/Delimitations of the Study
   G. Methodology
II. OUTLINE OF THE PROPOSED DISSERTATION
III. TENTATIVE BIBLIOGRAPHY

Research and Writing

All that has been said about research and writing applies here. A PhD student lives, breathes, and sleeps dissertation. If meticulous care in taking notes and organizing them was important in a research paper, it is triply so in the dissertation.

The relationship between a doctoral candidate and the adviser is of paramount importance. After you graduate, you will be your own boss. Until then, you need to practice submission to your adviser's wishes. Writing and defending a dissertation is not only a matter of dogged research and painful writing; it is a political feat as well. In fact, at the termination of the process, congratulations for a game well played are often in order.

An interesting and useful book by Ben Witherington III, *Is There a Doctor in the House?*, describes the challenges and opportunities of becoming a Bible scholar. In discussing doctoral programs, Witherington describes the differences between the European and American systems, especially in the writing process and the defense.[1]

---

1. Ben Witherington III, *Is There a Doctor in the House?* (Grand Rapids, MI: Zondervan, 2011), 34-36. Read the whole book; you will enjoy it.

Each school has its own rules for the interaction of candidate and dissertation adviser and committee. Obtain the handbook from your school and follow it closely, perhaps even blindly. There will be time to celebrate when the process is over.

Oral Defense

What has been said about the defense of a master's thesis holds for the ThD or PhD dissertation. After having written a masterpiece, you will be confident and your adviser will be thrilled to show you off. The defense will be a joyful exercise in which your achievements are made public. If, however, your work is merely acceptable and you have had uneasy moments with your adviser, you can expect the defense to be difficult. Given a choice, you will obviously choose the first route.

Specific guidelines for the defense procedure and the handing in of final copies of the dissertation are provided by individual schools. Become familiar with these instructions and follow them closely. You will be spared tears and grief.

At the defense, a doctoral candidate usually makes a brief presentation summarizing the research done. Practice this presentation as you did your first sermon. Make the presentation clear yet agile. Touch the high points, what the observers at the defense need to know to understand the dissertation without having read it. Use technology if it can make the presentation clearer and more enjoyable.

Asking and answering questions takes up the better part of the defense. Your examiners want to know how well you comprehend the topic and its ramifications. If you are not absolutely clear on a question (or its answer), ask the examiner to rephrase it. Doing so will give you a few seconds to think. This ploy cannot be used for every question, however. Answer the specific question asked, not one you wish the professor had asked. Refer to pages in your dissertation, especially when it is evident that the examiner did not read the document with great care. Whatever you do, do not argue with the examiners or contradict them. It is much better to say with a smile, "You may have a point there. I will be happy to consider it." When the questioning is over and the examiners sit in executive session to decide your fate, they may not remember what you said as much as how you said it.

Students usually have something to fix in or add to their dissertation. The adviser guides you through this and gives the final green light, after which you do the paperwork required by your school and pay for the copies and fees. When all is done, you can don your cap and gown and be legitimately called "doctor."

In conclusion, may your dissertation months be short and your joy at finishing your work be long.

One last type of paper remains to be discussed: the practical theology thesis or dissertation. That will be considered in chapter 8.

chapter eight

PRACTICAL OR PROFESSIONAL THEOLOGY DISSERTATIONS

The Doctor of Ministry or Doctor of Pastoral Theology, as it is sometimes called, is a professional program with an emphasis on practical theology. The variations between the two degrees are more likely to represent the differences between schools than between degrees. Both require theological reflection applied to a pastoral situation. DMin dissertations (aka projects) represent doctoral-level work but with a practical bent. Their aim is not so much to enlarge the fund of knowledge as to solve a problem in ministry and to provide the pastor-researcher an opportunity for personal growth.

Different seminaries have different requirements on the project or dissertation. However, there is an important similarity: the project will demonstrate the candidate's ability to find a problem in ministry, design an effective intervention, discover and use appropriate resources, and evaluate the results.

Timothy Lincoln describes the DMin project this way: "Written for an audience of persons engaged in ministry, the project should address an issue arising out of ministerial practice, use an appropriate research model informed by the social sciences, and interpret itself from the point of view of a Christian minister."[1]

The Doctor of Missiology dissertation is somewhat similar to the DMin paper just described. Both have a practical bent and involve the application of theory to practice.

1. Timothy D. Lincoln, "Writing Practical Christian Wisdom: Genre and the Doctor of Ministry Dissertation," *Theological Education* 36 (1999). 171.

Each seminary has its own rules—impossible to describe in detail here. However, we will attempt to give students (and teachers) an idea of what is involved in the final paper required for a professional seminary degree.

Types of Projects

DMin projects are as varied as the ministries of those who write them. Some are more practical; others can be more theoretical. Ministry or mission always figure prominently.

In-Ministry Project

A common model is the "in-ministry" project, described in chapter 5 as program development. In this kind of paper, students develop a program and apply it in their ministry setting. Preparation, presentation, and evaluation are all part of the process and the paper. The program may be as short as a weekend seminar or as long as a one-year church revitalization program. In the first case, the adviser or the DMin committee may require that the program be repeated, possibly at another location.

At Andrews University, the in-ministry project is defined in this way:

> It blends the theoretical and the practical, theology and ministry. The objective is to provide materials for the benefit of the church and to help pastors grow. The emphasis blends research, academic writing, skill development, and personal reflection. After presenting personal spiritual and theological reflection, analysis of the context, a theoretical and theological basis for the project itself, evidence of relevant literature, and description of appropriate research methods, the writer narrates and evaluates an intervention implemented over time, usually in a local church. The project document may be up to 125 pages.[2]

Descriptive research may be needed to demonstrate a need for such an intervention or to evaluate it (chapter 4). You need to know what the environment for your intervention is. You also need to be sure that you achieved what you proposed.

Your DMin project may be the place to employ action research (chapter 5). You want to use the expertise of others to plan, execute, and assess what you do.

---

2. Andrews University, Doctor of Ministry Program, "Handbook for Project Advisors and Readers," 2012, https://www.andrews.edu/sem/dmin/project/advisor_handbook/advisor-handbook.pdf.

Often the school that will give the degree requires that the adviser or mentor visit the place where the candidate is carrying out the program, sometimes at the candidate's expense. Find out what requirements your school has regarding advising of "in-ministry" projects.

More Theoretical Papers

The case study (chapter 5) is acceptable, as is the more theoretical study of a theological issue in ministry (chapter 3). There is no actual application or evaluation of a program, but ministry is at the heart of the research.

Among these more theoretical papers one could include church growth studies or strategies to reach an unreached people group. Again, descriptive research may be necessary (chapter 4). The application to ministry needs to be made clear.

Occasionally a DMin project may be more theoretical than the projects described in the two previous paragraphs. The history of a denomination in a certain country or region may be an acceptable research topic. Biographies of ministers or missionaries could also be done. However, this type of project requires exceptional writing skills and, usually, special permission from your school's authorities.

Two important parts complement each other in the project dissertation. There must be theory—the why—and there must be practice—the how-to. The proportion of each depends on the topic, the candidate, the doctoral committee, and the school. The theory includes the biblical and theological bases for the practical application as well as any explanations from the social sciences—sociology, psychology, education, economics, history, geography, culture—that may undergird the intervention. Practice is what you do, on the basis of the theory studied, to solve the problem addressed.

Stages of the Project

The DMin project, just like the thesis or dissertation, is done in stages: proposal, research and writing, and defense.

Proposal

The project proposal can be completed only after many hours of reading, thinking, and observing. Regardless of the shape of the study, the proposal is the initial and required step toward the coveted degree. Its indispensable parts—which may not be numbered from one to eight—are as follows:

1. Background information on the problem to be addressed to make the proposal clear to the readers and examiners
2. A statement of the problem
3. A statement of the task or purpose of the study
4. The justification for the study: the need for it and the contributions it will make
5. Any delimitations that affect the study (even your presuppositions, if they qualify)
6. The methodology or procedure to be followed, showing not only the areas to be researched in the library, but the practical application of the chosen intervention or program—the how. This part describes the candidate's war plan.
7. A detailed tentative outline
8. A preliminary bibliography (which in some seminaries must have at least 60 sources)

Normally a proposal for a DMin, DPTh, or DMiss does not exceed ten carefully written pages. Some schools may have different or additional requirements, such as length, a statement of intent, or a vita. Clear the requirements of your school with your adviser or program director.

The Written Paper

The project for a professional degree in theology demonstrates the ability to think creatively and to act decisively. The time spent in carrying out a plan, program, or intervention in ministry is usually not reflected in the number of pages of the project dissertation. How can you translate the hours you spent in evangelism, teaching, or administration into pages? The writing is important, but the doing usually takes precedence.

Most schools set a limit to the number of pages a project dissertation may contain. Usually, the body of the text (excluding appendixes and bibliography) should be under 150 pages. Again, professors are looking for quality rather than quantity. Be sure to follow the guidelines of your seminary or school.

The organization of the paper is similar to that of a dissertation. The first chapter introduces the topic, presenting the problem or issue, the task (or purpose) of the project, the benefits of solving the problem (justification), the approach being followed, definition of terms (if needed), and an overview of the rest of the paper. Chapter 2 normally is theoretical: biblical-theological-sociological-psychological. In fact, there may be two theoretical chapters, if needed. Other chapters depend on the topic. One must be dedicated to a narration of the intervention. The last chapter is always the same: summary, conclusions, and recommendations.

Bear in mind that often only the first and last chapters of a dissertation or project are read. Thus everything of vital importance must be in those two chapters: where you intended to go and what you found when you arrived there. Appendixes vary according to the project. For a seminar, for example, the outlines of the presentations, together with copies of the handouts and illustrations used, belong there. If there were questionnaires, they also belong in the appendix. A bibliography closes the paper.

Each dissertation is to be accompanied by an abstract, which is usually a 150-word summary of the dissertation. (Make sure you follow the instructions of your school!) The abstract includes the problem or issue, the findings, and the conclusions. The approval sheet follows the title page and is done according to the rules of your institution.

Working with Your Committee

The candidate's dissertation committee is made up of an adviser (your school may have another name for this person) and at least one reader or second member of the committee (different schools have different rules). Fortunately, the student is usually involved in the selection of the committee. The task of the adviser is to counsel and supervise the candidate in the preparation of the project. The adviser reads, marks, and returns the material to the candidate, who then rewrites and returns the material to the adviser, who reads, marks, and returns. Normally a candidate rewrites at least three times. The reader usually does not read a chapter until the adviser has approved it. Thus the adviser is far more involved in the preparation of the project/dissertation than the reader.

In working together, student and adviser should avoid pitfalls that might sour relations or delay the work. One of the dangers is that either party may forget what they said. A workable solution to this problem is for you to take notes of what your adviser said and write up a synthesis of the instructions. Give a copy of this summary to your adviser to make sure that you heard correctly. If you do this with a nice spirit, your adviser will probably thank you for making sure you both know what is happening.

Another issue that blights the project/dissertation procedure is delays, either by the adviser or the student. Suppose you work hard to complete a chapter, take it to the adviser, only to be informed that he has gone to Outer Slobovia for a series of evangelistic meetings. Or instead of finishing chapter 3 in April, you complete it at the end of May—and the adviser is up to her ears in a major writing project. The solution to this problem is to set up a timetable: when you will turn in your materials and how long you will have to wait for your adviser to read and return them. Obviously, there may still be glitches, but if you two agree, the battle is already won.

Defense

Once the project/dissertation is deemed ready for defense by the adviser and reader(s), a date is set for the oral examination, and copies are made available to the examiners—mostly online nowadays. At the oral examination you will make a brief and lively presentation of your research. You will then be asked questions about the research, its methodology, its findings, and your own conclusions. The project/dissertation may be approved as submitted, approved with revisions to be made and certified by the supervisor, or rejected. When the work has been carefully done, there is little danger of rejection.

After the defense, you and your adviser make the necessary adjustments to the paper. Then you submit the appropriate number of copies to the appropriate office—each seminary has its own rules—at the appropriate time, in preparation for graduation. Most seminaries in North America cooperate with Atla in the preparation of Research in Ministry (RIM). You can search this database at rim.atla.com. You or your school submits the abstract of your paper so that future students can refer to your work. As of spring 2019, new records can include a link to full text if available.

Other Kinds of Doctor of Ministry or Missiology Projects

This chapter has proposed general directions for DMin or DMiss projects or dissertations. In addition, specific information appears in other chapters. Three other possibilities are given as examples: a church-growth study, a church-planting project, and a strategy for reaching unreached peoples.

Church-Growth Study

A church-growth study may become an appropriate DMin project when it carefully studies the growth of a given church over time, analyzes the factors involved in its growth (or lack thereof), and designs appropriate strategies to enhance the church's growth. Occasionally, the study could include a group of churches.

Procedure

1. Become familiar with church-growth literature, both theoretical and narrative. Pay special attention to materials about churches similar to the one you are studying.
2. Investigate the growth patterns of the church over the last ten years. Get information from church records and other sources.
3. Study the climate and activities of the church during the last ten years. Read newsletters and reports; do surveys and interviews as needed.
4. Analyze the community in which the church is located. Find out about its people and its institutions, industry, schools, socioeconomic life, and traditions.
5. Come to tentative conclusions regarding the reasons for growth (or nongrowth).
6. Apply sound biblical principles of church growth, design a program for optimum growth for a specific church.

Written Presentation

The following chapters would constitute the study:

Chapter 1: Introduction

This should include a statement of the problem, justification for the study, definition of terms, and methodology used. A bibliographi cal essay or review of literature on church growth and church-growth studies pertinent to the study is appropriate here. This will give the reader the assurance that the candidate is indeed aware of what the literature says. (The scope of the review should be defined. For example, one might set limits on the time of writing or the type of church.)

Chapter 2: History and description of the church

The patterns in growth and finances are described, together with the history of the church during a defined period of time. Descriptions of current facilities, programs, activities, and membership demographics are also presented.

Chapter 3: Description of the community

This should include demographics, economics, religion, traditions, institutions, and the like.

Chapter 4: Analysis of the situation

This chapter analyzes the current church situation and possibilities for growth in light of church-growth theory, the history and statistics of the church, and the characteristics of the community.

Chapter 5: Strategy for growth

This chapter designs a strategy for sustainable growth by applying missiological and church-growth principles to the local situation.

Chapter 6: Summary, conclusions, and reflections

Appendixes

Bibliography

Church Planting

A church-planting project will take the planting of a new church from design through realization. This type of DMin project will naturally take much longer than bibliographic research.

Procedure

1. Study the literature on church planting.
2. Choose a location for the new church.
3. In collaboration with the adviser, design the plan and timeline for the church planting, together with the criteria for evaluating the final result.
4. Obtain support of church administration and members to be involved in the church planting.
5. Carry out the plan.
6. In collaboration with the adviser, evaluate what has been done.
7. Write the dissertation or project.

Written Presentation

The body of the paper (excluding bibliography and appendixes) should be around 100 pages long. The bulk of the work is in doing, not in reading or writing.

Chapter 1: Introduction

This should include the task, justification, plan, and timeline as well as the criteria for evaluation (all taken from the proposal).

Chapter 2: Theoretical basis

This chapter discusses biblical and theological principles and assumptions relevant to the project. It also gives a review of the literature on church planting under similar circumstances.

Chapter 3: Narrative of the church planting

This chapter carefully narrates the steps taken to plant the church, including dates, activities, programs, and participants. It shows how the objectives described in chapter 1 were met.

Chapter 4: Evaluation of the project

Chapter 4 narrates the evaluation process and presents its results.

Chapter 5: Summary, conclusions, and reflections

The summary is provided for those who read only chapters 1 and 2. The conclusions and reflections give opportunity for subjective evaluation of the process and suggestions for someone who might attempt to plant a similar church.

Strategy to Reach an Unreached People Group

This type of doctoral project is more common for a DMiss program than for other types of DMin programs. It is theoretical rather than practical. Such a dissertation is especially significant for those whose ministry brings them in contact with non-Christian peoples, but who are currently studying in a geographic area other than their own.[3]

Procedure

1. Read the literature on reaching unreached peoples.
2. Select a target group.
3. Study this group and its customs, beliefs, and socioeconomic situation.
4. Analyze any contacts the group has had with Christians in general and with your particular denomination.
5. Design a strategy for the specific group.
6. Write the project/dissertation.

Written Presentation

Since this is a theoretical paper, with no action, the number of pages will probably be greater than in a practical program.

Chapter 1: Introduction

This introduction states the problem, names the group and its location, justifies the study, defines terms and the methodology used, and so on.

Chapter 2: Description of the unreached people

---

3. My thanks to Bruce Bauer, missionary and mission professor, for this outline. Useful to this type of study are books such as the following: John D. Robb, *Focus! The Power of People Group Thinking: A Practical Manual for Planning Effective Strategies to Reach the Unreached* (Monrovia, CA: MARC, 1989); Bill Stearns and Amy Stearns, *Catch the Vision 2000* (Minneapolis, MN: Bethany, 1991). See also Edgar J. Elliston, *Introduction to Missiological Research Design* (Pasadena, CA: William Carey Library, 2011). See also Eric deGrove, "Joshua People Group Profile Research and Writing Guide," 2012, https://joshuaproject.net/assets/media/articles/profile-research-and-writing-guide.pdf.

Chapter 2 gives the location, culture, religion, history, socioeconomic status, health, and education of the target group. It also describes the people's interactions with Christianity in general and with your denomination in particular.

Chapter 3: Analysis of deterrents and bridges to evangelism

Chapter 3 studies factors that seem to make evangelism difficult and inquires into possible natural bridges from the group's culture and religion to Christianity.

Chapter 4: Proposed strategy

This part applies sound biblical missiological principles to design an implementable strategy for creating Christian presence among the group.

Chapter 5: Summary, conclusions, and reflections.

The summary is provided for those who read only chapters 1 and 5.

Appendixes

Bibliography

Now and then I hear people denigrate the DMin or DMiss project, comparing it unfavorably to a PhD dissertation. Such comments rankle my soul. Done correctly, this project has all the earmarks of research. It is based on solid theory—biblical, theological, or otherwise—and it contributes to the welfare of God's people as well as to the growth of ministry. May your DMin project bring satisfaction to you and glory to God.

chapter nine

WRITING FOR PUBLICATION

The two kinds of writing for publication considered in this chapter share many characteristics of research writing. Besides, professors frequently ask students to write book reviews that may or may not be published. At the doctoral level, an article accepted for publication is not an uncommon assignment. Both book reviews and publishable articles are part of the academic scene.

Book Reviews

In today's world, so many books are written and published that one cannot hope to read them all, even in the scholar's own field. In order to have an idea about the content of books you don't have time to read, you read book reviews. These give the thrust of the work, an evaluation of its contents, and an assessment of its importance.

Professors often assign book reviews to encourage students to read carefully and write thoughtfully. In some seminars, students read different books, then report on them in class so the group benefits, almost as if each had read every item. Students doing research can also benefit from book reviews as a prereading evaluation of potential sources, saving time and then focusing on the most promising.

As you can see from the preceding paragraphs, there are professional critical book reviews, as in scholarly journals, and reviews written by students. While they are different, they require similar skills. In fact, you might have an in-between review—one written for a doctoral-level seminar.

Writing the Review

Preparing a book review entails reading, taking notes, evaluating what you have read, and writing a summary, assessment, and comments concerning the book or article. That sounds like research, does it not?

A student's book review should contain four main parts: (1) a complete bibliographical entry; (2) information regarding the author(s) of the book, their academic training, position, and other books authored; (3) a summary of the book, which, depending on the length of the review, should be no shorter than one paragraph or longer than two hundred words; and (4) an evaluation of the book.

Bibliographical Entry

The format of the bibliographical entry for a student book review is the same as is used in a bibliography. Complete instructions on preparing this entry appear in chapters 20-23. For a book review, include the number of pages in the book. For reviews published in journals, the price of the journal is normally included.

Author Information

Information on the author may be obtained from the book, from biographical files many libraries keep, and from other sources, such as those mentioned in chapter 13. The Atla Religion Database also is a good source of information. Search by author to bring up the articles the person has written as well as reviews of books published. For books and some articles, try worldcat.org. These listings let you know how much an author has written, on what topics, and how the books have been received.

Summary

The summary of the book should synthesize the thrust of the book and its main arguments. Take care not to distort the emphasis given by the author. The length of the summary will depend not only on the length of the material but also on the complexity of its contents. Try to keep the summary to three or four paragraphs.

Evaluation

The evaluation of the book should be made first on the basis of the author's own objectives, as stated in the introduction. This mandates a careful reading of the introduction or preface. If the author said this book was a "simple sketch of the doctrine of the immortality of the soul," readers should not fault the author for omitting a record of the theological controversies of the Middle Ages on the subject. An author who states that the book deals with New Testament Christology would not be expected to deal with the topic in the subapostolic era.

The evaluation is often based on comparison. The content of a religious work may rightfully be evaluated by the Bible. It is correct to point out agreement with biblical teaching and any deviations. However, this must be done carefully, with documentation and an acknowledgment that the differences may be in matters of interpretation and presuppositions. At times it is appropriate to compare the book or article with another item written by the same author. This comparison may point out differences, similarities, and changes over time. A book or article review may compare the work of one author to that of another writer on the same topic. When making comparisons, one must describe the two concepts or items and then compare them. It is not enough to merely note that they are different.

The careful book review must document the author's statements, giving the page number where they were found. Sometimes a review quotes paragraphs that show the author's position. Be sure to keep in mind the author's context in order to avoid any distortion of the ideas.

Although one may disagree with the author and with the position he or she espouses, the language of a book or article review must be courteous. A well-documented analysis will be more convincing than a heated and emotional tirade. The language of a review written for a class assignment should be similar to that of research—cool, calm, and collected. Think of meeting the author of the book at a professional meeting and having him say in dismay, "So are you the reviewer who hit me so hard?"

Questions to Guide Evaluation

Broad questions to be answered are the usual journalistic queries:

1. What is the basic thrust of the author's work? In a nutshell, what is the author saying? You are given the chance to summarize the work in a few paragraphs.
2. Why does the author say that? What is in the training and background that leads the author to the conclusions expressed? It is important to place a book or article in its context; a person writing from a background of poverty and oppression will not write as would someone from a rich and privileged position. You need to be sensitive to the differences.
3. To whom is the writing directed and for what purpose? Is this work intended for children or scholars? The audience is vital to the tone and content of the piece. What is the author trying to achieve? The author usually does not keep you guessing, but lets you know.
4. For whom or what (or against whom or what) does the author stand? Answering question 1 should help answer this question. If the author states a position, you will have no trouble repeating it. If the author does

not, be careful to state this accurately. You know how you feel when someone accuses you of having said something you did not say—or mean.

5. How well has the author met the objectives? Do not judge an author by what you think should have been said as much as by what the author set out to do. You usually will find that information in the introduction of the book or article. If the idea was to write a brief introduction, you should not expect an in-depth treatment of the topic.
6. How does this work compare with other writings—either by the same author or by another author in the same field? You will have to read carefully and widely to answer this question. You may want to compare what the author wrote ten years ago and what was written now, or you may compare one author's work with another author's work.
7. What is your opinion of this work? What is it good for? Who will benefit from reading it? This kind of evaluation requires careful thought.

These questions are designed to help you analyze and evaluate thinking and writing. To evaluate content, you must be conversant with the topic. Perhaps professors assign reviews to motivate students not only to read the book but also to study the topic under consideration.

A Sample Review

Since "a picture is worth a thousand words," an example of a book review may be more useful than an explanation.[1] Please note that if your review is for publication (not a class assignment), you must follow the format stipulated by the journal where you want it published.

Sessoms, Rick, with Tim Brannagan. *Leading with Story: Cultivating Christ-Centered Leaders in a Storycentric Generation*. Pasadena, CA: William Carey Library, 2016. xxiv + 246 pp. Softcover. USD 14.39.

Rick Sessoms appears to be a widely-travelled author with an impressive website (www.freedomtolead.net). The subtitle of the book is Cultivating Christ-Centered Leaders in a Storycentric Generation. The book addresses the needs of leadership development in oral or, as he puts it, "storycentric" cultures. The reality is that this pertains to the majority of

1. If you were to put this review into the bibliography of a paper you are writing, you would format it as follows: Moyers, Bruce. Review of *Leading with Story: Cultivating Christ-Centered Leaders in a Storycentric Generation*, by Rick Sessoms with Tim Brannagan. *Andrews University Seminary Studies* 55 (Spring 2017): 154-155.

the world, increasingly so in the West, where more and more people are screen-oriented rather than book-oriented. The objective of his organization, Freedom to Lead, is to "bridge the gap between character formation and ministry development" (214).

It is not a simple task to impress such a literate audience as the readers of this journal with the realities of the majority-world, where learning is accomplished through story, poetry, art, and song rather than by reading books and articles. The reality is that a significant number of students in the Seminary where I taught come from storycentric cultures, where they are accustomed to learning in a very different format than formal classes with lectures. Another striking reality is that we are training pastors and leaders to work in an increasingly storycentric world, even in the West, Europe, and North America. Such is the new migratory world in which we now live. The importance of this may be seen in the recent national elections in the United States. Traditionally, politics were (assumed to be) rational and information-fed. We now are adjusting to a political scene that appeals far more to the emotions, fears, and feelings. People vote how they "feel" more than what they "read," in spite of the irrationality. For Christians, this may suggest why the charismatics and Pentecostal churches are so rapidly expanding, while the more staid, formal religious bodies shrink.

The first part of this book (chapters one to three) wonderfully alerts the reader to the importance of relating to a storycentric culture. For seminary teachers, this is an important reminder to be sensitive to the majority-world students in their classes, and to the need to speak, effectively, to post-modern congregations through their students. The first three chapters, in themselves, are worth the price of the book.

Unfortunately, the book seems to lose its storycentric push as chapters four through twelve move into the area of leadership development, with a strong emphasis on character development. There are only occasional references to the storycentric culture.

The bulk of parts two and three contain numerous illustrations, and perhaps this is Sessoms's nod to the importance of story. The author does give appropriate emphasis to the need for culturally appropriate leadership, important in our multi-cultural society and multi-cultural churches. A leader or pastor who understands that leadership can be different in different cultures is better prepared for the leadership role.

Sessoms gives excellent insight into the need for mentoring, as well as on-the-job training. He also stresses the need to treat people at the level of their potential, enabling and empowering nascent leaders.

One of the strong points of the book is the inclusion of a numbered summary at the end of each chapter. Actually, reading these before the chapter alerts one to the author's major points of emphasis.

In critique, I sometimes found Sessoms's stories and illustrations sufficiently vague to leave me wondering at their authenticity. They seem too "pat" to be genuine. Otherwise, he is very familiar with leadership, leadership training, and the minefields of culture.

The final chapter, "The Garden Project," is a very practical, very helpful recapping of the book. He does this by using his ministry, Freedom to Lead, as a model of what can and should be done. It ends with a very well done "Lessons Learned" section that pulls the rest of the book together.

Who should read this book? Missionaries and professors of missions are a major target of the book. They are on the front lines of cultural differences. However, in our migratory world, with its emphasis on multiculturalism, pastors and professors of leadership will also benefit greatly from this small volume. Homileticians would also receive benefit from this reminder of how important story, poetry, art, and song are in changing people's worldviews and cementing new insights into malleable minds.

Berrien Springs, Michigan *Bruce Campbell Moyer*
Used by permission.

Journal Articles

Now and then a professor may allow students to choose between writing a paper and publishing an article. Students may get through their classes without writing and publishing a paper; professionals must write for publication—their advancement depends on it. Therefore, it is appropriate here to talk about writing and presenting articles for publication in a professional journal.

When you think about writing for publication, you must take two items into consideration. In what journal will it be published? What is the content of the paper?

Periodicals Where Articles Are Published

Every journal or magazine has its own style. Some may publish research articles on the Bible or theology. Others publish articles dealing with pastoral work and may want articles that narrate how a certain process has been done. Some magazines want devotional material. Authors need to know exactly for whom or what they are writing.

Every periodical has its own style, its own requirements. You can go to the periodical's website to find "Writer's Guidelines" or something similar. Be sure to follow those guidelines exactly. These guidelines tell you what kinds of articles the periodical is looking for, how long they should be, and what the format for references is (in parentheses in the text or in endnotes). The editors may also ask the writer to submit a précis or abstract of the article.

In times past, all communications between a writer and the publisher were by mail, with printed copies of the article. Today, articles are submitted electronically—according to the publisher's instructions. By all means, follow the publisher's directions and do exactly as you are asked. Don't waste time or get upset by trying to be your own boss.

Writing an Article

The initial process for a journal article is the same as for a paper. Follow the steps of research described in this book. Once you have completed the research, you will write the article—following the publisher's rules.

Just as in research papers, articles in research journals must contain quotation marks and references. The references may be presented as in-text citations (see chapters 22 and 23) or be footnoted (see chapter 21). But you don't make the decision. The publishers do. Of course, you will have fewer issues with references if you are writing something devotional. Once again, in preparing an article for a specific journal, follow the instructions of the publisher exactly.

Publishers of periodicals want you to say what you have to say in as few words as possible. If you can say it in five words, don't use seven. People don't have time for any flowery expressions or preachy language.

The content of an article must be something new, different, beyond the ordinary. It is not a good idea to submit a viewpoint or analysis that has already been written, even if not in the periodical you are writing for.

To make sure that you have a good article, have a colleague read and critique it. Don't be afraid that you will be "criticized." A reader will only "critique" your work, which means you can learn how to do a better job from the reader's comments. I know it is sometimes hard to accept what others have to say about your work. Here's where humility is a virtue. I'd much rather hear the comments from my friends than from a publisher.

Once more, follow the rules in whatever guidelines the publisher has established. Don't try to change the rules. If you don't follow the rules, the publisher has no problem returning your work with a thanks-but-no-thanks note.

The Publication Process

When you send an article to a publisher, it is understood that you are not sending it to anyone else. There will be time to try elsewhere if your first publisher says no.

When your article gets to the publisher's office, its arrival is recorded and an editor looks at it quickly to determine to what reviewers it will be sent.

A copy of the article, with no indication of who wrote it, then goes to two or three reviewers who go over the article and send it back to the editor with their comments. A reviewer may suggest rewriting a section, adding or subtracting something, or not publishing it. In case the verdict is negative, the reviewer must give reasons for not accepting the article. When the reviewers have completed their work on your paper (often using "track changes" or an equivalent), they return it electronically to the editor.

With the comments of the reviewers in hand, the editor goes over the article and makes a final determination: publish as is, return to the author for improvements, or simply thank the writer for the effort. If the article is accepted, the editor decides who will do the editorial corrections, and the red ink process begins. When it is finished, the chief editor usually gives it a final look and sends it to the person who does the formatting. If the article is not accepted, the editor usually writes a note explaining what was wrong. The note to the author may simply state that "this article does not agree with our standards, style, objectives, or emphasis." With any luck, there are instructions for rewriting.

Well-known professionals may get their articles published easily. However, new writers can expect rejection letters. Please don't be discouraged if that happens to you. Consider any and all instructions and rewrite your article. By the way, your professor may be a big help. Professors probably have had articles rejected and understand how you feel. They can help you do better the next time. But please remember they are human. Because this kind of request is above and beyond their normal duties, they may not be free to spend all the time you need.

Now that you have learned how to put different kinds of papers together, you are ready to start writing!

Part Three

Carrying Out the Research

We have seen the different kinds of research a student in a theological program might be asked to do. We will now look at how to go about producing a good research paper.

Starting with an overview of research thinking, we will look at how to plan research, then how to find and evaluate sources—both in the library and on the internet. Chapter 15 deals with reading and taking notes, while chapter 16 describes research writing. The parts that a paper should have are the topic of chapter 17, and chapter 18 goes into detail on notes and bibliographical entries. To assist students in practical theology, chapter 19 presents the basics of statistics and their graphic representation.

chapter ten

RESEARCH THINKING

Research has a special way of thinking attached to it. Or perhaps it would be better to say that research is built on a particular way of thinking, which Sharon Rallis and Gretchen Rossman describe as inquiry. Inquiry is a "process of curiosity." Inquiry "includes elements of science (planning, deliberation, systematizing) and of art (curiosity, imagination, emotion)."[1] Inquiry, these authors point out, is "a planned, purposeful, and systematic process for collecting information, making decisions, and taking action as a means of contributing to knowledge."[2]

Much more could be said about the theory of inquiry. However, we have chosen to look at one application of inquiry in a fairly contextualized way, and for our purposes, we label it "research thinking." This includes a specific mindset, certain thinking processes, the asking of many questions, and the overarching issue of intellectual honesty within the context of "doing research" and writing the results.

Research Mindset

Researchers start their work from the premise that knowledge is attainable and that finding truth is possible. The quest may be long and difficult, but results are assured. Without this optimistic mindset, little research would take place. The research mindset is characterized by objectivity, focus, clearly set presuppositions, and logical organization. In a more biblical frame, it is adorned by humility.

Objectivity

A much-touted component of the scientific method of research is "total" objectivity, which states that researchers should be able to detach themselves from

1. Sharon Rallis and Gretchen Rossman, *The Research Journey: Introduction to Inquiry* (New York, NY: Guilford, 2012), 9.

2. Rallis and Rossman, *The Research Journey*, 45.

their preferences and convictions, and dispassionately consider the evidence. Our definition of research takes this expectation into account. Therefore, we define research as the grounded, intentional, and savvy analysis of an object. The object under analysis may be a natural object, such as an archaeological artifact; it may be an idea, such as the Trinity; it may be a social artifact, such as a religious text or a survey of church members. The foundational assumption is that the "object" exists outside of the researcher and is accessible by others. Where the conventional assumption about objectivity becomes challenging is when instead of analyzing the object, I construct my own interpretation according to my own desires. What I end up with is a piece of fiction or a work of art. What must be applied are grounding the analysis in collective prior knowledge, defining a particular method or intention, and understanding and following the conventions of analytical thinking skills. It is counterproductive to put aside all prior learning and life experiences, which are the conceptual frameworks through which we make sense of the world, even in research writing. Furthermore, it is shared life experiences that make the communication of our findings possible. The desired outcome of the research-writing process is, after all, the creation of a new textual "object." To the degree that readers are able to align their understanding of the "object" to that of the author, practical objectivity has been achieved. If the work is something only the author can understand, then it is indeed subjective.

While one might have to admit that "total" or, even better, "omniscient" objectivity is not probable, a researcher's goal is to provide as thorough an analysis as possible. This means that one must be sure that the presuppositions are reasonable and that preferences and prejudices are placed in abeyance. In constructing a credible argument, one must consider all the evidence—pro and con. When documenting our own ideas, we find it easy to weight the evidence in our favor. Objectivity demands that we look also at counterevidence. I once asked a student why he had not included a certain author in his paper. The answer was quick: "Oh, but he does not agree with me, so I could not use him." His objectivity score was very low, below passing.

Think of a courtroom. The prosecution makes a case. The defense makes a case. Arguments that take into account and provide a reasonable explanation of the counterevidence presented by the other side are strengthened. Arguments that ignore counterevidence will appear weak. It's up to the jury to decide.

Objectivity requires me to consider negative evidence, to analyze ideas that are foreign or different, to look at arguments that might upset my position. Being objective requires courage and humility; it demands putting pet ideas on hold while examining all the evidence; it insists on developing wisdom to consider every facet of a topic.

Finally, the direct benefit of objectivity in academic writing is that the end product is more accessible to the reader because the signal is clear and understandable. Subjectivity introduces noise that interferes with clear and accurate reception.

Focus

With Paul, a researcher must say, "One thing I do" (Phil 3:13), and focus on the problem and its solution. Research thinking must fly straight as an arrow, without deviating from the goal. For that reason, you cannot begin researching until you have determined exactly what your problem and purpose are—what needs fixing and how you are going to do it.

Some cultures (and languages) enjoy a way of thinking that repeats ideas and information. Take, for instance, the stories of the Hebrew Bible. In Genesis 24, the phrase "Drink, and I will water your camels" appears three times: when Abraham's servant prayed (v. 14), when Rebekah said similar words (v. 19), and when the servant told her family about it (v. 44). Repetition is natural and normal. However, in research, there is no space for saying the same thing twice. "Say it well, say it once" is good advice.

Another way of thinking allows for digressions, going off on tangents. You may find fascinating information, but if it does not further your argumentation, you will have to set it aside. Keep focused on your goal. As Deuteronomy 5:32 admonishes, "You shall not turn to the right or to the left."

Clear Presuppositions

A presupposition is a basic understanding that undergirds one's thinking on a given topic. Sometimes presuppositions are called "assumptions," what we take for granted. Such a presupposition appears in Hebrews 11:6, "Whoever would approach him [God] must believe that he exists." Attempting to approach God without believing in God's existence makes no sense.

Presuppositions are the givens, the things we do not need to explain—at least not to ourselves. My understanding—of life, of what I read, of what I judge—depends to a great extent on my presuppositions. If I believe in a recent creation, this basic understanding colors everything I read about theistic evolution. If I am convinced of the depraved nature of human beings, Rogerian counseling, with its emphasis on the neutral or good nature of human beings, makes me nervous. In both cases, the opposite is equally true.

At times authors do not state their presuppositions. They may, however, give hints through their choice of sources, their way of organizing information, or their commendation of ideas or authors. If authors do not state the presuppositions, readers spend unnecessary energy wondering what the author believes.

In the area of religious studies and theological education, presuppositions are usually strong, often considered matters of life and death, vitally important to who I am and what I say. To sweep presuppositions under the rug and pretend they do not exist is unwise and impossible. However, it may be difficult to articulate your presuppositions.

An important task in research thinking is to ask this question: "Which of my presuppositions affect the way I think and write?" Simple presuppositions deal with assuming that readers are familiar with the topic. For example, I assume that my reader can understand the Greek words I put into my paper. At a somewhat deeper level, I accept Paul as a historical figure, an apostle, and a writer of several canonical New Testament books; I assume my readers do too. Even more influential on my research outcome would be the acceptance of Romans as an inspired and authoritative book. These convictions will set the tone for my analysis of Paul's death-and-resurrection motif in Romans 6. To let my readers know what my basic assumptions are is not merely courteous; it ensures that they will understand what I say.

To understand a friend, I need to know "where she is coming from," to use a popular phrase. To know what my writing means, my readers must know where I am coming from and what my presuppositions are. It becomes my duty to explain to my readers the presuppositions that underlie my research. Before doing that, I will first have to bring my presuppositions into the open, list them, and decide which ones I must describe for my readers. My statement of presuppositions must be written in a way that explains my writing without making readers feel like I consider them to be heretics or fools if they do not share my presuppositions.

To summarize, presuppositions are neither bad nor good—they simply are. And readers have a right to know which ones are guiding an author's research and writing. It is frustrating for readers to wade through pages and pages of information wondering where the author stands on the topic.

Organization

When my mother would catch a glimpse of my messy room, she would remind me of Alexander Pope's assertion, "Order is Heaven's first law."[3] Whether order is the first or second law matters not; in research thinking, order and organization come near the top of the list.

3. Alexander Pope, *Essay on Man*, ep. 4, 1.49.

Organized thinking puts similar ideas and concepts together; everything has its own place. For example, a paper describing an unreached people group would describe various characteristics of these people: sociocultural, religious, political, and economic. You would not expect to find their history or the plans laid by mission societies to reach them under these categories. Nor would you expect to find a description of their diet under the heading "Religion."

Organized thinking places ideas, phrases, and words in a logical order, allowing the reader and hearer to guess immediately the criteria used to organize them. In other words, the order makes sense. For example, the organization could go from small to large, from deep to shallow, from important to inconsequential, from old to new—or any number of logical sequences. In history, for example, we expect to proceed chronologically.

Think of the organization of a zoo. Elephants and lions do not share the same enclosure. Song birds and birds of prey are not in the same cage. Cats and rabbits don't do well in the same space. There are good reasons for the "organization" of animals and birds and other creatures.

Yes, order should prevail in research thinking and writing—not only in my messy room. Samuel Smiles was right to urge, "A place for everything and everything in its place."[4]

Humility

Humility is a basic Christian virtue. Christ presented himself as "humble" (Matt 11:29) and indicated that those who humbled themselves would be exalted (Matt 23:12). Paul and Peter appealed for humility in the dealings of one Christian with another (Phil 2:3; 1 Pet 3:8; 5:5). James tied research and humility together by stating that "humility . . . comes from wisdom" (Jas 3:13 NIV).

When a book or an article exudes arrogance—a know-it-all, better-than-everyone-else attitude—readers soon lose interest. A wiser path is to write in a way that is humble, tentative, willing to learn. This kind of writing makes room for dialogue, for reaching solutions.

Above all, conclusions should be stated in language that shows humility—willingness to learn, to accept other possibilities. After all, few researchers, especially students, would be willing to lay down their lives for the results of their research.

---

4. According to "The Idioms" (https://www.theidioms.com/a-place-for-everything-and-everything-in-its-place), "The origin of this phrase is associated with many notable people in history including Benjamin Franklin, Samuel Smiles and Mrs. Isabella Beeton. It has been used in a story which was published in 1799 called 'The Naughty Girl Won' by the Religious Tract Society. In the Oxford Book of Quotations it is mentioned that the phrase has been in existence since the 17th Century."

Thinking Processes

According to Bloom's taxonomy of the cognitive domain of learning, knowing and thinking take place at different levels.[5] Knowledge is the simplest. Thinking about knowledge is more complex: for example, analysis and synthesis, evaluation and application require more complex thinking skills. The process of making deductions and inferences is important to research thinking.

Analysis and Synthesis

Both of these processes are indispensable to good research. Analysis could be exemplified by a small boy taking an alarm clock apart to find out what makes it tick. Synthesis is putting parts of three clocks together to make one functioning alarm piece.

Analysis is examining the evidence piece by piece. Analysis requires description and classification of each aspect of a topic, each piece of a history. Analysis demands considering what each piece is, what it does, and how it fits with the other pieces. Before deciding how to teach a history class, the new professor carefully analyzes the syllabi of the predecessor and of two colleagues who teach the same course in other universities. The professor looks at all the parts, all the details, and sees what each part is and how it fits with the rest.

Synthesis, by contrast, begins with two or more ideas or systems. After studying how each one works, you put parts of the old together to form a new idea or system. Our new history professor takes the pieces and parts of the three syllabi, adds his own ideas, and creates a new syllabus for the course. While it may be built on previous work, the course syllabus is a new creation, a wise combination of several sources, a synthesis.

Analysis and synthesis are mental activities. They may appear in writing, but they first take place in the researcher's mind. In a paper, analysis usually appears in the body of the paper, while synthesis is more evident in the development of a model or a program, or in the conclusions at the end of the paper.

Application and Evaluation

Application and evaluation are at the deepest level of Bloom's taxonomy. These are not lightweight activities.

Application refers to using information. One applies rules of Greek orthography to write Greek correctly. One applies exegetical principles to derive a coherent meaning from the text. One applies church growth principles

---

5. See Benjamin S. Bloom, *Taxonomy of Educational Objectives* (Boston, MA: Allyn & Bacon, 1984).

and procedures to add new members to a church. Application of information requires thought and insight. It answers questions such as these: So what? How can this be used? What can I do with this information? Knowing without applying could make for useless knowledge.

Evaluation does not use information to do something; rather, it uses information to decide whether something is of value. Evaluation requires setting up criteria by which to measure. One must not only answer the question, How good is this? but also, How do I know this is good?

Research must constantly evaluate. Is this evidence valid? Is this quotation good? Is it appropriate? Is there a better one? Does this idea fit well here? Are these the best words to use? Does this author's work deserve further attention? Finally, researchers should be able to evaluate their own work: Have I done a commendable job? Where could I do better?

Inductive and Deductive Reasoning

Both inductive and deductive reasoning are used in research, and both may be needed in the same paper. Yet if I use faulty procedures, both can yield invalid results.

Induction has been defined as the process by which people discover and prove general propositions. Starting from the particulars, we formulate conclusions, laws, and principles. Inductive reasoning is at the heart of the scientific method. Inductive reasoning undergirds surveys, polls, and advertising.

We are perhaps acquainted with "inductive" Bible study. We might carefully study the Sermon on the Mount (Matt 5-7) and then state the principles of the kingdom that Jesus taught in that sermon. In a similar vein, I could taste apples from a hundred different trees, noticing the color, the texture, and the flavor of the fruit. From my research I could induce that apples are a sweet-tasting fruit with whitish flesh and seeds in the center.

As useful as inductive reasoning is for research, it has pitfalls. One of the most serious is the use of limited observations. If I taste only red apples, I could conclude that all apples are red. Recently I saw a poll of students' favorite drinks on a certain campus. I was interested until I found that the report was based on the preference of fifty-five students on a campus of more than three thousand students. Furthermore, there was no information on how these students were chosen. Were they buddies of the researcher? Were they all women? What was their age? Did they really represent the whole student body? How could I be sure that a certain cola drink was truly the favorite?

Inductions will be more accurate the more thorough the study of the phenomena. To find out what Paul says about church elders, I need to study all the passages in his writings and in the book of Acts that touch on what elders should be and do. I need to analyze and compare them, especially where I see discrepancies. Only then will I be able to induce and synthesize what Paul says about elders.

Another important issue is the way I state my conclusions. Apples are sweet. Always? Could I have missed a variety that is sour? Perhaps, then, I need to state that apples are generally sweet. I leave room for further conclusions, technically called inductions, derived from studying other particulars.

While inductive reasoning goes from the particulars to the principle, deductive reasoning starts from the general, the universal. *Merriam Webster's Collegiate Dictionary* defines deduction as "the deriving of a conclusion by reasoning; *specifically*: inference in which the conclusion about particulars follows necessarily from general or universal premises"; and "a conclusion reached by logical deduction."

In philosophy and theology, deductive reasoning is more common than in scientific research. After all, we work from grand and everlasting principles. For example, God is love. Because God is love, we deduce that everything God does is loving. So we look at God's activities to understand what it means for God to be love. It is easy to see that this manner of thinking can lead to circular reasoning.

Asking Questions

Doubt is considered by some as basic to research. Others call the same principle criticism. Neither term sounds good to godly ears. However, asking questions is acceptable. Research asks hard questions—questions about the source of information as well as about the content and meaning of that source. See chapters 13 and 14 for further suggestions on asking questions.

My father-in-law read his Bible and the *Reader's Digest*. Whatever he read, in either source, was true. For many, what is printed is to be believed. Research thinking demands that I question the source of information. I am especially interested in the author and publisher. Questions about the author include: Who wrote this? Is the author an expert in this field? A recognized scholar? Who funded this research? Questions about the publication in which the material appears are also important: Is what I am reading published in a reputable journal? Is the book from a credible publisher? Just as important, does this publisher have an "angle"?

As I read critically, I need to question the content. What exactly is the author saying? Is it the same thing throughout the piece I am reading? How does this compare with other items this person has written? I will also ask what presuppositions undergird the argument, what research techniques the author is using. The answers to these questions will help me discern meaning.

I will also ask what the writer wants me to know and believe after reading this piece. Is the author trying to inform me or convince me? What is the writer's intention? Obviously, if I sense that there is an attempt to coerce my thinking, I will rebel.

Then, even after I have verified that the author is an authentic expert, that the argument is valid, and that the intentions of the author toward me as reader are appropriate, I must also realize the human limitations of documentary communication. Language is linear, one word must follow another. One idea must follow another in a sequence. It is not possible to absorb all the relevant concepts simultaneously. It may take multiple readings to make sense of all the author is attempting to communicate. A second limitation is space. The author, by necessity, limits the argument to a few selected points. These points probably represent a small fraction of the author's knowledge that, without space limitations, could have revealed so much more. In other words, no matter how helpful, wise, and complete a source may seem, that source can't be considered omniscient.

In my freshman English class, I read an article about the importance of an open mind. The author posited that the mind is something like a can. If it is closed, nothing comes in or goes out. If it is open on one end, ideas come in and go out. If the lid is used as a strainer, ideas coming in can be evaluated, straining out the bad and leaving in the good. Finally, a can that is open at both ends is of absolutely no use, for ideas flow in and out with no evaluation. Research thinking demands a mind like the can with a strainer lid.

One last metaphor. The research mindset is like walking along a path bordered by two deep ditches. The one ditch is a gullibility that trusts everybody; the other is a crippling skepticism that trusts nobody. The savvy traveler stays in the middle of the road, developing a sense of who is trustworthy and who is not.

At first, the research mindset may feel uncomfortable, uncertain. As you read, think, and write, you will become more and more comfortable and confident in this way of thinking. Your professors will notice the improvement in your writing. Learning to do research thinking is worth the effort.

Intellectual Honesty

What It Is

Honesty and dishonesty are defined in different ways by different peoples. Intellectual honesty and dishonesty are also defined differently in different cultures. In some cultures, to repeat the words of the masters shows how much one respects their wisdom. Borrowing from their writings is the only way to write. Quotation marks or footnotes add nothing to that reverence.

In other cultures, the flow and beauty of the words are far more important than any admission that someone else wrote them. Even the authors are delighted to have others use their words and ideas. Or if a sick baby keeps a mother up all night just before a difficult examination, her friend is quite happy to allow her to share his learning. As an act of compassion, he even places his paper so that she can see and copy what he has written. Cheating is a nonissue.

Without evaluating the honesty of the practices just described, we Western Christians emphasize that none of these practices fits in our research culture. Here I must recognize that whoever wrote before me opened the way. That work made mine easier. Therefore, I owe that earlier writer a debt of gratitude. I must acknowledge this debt by inserting a reference to that work, giving the writer's name. In a similar vein, the writers who said what they did in words so much better than mine (compelling me to use them) produced those words—their work, their art. I have no business taking what is not mine and using it as if it were mine. Consequently, I must put these wonderful words in quotation marks, recognizing each author's unique claim to those words.

Wikipedia—which represents today's cultural consensus—defines plagiarism as the "wrongful appropriation" of someone else's "language, thoughts, ideas, or expressions." Plagiarism is associated with "academic dishonesty and a breach of journalistic ethics." Not a "crime per se," but in academia "it is a serious ethical offense."[6]

An "ethical offense" is totally inappropriate for Christian students. Unfortunately, plagiarism does happen in seminaries and theological institutions. I know. As a teacher, I've discovered it and had to deal with it. However, my school, like most American schools (secular or religious), had a policy, and some of my students learned the lesson the hard way.

Research honesty precludes my putting my name to a paper taken from the internet, whether I paid for it or not. Honesty forbids me from using my name as the author of a paper when the piece is actually an article in an obscure journal. It is equally dishonest for me to quote an author in such a way as to distort the meaning. The epitome of such dishonest usage would be to say that a reviewer found a book "magnificent," not quoting the whole sentence, which reads: "The study is a magnificent exercise in futility." All these usages fall under

---

6. "Plagiarism," en.wikipedia.org/wiki/Plagiarism. Curious to see whether there was a different take on plagiarism in the Spanish version of Wikipedia, I checked it out. There I found that *plagio* in Spanish was more a question of infringing on an author's rights.

condemnation in the commandments: "You shall not steal," and "You shall not bear false witness."

For a Christian, there are two basic reasons to eschew plagiarism. One is the commandment "You shall not steal" (Exod 20:15). There is no doubt that plagiarism is taking what is not mine without permission. That is stealing. Furthermore, if we obey the Golden Rule (Matt 7:12), we will not do to others what we would not want done to us.

Intellectual honesty at times may require me to admit that I do not know something, or even that someone else has a better answer than mine. An admission of this kind is not dishonorable. In fact, it will be applauded as honesty.

Kinds of Plagiarism

Turnitin.com touts itself as the "global leader in plagiarism prevention." For a price, they check student papers submitted to them against billions of web pages. Turnitin also has a service to help professors understand plagiarism and help their students deal with it.[7]

Their list of ten kinds of plagiarism could help students avoid the pitfall.

1. Clone: Submission of someone else's work, word-for-word, as if it were one's own, with no reference.
2. Control-C: A paper that contains significant portions of text from a source, without alterations and no reference.
3. Find-Replace: The piece changes key words and phrases but keeps the essential content, without giving a source.
4. Remix: The writer paraphrases and copies from different sources, making it all fit together, and still gives no reference.
5. Recycle: This writing adds one's own previous work, perhaps from another course, to the passage cited, without giving any reference. This is "self-plagiarism."
6. Hybrid: Such work combines perfectly cited sources with copied passages, which have no citation.
7. Mashup: This paper mixes copied material from several sources without proper citation. Furthermore, the mix shows no skills in paraphrasing, synthesizing, or summarizing.
8. 404 Error: Here we find proper citations to nonexistent sources or inaccurate information about sources.

7. See https://www.turnitin.com/static/plagiarism-spectrum/.

9. Aggregator: Such a work cites sources properly but without much original work. This form of writing just piles up sources without paraphrasing or synthesis.
10. Retweet: The retweet presents proper citation, but relies heavily on wording or structure of someone else's writing.

What to Do about It

Here are some suggestions I have gleaned over years of teaching and writing. Following them can save you from plagiarism, an offense you want to avoid.

1. Read abundantly so you have a wealth of material on your topic—even more than you need.
2. Keep careful records of what you have read—note cards, computer database, whatever way you have chosen.
3. Think carefully about what you are writing—how you will organize it, how you hope to convince your reader.
4. Use your sources to back up what you want to say, but don't make them say it all.
5. Quote your sources accurately. Use quotation marks to show exactly what is theirs, so it is distinguished from what is yours.
6. Make proper footnotes or citations for each quotation of, or even allusion to, a source you have included in your paper. It is better to insert too many notes than to forget one.
7. Read what you have written, checking every quotation and its reference.
8. Reread what you have written, thinking of the Golden Rule.
9. Mentally (prayerfully) thank the authors that have provided material, recognizing that you could not have done the paper without them.
10. Rejoice that you have put together a paper that observes the Golden Rule and thus glorifies God.

While the outcomes of intellectual dishonesty may be fearful—after all, everyone who "loves and practices falsehood" is left outside the pearly gates (Rev 22:15)—the results of following an honesty-is-the-best-policy attitude bring their own rewards. Doing what is right for right's sake is always right. It is always best.

So, with your mind in research gear, bolstered by the conviction that truth must reign, you can go on to choosing a topic. This is discussed in chapter 11.

chapter eleven

CHOOSING A TOPIC

Topics come in many varieties: good and better and best, simple and complex, shallow and deep, interesting and boring, impossible and rewarding. Unless a teacher specifically demands a certain topic, students can make the most of a topic by choosing wisely. This chapter intends to help novice researchers make a good choice.

In high school, students do a paper on "The Amazon Rain Forest." Using an encyclopedia, a geography textbook, and two websites, they can construct a five-page description of the flora, fauna, economy, and human population of the area. For a college paper, they would need to concentrate on one of those aspects. At the graduate level, the paper would need to wrestle with an issue such as "The Effect of Global Warming on Deforestation of the Upper Amazon Rain Forest." This is an example of how a topic goes from shallow to deep.

The same occurs in papers specific to the area of religion. A paper on "The Divinity of Christ in the New Testament" would be general. You could make it more specific by limiting the study to "The Divinity of Christ in the Gospel of John." Even this might be too involved for anything less than a doctoral dissertation. Much better would be "Christ as the Bread from Heaven in John 6." Not only does the topic go from shallow to deep, but it also goes from impossible to feasible.

Important steps in choosing a topic are reading, asking questions, and narrowing the scope. These steps feed on each other. Reading raises questions; questions take you back to reading. Even when the topic is assigned, following these steps can result in a better topic and, hence, a better paper.

Reading

A topic cannot be chosen in a vacuum. You cannot research an island in the sea of your ignorance. General knowledge of the area is basic. When you know how to find sources (chapters 13 and 14), you are ready to comb the library and the internet for ideas for your topic.

Textbooks are a good place to start. Dictionaries and encyclopedias may also be helpful. They do not provide topics as such, but they can help to clarify parameters and provide basic information.

The following sources provide a starting place. The first two are good, however dated, general religious encyclopedias. The third and fourth are more up to date:

Hastings, James, ed. *Encyclopaedia of Religion and Ethics*. 12 vols. and index. Revised and corrected edition. Edinburgh: T&T Clark, 1994.

The New Schaff-Herzog Encyclopedia of Religious Knowledge. 12 vols. and index. New York, NY: Funk and Wagnalls, 1908-1912; reprint, Grand Rapids, MI: Baker, 1955. (Available online.)

Jones, Lindsay, Mircea Eliade, and Charles Adams, eds. *Encyclopedia of Religion*. 15 vols. 2nd ed. Detroit, MI: Macmillan, 2005.

Betz, Hans Dieter, ed. *Religion Past and Present: Encyclopedia of Theology and Religion*. 4th ed., English ed. Leiden: Brill, 2007-.

These encyclopedias give denominational slants to the information provided:

New Catholic Encyclopedia. 2nd ed. 17 vols. Washington, DC: Catholic University of America, 2005.

Encyclopedia Judaica. 16 vols. New York, NY: Macmillan; Jerusalem: Keter, 2007.

Global Anabaptist Mennonite Encyclopedia Online. Online at www.gameo.org/. This site is continually updating and replaces the old *Mennonite Encyclopedia*.

Seventh-day Adventist Encyclopedia. Commentary Reference Series, vols. 10, 11. Hagerstown, MD: Review and Herald, 1996.

Among the many Bible dictionaries, the following could prove useful:

Ballentine, Samuel E., ed. *The Oxford Encyclopedia of the Bible and Theology*. 2 vols. Oxford: Oxford University Press, 2015.

Freedman, David Noel, ed. *Anchor Bible Dictionary*. 6 vols. New York, NY: Doubleday, 1992.

Sakenfeld, Katharine Doob. *The New Interpreter's Bible Dictionary*. 5 vols. Nashville, TN: Abingdon, 2006-2009.

For general church history, the following may be consulted:

Oxford Dictionary of the Christian Church. 3rd ed. rev. New York, NY: Oxford University Press, 2005.

For theological topics, the following provide good overviews:

Kurian, George Thomas, ed. *The Encyclopedia of Christian Civilization.* Malden, MA: Blackwell, 2011.

Patte, Daniel, ed. *The Cambridge Dictionary of Christianity.* Cambridge, MA: Cambridge University Press, 2010.

Treier, Daniel J., and Walter A. Elwell, eds. *Evangelical Dictionary of Theology.* 3rd ed. Grand Rapids, MI: Baker Academic, 2017.

On topics related to mission and mission history, consider:

Moreau, Scott. *Evangelical Dictionary of World Missions.* Grand Rapids, MI: Baker, 2000.

Barrett, David B., ed. *World Christian Encyclopedia.* 2nd ed. 2 vols. New York, NY: Oxford University Press, 2001.

As you read, take note of information on your sources. You will want to be able to find the items again. Also make notes on what you read. See chapter 15 for specifics on taking notes. Be especially attentive to questions that your reading brings up.

Asking Questions

Asking questions—of yourself, of your peers, of your professors, of the books you read—can help you determine whether you have a good topic. Questions can also help you narrow the topic and focus on an issue to research. Ask questions as if you were a five-year-old. At this point, questions concern content and feasibility.

Questions on Content

Some important questions regarding the organization of the topic might be: What are its parts? Of what larger whole is this topic a part? You can find the parts of a topic in the subdivisions of an encyclopedia article or in the table of contents of a book. For example, the *New Schaff-Herzog Encyclopedia of Religious Knowledge* divides its article on "Sun Worship" in such a way that I can see that one part would be enough for my class paper, perhaps sun worship among the Hittites.

I. Among the Hebrews
  Names and Titles
  General Conceptions
  Worship
  Date of Introduction
II. In Other Lands
  1. In General
  2. Babylonians
  3. Egypt
  4. Aramea, Syria, and Phoenicia
    Place Name
    Personal Names
    Monumental
    Testimony
    Arabs, Nabateans
  5. The Hittites
  6. India
  7. China and Japan
  8. W. Indo-Europeans
  9. Primitive Peoples

Other questions to ask regarding the history of the topic include: What has been written on this topic? Is this a controversial topic? Are lines clearly drawn between two opposing sides over this topic? What can I add to this history? For example, the discussion on Paul's intention when he informed Timothy that women should not teach (1 Tim 2:12) has a long history. Positions have been taken—on both sides. Is there something new that I can add to this history? Or will I merely be repeating what others have said and I could learn from reading?

Given the hours and hours you will spend researching and writing on your chosen topic, ask yourself: Do I find this topic interesting? Can I get excited about it? It makes no sense to commit yourself to sixty hours (for a serious twenty-page paper) with a topic about which you could not care less.

The ultimate questions involve the usefulness of the topic. What good is this topic? How can I use the results of my research? Besides me, who else will benefit from my work?

Questions on Feasibility

While you might be inclined to make heroic efforts to research the topic of your choice, certain practical considerations must prevail. The following questions deal with the feasibility of a topic.

1. Do I have the necessary sources to do this research? If the topic chosen must be researched from original documents in Bombay, a student in Buenos Aires would have difficulty finishing the task. If the chosen topic is a word study of the Hebrew word *niṣdaq*, the researcher must

have access to Hebrew dictionaries, lexicons, and word studies already done on *niṣdaq* as well as articles published in journals.

2. Am I qualified to do this research? A researcher who has chosen to study the word *niṣdaq* in Daniel 8:14 but knows no Hebrew will not be able to write a good research paper. Sometimes it is possible to acquire the skills needed to complete a research project—languages, statistical expertise, or thorough knowledge of a specific area in a discipline—but often there is not enough time to do this.
3. Do I have enough time to complete the research of this topic by the due date? This question is of prime importance to students, especially in intensive courses. If one needs to travel halfway around the world to get information to write the paper, it may be impossible to finish by the end of the semester. Some students choose topics that require interviewing someone who lives at a distance. Interesting as that research might be, one must count the cost—in time or money—before embarking on the project.
4. Does this research demand finances I do not have? The cost of mailing questionnaires or traveling to complete research can become high. The expense of typing a paper (or worse, having it typed) must also be considered. Today, computer and internet expenses must be factored into the total cost. Of course, it is not possible to escape all financial burdens, but one must take finances into consideration before settling on a topic.

In synthesis, one does well to ask Jesus' question recorded in Luke 14:28: "For which of you, intending to build a tower, does not first sit down and estimate the cost, to see whether he has enough to complete it?"

Narrowing the Topic

Congratulations for having chosen a good topic! Now comes the narrowing, the task of making the topic even more specific.

The questions asked about feasibility point to limitations: reasons why something cannot be done properly or done at all, and limits placed on the research by circumstances. Once a topic is chosen, limitations no longer count. Now we speak of delimitations—self-imposed limits that make the topic better, clearer, and more manageable.

Delimiting a study is indispensable because in doing good research, the researcher is responsible for turning up and examining every single piece of information on the chosen topic. It is as if one were putting a fence around a certain piece of land and agreeing to turn up every stone and investigate every plant enclosed in that fence. If the piece of ground is too large, the task cannot be completed. It is better to fence a small piece of ground and examine every pebble and blade of grass on it—not forgetting the small insects that might be hiding under the surface. In doing research, one must become a specialist in the chosen area.

One delimitation could be that of a time period. A research project studying the chronology of the kings of Judah would take several years to complete. It would be wiser to study the chronology of the reign of Josiah. Considering the chronological problems involved, it might even be better to study only the date of the death of Josiah. Because you set forth this time delimitation, no one will ask why you did not include other kings.

Another delimitation might have to do with sources you will use. Your topic could be an examination of the "kingdom of God" concept in the works of G. E. Ladd. Unless you are writing a dissertation, you will want to delimit the sources to one work by Ladd. In a paper comparing the divorce passages in Matthew 5 and Mark 10 you could appropriately delimit yourself to the biblical passages and commentaries on those passages. Thus you would protect yourself from accusations of not having taken into account the latest Christian book on divorce.

A paper could be delimited to include only certain aspects of a topic. For example, in writing a paper on the theology of worship, you might choose to exclude the issue of whether contemporary music is appropriate for worship. The topic would not have room for that discussion. You could, for example, state that "this study is limited to the nine texts containing the same Hebrew verb form," or that "the research confines itself to a study of the general body of Rastafarians, ignoring the splinter groups," or that "only those members whose names are on the local church books are taken into account in this study."

You will often see the phrase "This topic is beyond the scope of" this paper/thesis/dissertation. That simply means that the author has chosen certain parameters that eliminate some aspects of the topic. Of course, too many delimitations might suggest that your topic is too narrow. Choose your delimitations with care. Be sure they make as much sense to your readers, of whom your adviser is the first, as they do to you.

Selecting a Thesis or Dissertation Topic

Most of what has been said about selecting a research topic is as valid for a thesis as for an undergraduate term paper. However, a master's thesis is expected to cover more ground. The fenced-in area is larger, and the student is expected to more carefully examine the soil turned over by the researcher's spade. Normally, it cannot be simply a survey, no matter how well organized and presented, of what others have already written.

The selection of a topic for a thesis must be made in close communication with the adviser or committee. The students make the final choice, and the preliminary reading is their responsibility—but listen carefully to your adviser! Before seeing the professor about a topic, complete the initial pre-research and write down ideas on two or three possibilities. If you write out problem and purpose statements before seeing your adviser, the professor can give you more helpful advice. More information on theses can be found in chapter 7.

Just as the thesis is more complex than the term paper, the doctoral dissertation is deeper and broader than the thesis. The dissertation in theology or religion may have a practical or theoretical orientation, depending on the degree pursued. A doctoral dissertation is expected to break new ground, to provide something original. Dissertations are discussed in chapters 7 and 8.

Once a viable topic has been chosen and approved, the research plan can be implemented. Now, before looking at how to go about finding resources in chapters 13 and 14, let's consider in chapter 12 how to plan your research.

chapter twelve

PLANNING RESEARCH

Writing a research paper takes time. Some scholars find that for every finished, double-spaced, typewritten page, with its appropriate footnotes, they need at least two hours; most need three hours. On that basis, a twenty-page paper would take some forty to sixty hours to complete—from choosing the topic to handing the paper in. A dissertation may take as much as five hours for every page of the final version. If the professor requires rewriting, even more time must be allotted. Of the total time, about two-thirds is research time; one-third is writing time.

Planning takes time but is well worth the effort. The first step in planning is to define the problem to be addressed and formulate the purpose of the research. Then comes the methodology—the road map for the process. These elements go into the proposal, along with other items, such as a tentative outline and a preliminary bibliography. Some professors request a proposal even for a term paper; others want a proposal only for a thesis or dissertation. Even if the proposal is not required, the time spent in preparing one is amply repaid because the proposal brings the whole project into focus and saves time in the long run. A proposal is always required for a thesis or dissertation.

This chapter explains the first three steps: problem, purpose, and methodology. Having accomplished these steps, you will be able to write the proposal and outline the contents of your paper.

Basic Steps

Step 1: Define the Problem

Once you have a research topic in hand, you must define the problem. The problem should point to a gap in knowledge, an unclear situation, an unresolved question, a lack of information, an unknown, a specific question to be investigated and answered, or a problem to be researched and solved. It is important to state the problem because this statement guides the research. It also helps the professor give appropriate guidance. Those who do not like the term *problem* because of its negative connotations could just as easily think of the problem as an issue or even a research question.

Whether a problem is simple or complex, it must be clearly stated: Exactly what is wrong and needs fixing? In most cases, the problem is expressed in a full sentence. Note these examples:

- There is disagreement regarding the exact date of the death of Josiah.
- There is only scattered information on the beginning of the Methodist mission in the Solomon Islands.
- Lay members are frequently uninformed concerning their function in the church.
- Women in some churches in Zambia are not permitted to preach.

Often the problem, especially for a short paper, can be expressed in a question to which a direct answer may be given.

- What is the relation between tithing and the receiving of God's blessings?
- Which kind of Christian mission has won the most converts among the Muslims of Mindanao?

Regarding the transmission of religious heritage in the Jewish faith, the problem could be expressed:

- What is the role of the Jewish family in the transmission of the religious heritage from one generation to the next?

A student, writing on the history of the Guadalajara Sanitarium in Mexico, the first Adventist medical institution outside the United States, stated his problem in the following terms: "In 1897 Seventh-day Adventist leaders declared that this sanitarium was the 'most important and the most promising enterprise of the sort to have been undertaken in modern times.'[1] However, by 1907 it had been closed. Why did the Guadalajara Sanitarium fail?" (The footnote reads: [1]J. H. Kellogg, "An Appeal for Mexico," *Review and Herald*, 29 [June 1897]: 408.)

A dissertation proposal lists the following problem: "Few terms in the Old Testament have caused as many differing opinions and misunderstandings, which have been so disturbing and controversial as to lead scholars to fierce polemic, as the Hebrew word *šᵉʾôl*. In spite of valuable contributions by many scholars, there is no consensus in regard to the nature, function, and purpose of the term."

Another problem, elaborated for the dissertation proposal seminar, contains some background elements, which make the problem clearer:

> Evangelicals have assumed that while methods of evangelism may be changed, the evangelical salvation formula is the essential message of the gospel and therefore must remain the same. Thus when a spiritual seeker asks, "What must I do to be saved?" an evangelical Christian is likely to respond with terminology and concepts that have remained relatively unchanged for decades. Evangelistic presentations may now be accompanied by multimedia pyrotechnics and contemporary Christian music, but when a seeker wants to know how to cross over from death to life, the message is likely the same one the seeker's parents heard years before. This traditional way of describing the way of salvation, however, no longer elicits the positive response it once did. It seems to fail to communicate to the postmodern mind with clarity and impact.[1]

Only half in jest, it has been said that a research problem that can be written on the back of one's business card is the most apt to be solved. If the question is clear, the answer will also be clear. Time spent on clarifying the statement of the problem is never wasted.

Step 2: Determine the Purpose

At this point you must determine what to do with the problem. Are you going to analyze? Compare? Reconstruct? Synthesize? Design a program? Any of these may be a valid option, depending on the problem and what you want to accomplish.

Determining the purpose follows on the heels of defining the problem. It tells the reader (and the professor) what you are going to do about the problem. If the problem is a lack of information, the purpose will be to find that information. If the problem is a disagreement between two of Jesus' sayings on peace, the purpose could be to try to bring harmony or to understand the difference. Some examples of purposes: to reconstruct the events of a given historical period,

1. Paul Brent Dybdahl, "The Stairway to Heaven: A Critique of the Evangelical Gospel Presentation in North America" (PhD dissertation, Andrews University, 2004), 2-3, https://digitalcommons.andrews.edu/dissertations/44/.

to compare two theories, to organize certain information, to determine the relation between two events, to synthesize, to discover, or to formulate.

The purpose for the dissertation on the evangelical presentation of the gospel was described as follows: "The purpose of this dissertation is to critique the typical evangelical response to the question, 'What do I need to do to be saved?'"

The purpose of the *šᵉʾôl* dissertation was straightforward: "To examine the sixty-six occurrences of the Hebrew word *šᵉʾôl* in the Old Testament in order to discover the nature, function, and purpose of this term."

Suppose the problem is that the Christian church is not growing in the Czech Republic as it did in the first years after the fall of the Communist regime. The purpose might be to describe the growth patterns of the church or even to consider the factors affecting church growth. It might be to compare the growth of the church in the Czech Republic with the growth of the church in another post-Communist country. In a recent dissertation, a student proposed "to explore the contextual and institutional factors of the current Czech situation in order to develop a strategy rooted in Czech culture for revitalization of local congregations."

After completing this step, two things are settled: What the issue is and what is being done about it. The next question is how to go about solving the problem.

Step 3: Design a Methodology

The "method" of solving a problem is called "methodology." It is the way you go about achieving the purpose stated. This is the process you will follow. You must ask: "How am I going to do this?" In a class paper, you need to convince only the professor. In a thesis or dissertation, the adviser and/or committee need to be convinced that the route chosen will lead to a successful solution of the problem.

In theological, biblical, or ministerial research, methodology is not so clearly set out as in social science research. In fact, scholars on that side of the campus may look at the "method" used in seminary research and find only "madness." Various methods are used in seminary research. Imagine the difference between the method to uncover the meaning and function of *šᵉʾôl* and the method to develop a premarital seminar as part of a DMin dissertation. Any good research must have a clear and logical method—a way to get from here to there.

Sometimes it might be helpful to reflect on the object of the research and rely on conventional methods as indicated by the object. Our friends in the natural sciences are analyzing a physical object, whether it be a cell, a manatee, or a galaxy. Their methods revolve around measurements and descriptions, interactions with variables, and so on. Except for some archaeological work, seminary research may not use many of these methods. Much more common are projects in which the object under analysis is an idea or a concept. In that case, the method engages the practice of logic and reasoning. An example might be some aspect of the Trinity. Another common example is when the object of research is a socially created text, and the methods turn to literary analysis. An example might be the Trinitarian texts of Athanasius. In some ministerial research projects, the object of the research is people. How do young people in a local church understand the Trinity? This is where some of the social science methods are helpful. Most research projects end up being some form of mixed methods, involving texts, ideas, and people.

If your research is to be done in the library, decide where you are going to start and where you will go next. Will you trace the history first? Or will you do the exegesis of your text first? You will also need to tell your professor how you plan to use your sources. Will they be outlined? Compared? Analyzed? If the research is other than bibliographical, the methodology of the survey or experiment to be used must be even more clearly spelled out. The instrument you plan to use to gather data also must be described and/or prepared. All steps of the research must be clearly enunciated. In some cases, the section on methodology may become an entire chapter of the paper.

Some examples should help to clarify the idea. The method of the dissertation on the presentation of the gospel was expressed this way:

> I begin my study with a survey of the overall content and central themes contained in the typical evangelical gospel presentation. Thus I attempt to answer the question, What do evangelicals usually say about how to be saved? I then critique this typical presentation from two perspectives, by asking: (1) Does the evangelical response employ sound communicational principles so that it can communicate with impact in contemporary North American society? (2) Is the evangelical response true to the New Testament teaching on the steps one must take in order to be saved?
>
> In order to arrive at an answer to the first question, I explore the basic principles of communication theory. Since sound communicational strategies are receptor based, I also study the basic characteristics of North American popular culture.
>
> The second question is answered from the New Testament itself. In a number of instances (explicit and implicit) Jesus or the apostles were asked, "What must I do to be saved?" I look carefully at these instances and then critique the contemporary evangelical presentation in light of the biblical response to those who wanted to receive salvation.

> Finally, I summarize the results of my study and suggest biblical modifications to the traditional evangelical salvation formula that may communicate with more clarity and impact in contemporary North American society.[2]

A church growth study of an inner-city church could have the following methodology: (1) review current literature on inner-city church growth, including theory and practical examples; (2) analyze the community in which the church functions; (3) study the church, its growth history, its activities, its climate, its membership; and (4) design, implement, and evaluate a suggested church growth strategy for this church, based on the three previous points.

Before writing the methodology in beautiful prose, simply list the different steps. What will you do first? Second? Third? Make sure the steps are completely logical for the problem as presented and the purpose as intended. Consultation with your professor or adviser is indispensable. Additional reading may also help to clarify the steps you must take.

The Proposal

As noted above, the preparation of a project or paper proposal, even when not required by the professor, is a valuable exercise. Not only does the proposal provide a clear guide for the research process but it also becomes the basis for the introduction to the paper.

The proposal described here is appropriate for a class or term paper. A thesis proposal will, of necessity, be more complex and extensive. Proposals for theses and dissertations are described in chapters 7 and 8.

Generally speaking, the research proposal needs to include the following items. (In this outline, items that have been described in the first part of this chapter are merely enumerated.)

1. Background of the problem. This section may also show the scope or extent of the problem. It will help the reader to understand the issue.
2. Statement of the problem.
3. Purpose of the research.
4. Significance of the research (also called "importance"). Although a student paper may not have far-reaching consequences, any well-prepared

2. Dybdahl, "Stairway to Heaven," 6-7.

research paper should be useful to someone. In this section of the proposal, the following questions should be answered: Who will benefit from having this problem solved? How will they benefit? How important is it to answer this question? What is the value of this research to a given discipline? Why is doing this research important? No rule prohibits the writer from being one of the beneficiaries. One value or objective of research on Christian work for people with disabilities might be its "use by the writer for ministering to disabled people."

5. Definition of terms. An author should clearly indicate the precise meaning of terms that might not be common to the readers or might have more than one meaning. A writer might define "emerging adults" as "persons of either gender between the ages of 18 and 23." Thus the reader is informed of the exact meaning of the term in this paper. It is important for everyone—writer, professor, and readers—to be given the exact meaning of a term. If a paper is to be read by those not familiar with denominational or local terms, it is imperative for these to be clearly defined. A precise definition of theological terms characteristic of one's own tradition may be needed for noninitiated readers. Not all papers need definitions of terms.
6. Limitations of the study. Here the researcher honestly states the limits imposed by shortness of time, lack of library facilities, or language limitation. Too many limitations may suggest that the wrong topic was chosen or poor research is underway. Stating the limitations is especially useful in the rough draft of the proposal because they show your honesty and foresight. These usually are left out of the actual paper.
7. Delimitations of the study. Not to be confused with "limitations" (see above), delimitations are parameters chosen by the researcher. "While the problem of elders who do not know how to preach proper sermons is common in the whole of Tanzania, this paper will study only the issue in the Arusha Central Church."
8. Methodology. The researcher must clearly show what steps are to be followed to complete the research.
9. Tentative outline. Give chapter titles with their main sections and subsections.
10. Working bibliography. This is a list of sources already consulted and found useful to the topic. This list will grow as the research progresses. The tentative bibliography helps the professor gauge the student's familiarity with the topic.

Another item, the hypothesis, may or may not enter into the proposal of bibliographical research, but usually is present in other kinds of research. A hypothesis is the researcher's tentative solution to the problem, an indication of the expected result of the study. Sometimes called a "thesis," it is the proposed solution to the problem. If a hypothesis is clearly going to direct the research, it must be stated.

For example, in a study of the history of the early change from Sabbath to Sunday observance, the hypothesis could be the following: "Second-century Christians replaced Sabbath observance with Sunday observance because they did not wish to look like Jews." The research would present all the information to substantiate that position—without neglecting evidence to the contrary. The hypothesis could be proved or disproved by the evidence accumulated. The danger in blindly following one's hypothesis is that one might fail to see adverse evidence in the pursuit of a solution one has already decided on. If the hypothesis keeps the research on track but does not dominate it, it can be useful. See chapter 10 on "Research Thinking."

Sometimes a section on the need for the study is appropriate; it may be used as background material to the statement of the problem. However, a researcher may choose to write about the need as a separate item. Need may also be put together with the significance.

A proposal for a class paper can be written in one or two pages. A thesis proposal will be much longer and will reflect a great deal of study and research already completed. Some graduates have indicated that of the total time spent on the thesis or dissertation, one-fourth had gone into the proposal. For a thesis or dissertation, the professor (or committee) usually asks for a review of literature or equivalent evidence that the student has already read amply on the topic. On thesis and dissertation proposals, see chapters 7 and 8.

Tentative Outline

Some professors ask for a tentative outline early in the research process. Even if they do not, you should prepare one before proceeding with the research. As you read, new information may change details or even sections of the outline, but the foundation usually will remain the same. When you have finished the research and are about to write, you will produce a final outline.

The outline is the backbone of the paper. It provides the basic organization for the research report. It is also the basis for the table of contents. Each chapter must be so well outlined that student and professor can clearly follow the development of the topic. Outlines can be written using complete sentences or only phrases. The model given here is of the second kind. Parallelism in form is important. Each item that subdivides at all must have at least two parts. All subdivisions of a topic must clearly relate to the heading of which they are a part.

The following outlines, from the proposal of a DMin project on the Bhakti way of philosophical Hinduism, show that the researcher (a blind Indian professor) already has a good knowledge of the topic. The first outline is done in the traditional form, using a sequence of Arabic numerals, capital letters, lowercase Roman numerals, and lowercase letters. The second outline uses Arabic numerals and the decimal system, in a style employed in many areas of the world. Both forms are correct and acceptable since they give a detailed outline of the study. Either model should be followed precisely, including all items, such as indentations, sequence of letters and numbers, and alignment of periods. Do not mix the two systems.

1. Introduction
2. Bhakti Yoga
    A. Definition of Bhakti
    B. Ninefold Bhakti
        i. Passive Bhakti
            a. Sravanam
            b. Kirtanam
            c. Smarmam
        ii. Active Bhakti
            a. Padasevanam
            b. Archanam
            c. Vandanam
        iii. Relational Bhakti
            a. Dasyam
            b. Sakhyam
            c. Atmanivedanam
    C. Madura Bhakti
        i. Symbolic Nature
        ii. Allegorical Interpretation
3. Barriers to Bhakti
    A. Women
    B. Wealth
    C. Wrong Company
    D. Wrong Emotions
        i. Lust
        ii. Anger
        iii. Greed
        iv. Attachment
4. Summary, Conclusions, and Reflections

Notice that Roman numerals, so traditional in yesteryear, are no longer used as chapter numbers. That has to do with the difficulty of aligning the dots following them. A Roman numeral may occupy one space or four. Evidently, at the third level they are not so problematic.

The second form, much more common in Europe and Asia than in the United States, is as follows:

1 Introduction
2 Bhakti Yoga
2.1 Definition of Bhakti
2.2 Ninefold Bhakti
2.2.1 Passive Bhakti
2.2.1.1 Sravanam
2.2.1.2 Kirtanam
2.2.1.3 Smarmam
2.2.2 Active Bhakti
2.2.2.1 Padasevanam
2.2.2.2 Archanam
2.2.2.3 Vandanam
2.2.3 Relational Bhakti
2.2.3.1 Dasyam
2.2.3.2 Sakhyam
2.2.3.3 Atmanivedanam
2.3 Madura Bhakti
2.3.1 Symbolic Nature
2.3.2 Allegorical Interpretation
3 Barriers to Bhakti
3.1 Women
3.2 Wealth
3.3 Wrong Company
3.4 Wrong Emotions
3.4.1 Lust
3.4.2 Anger
3.4.3 Greed
3.4.4 Attachment
4 Summary, Conclusions, and Reflections

Your word processor can help you do these, but make sure to choose the format your professor wants. Also regarding outlines, any part that divides must have at least two parts. Have you ever been able to cut an apple into one part?

Although the formulation of a research plan—including the writing of a proposal and the preparation of an outline—follows on the heels of choosing a viable topic, this activity takes place at the same time as the initial bibliographic search. Now that we have talked about the organization of the paper, we turn our attention to finding information in chapters 13 and 14.

chapter thirteen

FINDING AND EVALUATING RESOURCES IN THE LIBRARY

Now that you know what research is (and is not) and you have narrowed down your topic, you are ready to start on your adventure. And you suddenly face many questions: Where will I get information? How can I keep together all the information I find? How will I organize it into a paper that will get me a good grade? Activities described in chapters 10 through 14 may happen at the same time. (The order of these chapters is arbitrary to facilitate organization of this book.)

Whatever you do, consider the library basic to choosing a topic, finding the right sources, and gathering the information needed. True, the internet is an important source of information—and will be considered in chapter 14—but the library is the traditional beginning point of an investigation. It remains the cornerstone of research not only because there are thousands of pages of resources, but because these materials have been handpicked for you, chosen by experts to support the course work offered at your school.

However, because of the rapid development of digital resources, the library has become much more than a building with stacks of books. The library now encompasses a vast range of sources that can be accessed over the internet. Some degree programs are completed far from the physical library, and many of the essential sources are accessed without setting a foot into the campus library building. Because of this expansion of the library into cyberspace over the internet, the line between the traditional library and the open internet may seem fuzzy. One way to make a distinction is to determine who is paying for the information. Library resources are paid for out of student tuition and institutional support on your behalf as a user. The open internet is paid for by the producer of the information. Using the library effectively means making the most of your investment.

Using the Library

The first task is to become acquainted with your home (school, seminary, university) library and all its departments. Read the library handbook, if there is one. Study the library's website. Walk through the library, noting where different collections are housed—reference works, media, special collections. Find out where the reference and circulation desks are located and what services they offer. Do not forget such basic services as restrooms and drinking fountains. Sign up for whatever library orientation programs are offered, especially if they are not required. Make sure you understand the loan policies of the library, including those for interlibrary loan. If you are an off-campus student, review the library policies that concern your access to the library materials. You should also make sure you are able to authenticate yourself as a user and that usernames and passwords get you into the resources you need. It is better to do this now before needing them becomes a crisis.

One of the best resources for using the library is the library staff. Get to know them, especially the person responsible for choosing the books in theology and religion. They will be able to answer many questions not covered in general orientations.

This section on the library will begin by describing the library catalog, including some general principles for using it. This will be followed by descriptions of the departments, such as periodicals, reference, media, and the rare book room.

The Library Catalog

Efficient use of the library begins at the catalog. While browsing the stacks is a pleasant pastime and may result in some serendipitous discoveries, the catalog is the key to locating specific resources. Most libraries now use a computer-based catalog, though some smaller and more remote libraries may still use a card catalog of some type.

One gains access to the materials in a library through the catalog, where all holdings (library jargon for books, journals, and other materials) are listed. While all the information about books is provided, the library catalog lists only the titles of journals. It does not provide access to titles of individual articles or author names. (Those will be addressed in the next section.)

Library online catalogs have become the norm for academic libraries. Protocols for metadata (information about an item added to a record) make the search process user-friendly. New ways to keep track of records for items you wish to consult are being added. More standardized features are showing up, such as "shopping carts," the contents of which can be saved, printed, or exported. Typing and computer skills are a must. Overall, catalogs are following the kinds of uses that are the most popular, such as shopping and social media.

WorldCat is an online catalog that aggregates all the records in participating library catalogs into a single catalog. Most North American libraries and a growing number of international libraries participate. If the holdings of your local library are limited, doing searches in WorldCat will provide you with options such as interlibrary loan.

Each record in the catalog divides the bibliographic information into fields. These include author, title, publication information, and many more. When you know the author of a book, it is possible to search just that field to find all the books by a single author. The same is true for the title of a book. There are also fields for location, such as the reference area, and the call number, the address on the shelf. It is also possible to search for items on a topic, but this type of search is more complex.

To better understand the online searching of a library catalog on a topic, two strategies need to be understood. A thorough search requires both.

Thinking Like a Computer

A computer is a machine that is able to process bits and bytes. To maximize the efficiency of searching a library catalog, you need to think of using code. Each letter of the alphabet is part of that code. The computer is particularly good at finding strings of attached letters separated by encoded blank spaces anywhere in the catalog. We will label these strings as "terms." The burden is on you to use terms that will pull up the records you are seeking. This form of search is known for generating many results, or redundancy, and it has a problem with relevance. Although many results won't match what you were expecting, it is still worth your time to skim the top 10 or 20 results. Relevancy algorithms are improving. Or sort by date for the most recent results. The efficient use of this form of search depends on knowing the most precise and unique terms for your topic. But if terms are too unique, you risk missing some pertinent materials.

A reasonable goal for this type of search is 20 to 50 results because it is not overly tedious to read quickly through that many sources. If you end up with way more or hardly any, several modifications to the search can be tried.

One way is to understand the relationship between terms. Some terms are broad, for example, "pet." A narrower term would be "dog." An even narrower term would be "collie." If the term "collie" does not come up with adequate results, try "dog." And if that does not suffice, try "pet." Moving up and down the terminology hierarchies will expand or narrow your search. You may also need to consider related terms, for example, teenagers and adolescents. You might need to do a series of searches to find the best resources. That is one of the benefits of the online catalog. It is almost too easy to do another search.

Boolean operators provide an additional method for finding more relevant results. The most familiar are these:

- Cats AND dogs brings up only records that have both terms.
- Cats OR dogs brings up any record that has one term or the other.
- Cats NOT dogs brings up any record that refers to cats but does not also refer to dogs.

The best way to use Boolean operators is to find the Advanced Search screen in the library catalog. This is characterized by a separate dialog box for each term, separated by a pull-down menu for the Boolean operator. In a Simple Search dialog box, AND is usually the default operator, but some databases may have OR as the default. You will need to experiment.

A third way to expand a search is to use term truncation. In English, tense and number are indicated by a suffix to the root word. There are also many compound words. The standard truncation symbol is the asterisk "*". For example, teen* could include teen, teens, teenaged, teenager, teenagers, and teeny.

Phrases can be kept together by using quotation marks. "English Reformation" is more precise than retrieving "English" somewhere in a record and "Reformation" somewhere else in the record.

Another recent trend is integrating the search of the library catalog with other databases. This is called a "discovery layer." So now a single search using terms as described above will bring up results in the library catalog and simultaneously from any number of other databases selected by the library. These searches can then be narrowed in a variety of ways, including language, year, format, location, and, in some catalogs, cloud tags. I have found this type of search somewhat frustrating for keeping the number of results manageable. But when I have a precise term(s), with only one meaning and one use, such as an uncommon place name, then useful and manageable results are achieved. For example, I did a discovery layer search on the Andrews University library's system for "Coptic" AND "Gnostic*". I had 79 results for books, and 219 results for articles. Of these books, 60 were written in English, well within my target for a practical search.

Thinking Like a Person

The second strategy for efficiently using a library catalog is to think like a person using "controlled language" subject headings or descriptors. In English-speaking countries, many of the larger academic libraries use the Library of Congress Subject Headings, while many smaller libraries use Sears List of Subject Headings. These systems arbitrarily choose one term to represent a class of related terms. For example, all the different ways we have to describe church planting are incorporated under the Library of Congress (LC) subject heading "Church Development, New." This in turn can be delimited by denomination or geographic location, that is, Church Development, New—Mennonites; or Church Development, New—Texas. Other relevant delimiters include type of work, for example, Church Development, New—Biblical Teaching; or Church Development, New—Case Studies.

Of particular interest to seminary students is how to search for commentaries and studies of the Bible. While "Leviticus" might work; "Job" or "John" or "Numbers" do not fare well as standard search terms. But a subject heading search for "Bible—Job—Commentaries" or "Bible—John—Criticism, Interpretation, etc." will yield results right on target. The only additional detail essential to following the pattern above includes Bible books that have a first or second: for example, Bible—Peter, 2nd—Commentaries. It is a useful strategy to pay close attention to the subject headings whenever you find a book that is relevant for the topic. This form of subject linking is a powerful tool for achieving results with high relevance and low redundancy.

Another strategy for finding books while "thinking like a person" is to become familiar with the call number system. This number represents the informed classification of the item and was carefully chosen by a library professional with the intention that books on the same subject sit on the shelf together.

Most libraries use one of two popular classification schemes: Dewey or Library of Congress. The Dewey system uses only numbers, while the Library of Congress uses letters and numbers. In the Dewey Decimal System, most of the books on religion and theology are found in the 200 Class. For example, the number 223 refers to the Old Testament poetic books and wisdom literature. Job is further classified by 223.107. So it would be reasonable to presume that most commentaries on the Old Testament book of Job would have that call number.

Using the Library of Congress Classification, the commentaries on the biblical book of Job have a basic call number of BS1415. This basic number groups books on Job to books published prior to 1950. To these are added a decimal point to divide into types of books published since 1950.

BS1415.2—Criticism, Interpretations, etc., 1950-1999
BS1415.3—Commentaries, 1950-1999
BS1415.52—Criticism, Interpretations, etc., 2000-
BS1415.53—Commentaries, 2000-

Once you find one book right on target for your topic, you can browse the shelves around that book for others that you might not have found using the search you used. Another way to maximize the use of the classification system is to search by call number. For books on the topic Church Growth, try BV652.25.

To summarize, a complete search may begin with keyword searches in the library catalog or in a discovery layer, which includes other databases and the library catalog. The terms you think of are probably used by other authors as well. You can anticipate, however, many hits (redundancy) with a low level of relevance. As you complete a few searches, pay attention to the subject headings/descriptors and call numbers. Using these will give highly relevant results with low redundancy. You may still miss the occasional book that may be mostly about something else, but which does speak to your information need. That is why both strategies have a place in your search of library resources.

Ebook Databases

In 2004 Google launched its Google Book project. In cooperation with major libraries, millions of books have since been scanned. Copyright debates and lawsuits have limited the full text availability of books to pre-1924 titles and those with specific author/publisher permissions.

In addition, many publishers have partnered to make some of the content of their books available through the database, marketed as a preview. Using the preview feature is like walking into a bookstore, picking up a title that looks interesting, and scanning the table of contents and a few pages here or there. Using the database can help you find which books have useful content based on specific search terms. It will take you to the exact page on which the term is used. If on further reading you determine you need the entire book, you can look for it in a library.

Subsequently, libraries that participated in the Google scanning project have made their digital copies of the scanned books available through HathiTrust.org. This has become a premier database of books in the public domain.

A recent initiative is the Open Access Digital Theological Library (http://oadtl.org/). Using a user-friendly interface, the OADTL curates records from WorldCat that have linked open access content in the field of religious studies, broadly conceived. At the time of this writing, the library includes more than 190,000 items.

The Digital Public Library of America (http://dp.la/) links the digital resources from a growing number of libraries, archives, and museums through a specialized search engine. European counterparts include Gallica (French) and Europeana.

Libraries have begun purchasing ebooks, and you can access them and search them through a database such as Ebook Central from ProQuest or eBook Collection from EBSCO. Depending on your library's acquisitions policies, there may or may not be much of use for religion and theology students. Most of the relevant works are from university presses and large commercial publishers.

Subscription databases of older materials include the *Early English Books Online*, *eHRAF World Cultures*, and *Early American Imprints*. These databases tend to be somewhat expensive, so only the larger libraries will have them. They do have advantages for comprehensiveness and detailed searches appreciated by advanced researchers. However, for those who do not have access, many of these works can still be found in databases like HathiTrust, Gallica, and Europeana, and even more specific titles can be found in local institutional digital libraries.

Periodical Literature

The library online catalog provides access information for library holdings and will provide records for books, media, journal titles, local dissertations, and so on. But the library catalog does not provide access to article information within journals. This level of record is found in periodical indexes. Most such indexes are now available online, and for simple clarity, we will refer to these as databases, though the content is similar to older print indexes. For the period and topic each one covers, they are the preferred access tool. However, for some more historical literature reviews, it may be necessary to consult the older print indexes and bibliographies.

In addition to the journals to which the library may provide access in databases, it will also subscribe to a number of key journals in paper format. These are displayed and preserved in the Periodical Department. When you have a citation to a specific article and the library only has access to it in their paper-based collection, you will need to go to that area of the library and find it on the shelf. The most common way libraries shelve periodicals is alphabetical by journal title, though some assign call numbers according to the subject content. Browsing the current paper copies of the journals your library continues to receive can prove to be a useful method of finding interesting articles not yet indexed as well as to keep you informed of the latest issues.

Online Databases in Religion and Theology

Because periodical literature is a critical form of scholarly communication, it is important to be able to search it effectively for sources. Some indexes are the work of trained professionals who carefully classify and consistently organize the entries over decades. Because these indexes represent a significant investment of time and money to create, they are paid for by subscribing libraries. You can have access to them only as an authenticated user of the subscribing library. Consult these indexes first because they represent a vetted disciplinary standard, besides your tuition money pays for them. Thanks to a general trend toward search standardization, you will find that these databases use similar search and listing screens, so once you work through one, you will understand how to work through the rest.

In the field of religion/theology, the Atla Religion Database with AtlaSerials Plus is the best place to begin. The American Theological Library Association has been a leader in library support for academic religious/theological education, and it has maintained this subscription index for seventy years. They are also aggressively adding the full text of the articles to the records, and at the time of this writing they have over 500 full-text journals available online, with new titles added regularly. One unique feature is the Scripture index, which makes it possible for you to retrieve all the articles that refer to a specific verse of the Bible. A comparable product is ProQuest Religion, which is a subset of their full database.

Religious and Theological Abstracts provides abstracts and brief descriptions of the articles and uses a standard internet search interface. The abstracts are helpful because you can find articles with search terms that may not be in the title or in a formal subject heading. This index does not link to the full text of the articles.

Several other online databases of interest in the field of religion and theology include some that focus on a topic. New Testament Abstracts and Old Testament Abstracts survey a broad range of publications, and then list and abstract only those relevant to the field of study they represent. Other databases represent the literature of a religion or Christian denomination: Catholic Periodical and Literature Index, Seventh-day Adventist Periodical Index, RAMBI: The Index of Articles on Jewish Studies, and the Index to Jewish Periodicals.

If you need to search in areas related to theology/biblical studies—for example, anything dealing with the education of young people—take note of ERIC, Education Resources Information Center. You may also need to check PsychInfo for materials on psychology or counseling. If your paper requires the latest medical information (such as something on HIV/AIDS), you will want to use Medline or PubMed. Most areas of study have similar databases with specialized content.

Aggregator Databases

Most academic libraries subscribe to a multidisciplinary mega database that aggregates in one place thousands of journals. These include journals and articles that were "born digital," so they do not have much coverage from before the 1990s but do have the full text of many articles only a click away. These databases are dependent on financial arrangements made with the publishers and often include a one-year embargo on the full text. That means that the most recent articles from a journal are not available. Examples of widely used aggregator databases include: Academic Search from EBSCO, Academic OneFile from Cengage Learning, ProQuest Central from ProQuest, and Ingenta. All include significant content in Religion/Theology, though not as thoroughly as the discipline-specific databases. They can be helpful because there may be articles relevant to your topic that are in titles that primarily serve other disciplines, for example, in religion and culture themes or historical topics.

JSTOR is an archival journal database. For the journal titles included in it, the full run from the beginning is available up to a contractual date of three to five years ago in full text. As such, it is more useful for a historical literature review. The coverage of religion journals is growing, but it is still somewhat limited (currently only 147 religion titles are listed). This database is most useful for finding the article from a citation provided elsewhere. It provides partially open access for noninstitutional users who can register to use whatever is available—which is only a small percentage of the standard licensed JSTOR. This does include some key journals in religion and theology as well as history and philosophy, so it is worth the effort.

Each of the databases listed above has person-created metadata that can be used to refine and focus searches. Another form of database has been developed, compiled by machine-based web crawlers, so these do not have the same level of useful metadata. But neither do they require a subscription fee, so they can be used anywhere by anyone with an internet connection. These only accommodate keyword or term-searching strategies. For these, the coverage is extremely broad, and often the full text of the articles is searched, so typical search terms tend to produce huge numbers of hits. The most useful strategy with these is to find unique terms, or to combine the terms in complex patterns and phrases on an advanced search screen. The two principle databases in this category are Google Scholar and Microsoft Academic Search. While some results may include a link to full text, most results will require that you record the citation and then find the article in one of the subscription databases or in paper format.

Another tool that advanced students may wish to explore is a journal table of contents alerting service such as JournalTOCS. After selecting any number of journals that are of interest to you, you will receive either in an email or in an RSS feed[1] a list of article titles with links to the abstracts as the journals are issued. Many publishers also provide this service for their journals, for example, Oxford University Press and Sage.

Reference Materials

Reference materials such as dictionaries, encyclopedias, and concordances are useful in the *initial* search for information. Later on, once the topic has been defined, these general works are less important but still may be helpful to clarify details. In addition, their bibliographies may contain valuable references. By definition, the reference section for print materials should be rather small in a typical library, so it is worth the time to browse the whole section, taking note of all the classes of material that might be helpful for your project.

As with periodical literature, libraries have the option of providing online access to many academic reference works. If your library has purchased this option for a title, you will need to authenticate yourself as a valid library user to access it; for example, at Andrews University we provide this for *Encyclopedia of Religion*.

The best-known general online reference work is Wikipedia. For a brief overview of a given topic and some bibliographic references, this is a reasonable place to begin, particularly for factual information on a topic for which you have little prior knowledge. In spite of its bumpy history and early problems with poor editing practices, it has proven to be generally reliable for noncontroversial details. However, it needs to be used critically, and important points in your paper should be validated with more substantive sources.

Dissertations and Theses

When it comes to reading, dissertations and theses can be especially tedious. But because they often deal in depth with very specific topics, they make good resources for research. The chapter on the history of interpretation or literature review is particularly helpful for understanding the literary background of a question, and the bibliographies can highlight further resources that might not have been found otherwise. Of course, doctoral-level students will need to defend a proposal, and one facet of doing that is to demonstrate their unique

---

1. This explanation is from Wikipedia: "RSS Rich Site Summary (originally RDF Site Summary, often dubbed Really Simple Syndication) is a family of web feed formats used to publish frequently updated works—such as blog entries, news headlines, audio, and video—in a standardized format. An RSS document (which is called a 'feed,' 'web feed,' or 'channel') includes full or summarized text, plus metadata such as publishing dates and authorship," http://en.wikipedia.org/wiki/RSS.

contribution to the topic, and that includes giving evidence that no one else has already written that thesis.

The primary database for North American dissertations is ProQuest Dissertations and Theses Global. This is a subscription database, so you will need library authentication to access it. It covers all participating schools going back decades. However, there is a recent subset of the database, PQDT Open, which includes open access full-text dissertations licensed by the author, with coverage beginning in 2007. Anyone can access these from anywhere with an internet connection. There are also a number of national dissertation databases that provide open access. Examples include Theses Canada and The British Library's EThOS: Electronic Theses Online Service. Many universities are including full-text access to their theses and dissertations in open-access repositories.

A disciplinary focused database of Doctor of Ministry dissertations and projects has been compiled by the American Theological Library Association, Research in Ministry (RIM). Formerly, this database included only citations and abstracts; however, enhancements made in 2019 now provide for the option to include links to the full text for new entries. The Theological Research Exchange Network (TREN) is a commercial entity that sells, at a reasonable cost, both paper and digital (since 2000) copies of these dissertations and projects.

Special Departments

Archives, rare book rooms, heritage centers, manuscript centers, media centers, music libraries—these can be sources of valuable information. Usually, materials held in these special departments appear in the library catalog. If not, there will a departmental listing of some kind. You may need to visit each department to find out what it can offer to your topic.

Interlibrary Loan

No library has the capacity to hold all the books and journals ever published, so there has long been a cooperative understanding about borrowing and lending materials between libraries. When you have a citation for a book or journal article that is not available in your library, the interlibrary loan office will try to get it for you. You need to find out your library's interlibrary loan policies and procedures. Often you make your request and supply the information online.

Some Final Thoughts

The information resources essential for your learning success reflect the investment of time and expertise of the author/creator. For you to have access to these outputs, some form of technology is needed, whether ink on paper or bits and bytes on a server in the cloud, and some publisher must be financially responsible to make this happen. A distribution system of some type delivers the information to you, whether by trucks and airplanes, or fiber-optic cables, or satellite communication systems.

Each of these facets involves major investments of capital. Information is not free, and a significant portion of the tuition revenues to which you have contributed are invested in library resources. For the system to keep working, each of the players—whether creators, producers, or distributors—must be financially stable and be able to trust the other players to fulfill their obligations. For that reason access is made possible through license agreements between the different parties: authors and publishers, publishers and distributors, distributors and users.

This means that, as a user, you must have a license to be able to use these resources. This license is normally provided to you as part of the financial arrangement you have with the higher education institution you attend. You can expect some form of verification of institutional status, such as a username and password, will be required to use the resources, including the electronic resources, now generally available from anywhere with an internet connection.

Knowing your way around the library and being familiar with its services and resources will aid your research and enrich your student life. And now, on to some information on deciding which materials are the best for your paper.

Evaluating Your Materials

You could read for years—in books, journals, and online—for there is much written on almost every topic. However, not all written materials are of the same value, even if they deal with the subject you are researching. Here are fourteen questions, the answers to which can help you weigh the potential value of a work before you invest time in reading the entire work thoroughly.

1. Who is the author? Information about the author may be found on the back cover, on the dust jacket, or in the preface. You will find the author's qualifications and a list of other books by the author. Most authors who are currently employed as professors will have an institutional profile. If you cannot find information about an author, ask your professors, who know most of the important people in their area of study. Check the Atla Publications and WorldCat for items this person has written.

Go online and consult Google Scholar. You can also explore the scholarly social media sites, ResearchGate and Academia.edu, where scholars post profiles and bibliographies of their work. These sources will show you authors' areas of expertise and what journals and publishers carry their work.

2. Who is the publisher? Not all publishers are equally academic or scholarly. Some specialize in learned books, while others publish popular works. Whether the book was published by a Protestant or Catholic publisher makes a difference if you are interested in a certain approach to your topic. If a book was published by the author or has no imprint, it is appropriate to question whether a publisher was unwilling to take the manuscript. Or would the author have chosen to self-publish because the financial remuneration was better? Publishing companies that produce works for the highly educated academic and professional audience are careful to have their imprint only on quality books. Ask a librarian or a professor about publishers.
3. If the source in question is an article, is the journal in which it appears recognized as a specialized and serious journal? An article about an archeological finding in *Time* is not worthy of as much confidence as one on the same finding in *Biblica* (from the Pontifical Biblical Institute in Rome) or *Biblical Archaeologist* (from the American Schools of Oriental Research). Somewhere between the two extremes would be an article in *Biblical Archaeology Review*, which admits its purpose is the popularization of biblical archaeology. Popular magazines, such as *Reader's Digest*, *Newsweek*, *Christian Woman*, or even *National Geographic* are not usually good research sources—unless your research is unique. You need to take the time to become acquainted with the specialized journals in your field.
4. What is the date of publication? If you are looking for a source that includes the latest research on a Hebrew language problem, the date needs to be recent. A 1907 book may be useful to know what authors wrote then, but it will only be of value to understanding the history of your problem. On the other hand, if the research concerns the history of Presbyterians in Korea, a book written in Korea in 1907 about Presbyterian mission activity would be a valuable primary source. The date that counts is that of the copyright or edition, not that of a printing, when no substantive changes are made to the book.
5. What is the author's purpose? Generally the introduction to a serious book will give the author's basic philosophy, the purpose for writing the

book, the audience to which it is directed, and maybe even a hint on the conclusions reached. You can safely judge a serious book on the basis of its introduction (written by the author, not to be confused with a foreword written by someone else). After reading the introduction to some books, you may decide to drop them from the list of potential sources.

6. Is the style of writing popular or serious (that is, scholarly)? This question is answered by reading a little here and there. If the answer is "popular," the source may not be valuable for serious study. That does not mean that research writing is all dry. It does mean that books written for entertainment may sacrifice content to readability. Items written with quoted conversations, colorful language, or abundant contractions are suspect.
7. Is there a bibliography? How extensive is it? Are there footnotes? Are they complete? The presence of these items indicates the writer has done a serious piece of work. Notes and bibliography show that the author took the time to look at other people's work and was honest enough to note what was borrowed.
8. Are there tables? Graphs? Maps? Not all sources need these items, but a book that contains well-made graphs and tables, together with the source and date for the information presented in them, usually can be considered a serious work. A map can say something about the book. If it is sloppily made, or a copy from a lesser atlas, it may indicate carelessness. Note that pictures in a book—unless the topic is archaeology or something of that sort—do not enhance the research value of a source.
9. Is the table of contents detailed? Is there an index? Much information may be obtained by reading the table of contents. A sketchy one may suggest lack of precision and care for detail—unforgivable flaws in research. In modern English-language books, the index is often a mark of a good research source. The same cannot be said for other languages. An index facilitates research and is to be considered a plus.
10. In the footnotes and bibliography, are the works recent and the authors specialists in their fields? Sometimes a fairly recent work quotes rather old sources. This would indicate that the research was done some time ago and the author did not take the trouble to update the material. If the authors quoted or consulted are not specialists, it is fair to wonder if the writer knew who the specialists in the field were.
11. What is the tone of the writing? Is it sober and objective? Or is it emotional? How are adjectives and adverbs used? Are epithets applied to people? Some authors are not able to convince their readers by the

information they give or by their logic, so they use emotional phrases that appeal more to the heart than to the mind. When the language is strong, the content may be weak. If authors need to tear down an opponent in order to build up their work, there is a problem. The best research sources are clearly written in an objective style.

12. Is the style of writing clear and easy to read? Is the phrasing concise? Is the vocabulary as simple as the topic will permit? There is no virtue in using long sentences and unnecessarily difficult words; in fact, such writing may suggest the author is hiding ignorance behind fancy language. Good research writing is simple and straightforward.
13. Has this source been translated from another language? How many editions has it had? An item translated from another language has been considered important enough to receive wider dissemination. A book that has been reedited for a subsequent edition has evidently been deemed significant. A positive answer to both questions suggests a good research source. One additional suggestion: in choosing between the original and the translation—if you can read both—choose the original.
14. Is this a primary source? A primary source on Vatican Council II would be the documents put out by the council. A secondary source would be a book that comments on or interprets those documents. In a secondary source, authors can include their own ideas and thus color the reader's understanding of the original. For example, what the Latter-day Saints say about themselves is a primary document; what someone else says about them is secondary and liable to include bias and distortion. Using primary sources minimizes the danger of misinterpretation.

Now that you have been enriched by your search in the library, let us turn to another, ever more important source: the internet. After all, there is more to the internet than Facebook and email.

chapter fourteen

TAMING THE INTERNET: USING AND EVALUATING ITS RESOURCES

Many library resources are delivered and accessed over the internet. This chapter will focus on internet-based resources that do not fit neatly into the categories covered in the previous chapter about library-based resources. First, a brief overview of using the internet. While this may seem familiar and obvious to regular users, it sets the stage for finding and evaluating sources that may be appropriate in an academic paper.

Using a Search Engine

Someone wants to make information available to others by using the internet. After creating a document of some sort, the document is digitally stored on a server that is connected to the internet. Each document has a unique address, called the URL, the Uniform Resource Locator. Browsers are computer programs that are needed to connect to the internet. These include products such as Chrome, Internet Explorer, Firefox, and Safari. But to find and access the document, special computer software is needed, and these programs have been called search engines. Many such search engines have been developed. Popular examples include Google, Bing, and Yahoo. Billions of users can search millions of servers for trillions of documents. Just the enormity of the content alone presents a whole range of challenges, to say nothing about the problems associated with evaluating the resources. In spite of all this, good information can be found by the astute searcher when using the right tools efficiently.

Your primary portal to the wonders of cyberspace is the search engine.

Google is currently the most popular. It uses a special algorithm to rank the sites where it finds your search string. Of these sites, the ones that are linked to by the most other sites float to the top of the list. The end result of this algorithm is that the first sites listed in your search tend to be general information sites that appeal to the widest audience, from elementary students to retired senior citizens. This is a form of "crowd sourcing" reliability monitoring. A typical search yields millions of results, and so the first hundred or so provide general, reasonably reliable information, most likely readily available elsewhere and easily verifiable should the need arise. The farther down the list you go, however, the ratio of nonrelevant hits increases, and the "crowd sourcing" reliability cushion gets thinner. While somewhat helpful in that you may actually find good information, for the most part, stumbling on anything uniquely valuable will prove to be serendipitous.

Complex searches using Advanced Search features can improve the result lists, but you will still find high levels of redundancy and low levels of relevance, with an even thinner reliability cushion. The standard Google search works best as a convenient "quick reference" source for objective "common knowledge" facts and not as a resource for in-depth, focused discussions of complex topics. You cannot write a credible research paper with sources found simply by Googling your topic. Critical points in your paper need to be carefully documented in recognized and reliable sources.

In spite of this ambiguity, there is a growing wealth of information available for free on the internet that may not be available any other way, or at least not as conveniently. These types of sites can be found using any search engine by searching on specific titles and names. Three types will be highlighted to illustrate.

1. The historical documents of virtually every religion are available on the internet, from the Christian Bible to the Qur'an to the Buddhist Sutra Texts. One of the easiest ways to find them is to look up the relevant article in Wikipedia and, at the bottom of the article, links are provided. In addition to the various Scriptures, other historical literatures of the religions are available. Christian history is particularly well represented. One pioneering site that has been available and routinely updated since the earliest days of the internet is the Christian Classics Ethereal Library. It includes a broad spectrum of texts beginning with the earliest church fathers down to the beginning of the twentieth century. Codex Sinaiticus, one of the earliest copies of the Greek Bible, can be studied online. The site includes a photographic reproduction of the pages with a transcription into a current Greek font, and a translation into several different languages. These sites not only provide a readable copy of the ancient literature, but

allow a research strategy commonly known as "text mining," a computerized indexing of a specified word or phrase across a body of literature.

2. Denominations, universities, publishers, local congregations, parachurch organizations, charities, museums, archives, and businesses all have web pages as a means to communicate with their constituencies and to promote their causes and products. A good example of a rich and pertinent organizational site is that of the World Council of Churches. The wealth of material on all facets of ecumenism available through the site is astounding. The web presence of Zondervan includes helpful prereading information on the many books they publish and their authors. The same applies for most other publishers. University faculty pages include lists of publications by their faculty, and some even include links to unpublished materials that they are currently working on.
3. If you are doing a research paper on the problem of HIV/AIDS in South Africa, the South African Department of Health site has some of the best resources on the topic. Many other governments also are turning to the internet to publish their documents on all areas of public interest, some of which may provide important sources of up-to-date local information. One class of seminary-based writing that should consider these sources is contextualized Doctor of Ministry dissertations/projects, particularly if the project is based in a nation other than the United States.

It is simply not practical to list all the useful websites; such a project would be out of date as soon as it was published. For research purposes, it is a best practice to preserve, either in print or digitally, a copy of the web pages you cite in a paper. Tomorrow, the content may change, the server may crash, or the institution may update its website; any number of destabilizing events could mean that the information you found today is not there tomorrow. One form of this problem has been labeled "link rot." These are links that no longer work because no one thought to update them. So keep yourself covered by archiving a paper copy of whatever you use (it is hoped you appreciate the irony). Turabian 9 does not require the access date on your paper, but you should have it recorded—just in case.

Institutional Repositories

Around the turn of the century, universities and some professional organizations began experimenting with a new way to manage their "digital assets." These became known as "institutional repositories." The idea was to provide a place where students and scholars could make their work available. Early repositories primarily included local dissertations and theses. Additional formats of work have become more and more common. Many high-ranking commercial journals now permit publicly funded research articles to be added to a local open access repository because government and other public funding organizations are requiring it. Non–North American institutions have been more intentional in establishing these repositories as a way to showcase national research initiatives.

A particularly significant repository launched in 2011 for the study of religion and theology is associated with the World Council of Churches and financially supported by many international church organizations. GlobTheoLib requires individuals to register for a free account to use the resources. Content is carefully screened before it is added. While much of the licensed content made available through the site is readily available in North America and Europe, this repository is showing high use in the rest of the world. It is also showing promise as a repository of choice for theological scholarship from the global South.

Open Access Publishing

One of the hottest topics in scholarly publishing is the question of open access. One way or another, this form of publishing is making strong inroads into journal publishing. For scholarly books, the practice is still in the experimental phase. This is not to be confused with publishing online or in an electronic format. Rather, this form of publishing values free access to the work and covers production costs in other ways.

Three categories of article-level open access publishing predominate. The first includes those journals that are born digital and open access. That is, this is the only way the articles have ever been published. The second includes journals originally published in traditional paper formats, but whose editors have chosen to make the archives available online with open access. These two classes of open-access journals are well represented in the Directory of Open Access Journals (www.doaj.org). At the time of this writing, there were 12,812 titles in the list. DOAJ lists 142 journals in psychology, philosophy, and religion. The third represents commercial publishers who make articles open access through author fees, either for the complete journal issue or for selected articles within an issue. While there may occasionally be reasons to go to the DOAJ and use its rudimentary search engine, or to publisher home pages, searching for content in virtually all of these journals can usually be achieved through Google Scholar or Microsoft Academic Search.

Public domain books with their copyright expired (published before 1923) can be found online and read without economic restrictions. As noted earlier, there is a collective rush to make these works available. Recently a number of new experiments have been launched to provide current books in open access publishing. For example, the University of Nebraska–Lincoln libraries have launched an open access ebook collection, Zea E-Books, that includes a variety of works that do not fit into conventional publishing models..

Another experiment is the Directory of Open Access Books (DOAB) (http://www.doabooks.org) initiative. A number of academic publishers have contributed content for this database. As of this writing, this digital library includes more than 26,288 books from 365 publishers. These works were originally published in a paper format, but rather than simply going out of print, they are now licensed for distribution online. You can anticipate more such initiatives to emerge as alternative funding methods are developed to meet publication costs.

Social Media

The current fad for social media includes digital online programs like Facebook and Twitter. An older form many participate in is the web log, or blog. Scholars are beginning to use similar products more suited to their needs. Some examples include Academia.edu and ResearchGate. Many full-text papers, citations, and much more can be found on these sites. A recent entry into the blitz of academically useful resources is the MOOC, or Massive Open Online Courses. Leading professors at major universities are recording their lectures, some only in audio, some including video, and making them available online for anyone who wants to take the time to listen or watch. Of course, there is no academic credit for listening to the lectures, and no one will grade your papers for the course, but this is one more online resource you can access.

Whether you wish to mine the internet for potential sources is a question of personal preference. In spite of the ease of using the internet, for most topics in religion and theology, it is inefficient compared with a good nearby library. One more cautionary note: a term paper is not a better paper because it cites exotic or previously unheard of sources from obscure websites. What makes it a good paper is the quality of the writing, the quality of the argumentation, and the reliability of the sources.

Evaluating Internet Sources

With so much material so readily available only a click or two away, a prereading strategy is needed to delimit and prioritize which sources are the most likely to meet the expectations of the assignment and should be read first. Here are some helpful questions.

1. What is the purpose of the website? Is it for entertainment? Information? Research? To keep the family together by sharing information? Does it want to sell you a product or an idea? Your commonsense answer to this question will start you on the right track.
2. Who sponsors the website? A credible organization, such as a university? A professional society? An advocacy group? Or is it a company trying to sell something? An individual interested in the topic? Obviously, the first is better than the last! But sometimes you can use a less valuable website to gain access to serious information. Researching the history of deaconesses through the centuries, I found useful materials at womenpriests.org—a site that advocates the ordination of Roman Catholic women to the priesthood. The site served as a portal to historical resources.
3. For evaluation, you need to know when the material was written. You may have to search various pages to find the date. At times, the best you can do is to find when the site was updated. There's nothing wrong with old information; in some cases it is very good.
4. Who wrote the piece you are reading? A professional? A student? Just somebody? I do not mean to denigrate nonexperts, but we are talking research, serious study. Maybe there is no author named, suggesting that the piece may have come from elsewhere or that no one was willing to take credit for that piece. If you cannot find the author's name, make sure you know who or what organization is responsible for the website.
5. What are the author's qualifications, either academic or professional? Is the writer an established author? An amateur? Use the web to find more information about the writer. Use Google Scholar (scholar.google.com) to learn what else the person has written, if anything. For example, searching for Nancy (or Nancy J. or Nancy Jean) Vyhmeister, will grant you more than 100 hits that include articles and books as well as citations in the writings of others (friends and foes!) and course lists that use *Quality Research Papers* as a textbook. (This works well with an uncommon surname like mine. With a surname like Robertson, it takes the full name "Terry Dwain Robertson" to get useful results.)
6. Is this material available elsewhere? On the web? In a printed source? Use search engines to find out.

7. What is the tone of the material? "I know it all"? "You are stupid if you do not agree with me"? "This is an observation I have made"? Does this sound like someone searching for truth or simply pushing an idea?
8. What company does this piece keep? If there are hyperlinks in the piece or on the site, what are they about? Whom does the author cite? Recognized scholars? Journals and recent books? Or, citing no one, is the author the ultimate authority?
9. How do you think your professors will rate this information? Ask them. Get help to evaluate websites and web authors, especially if you are a beginner.
10. Never stop asking questions—about websites and everything else. After all, questions form the basis of good research.

In an ideal world, with no time limits, it would be wonderful to read everything and evaluate the content based on your thorough prior knowledge of the topic. But since that is not reality, these helpful prereading criteria can make your writing project more manageable—particularly for term papers due in a few weeks. All of these points contribute, whether the work is a book, a journal, or a website; whether you find the work in an academic library or as an ebook from an online vendor, or as a blog or MOOC. These are not hard and fast rules, only guidelines, because what really matters is the credibility and usability of the content. That can only be fully assessed *after* reading the work carefully and reflectively.

Now that you have located resources of all different kinds, it is time to sit down and read. Chapter 15 guides you through the process of reading and taking notes.

chapter fifteen

RESEARCH READING AND NOTE TAKING

Reading for a research paper takes time, thought, and skill. Research reading requires the implementation of the advice given in chapter 10, "Research Thinking." To get the most benefit from this major part of the research activity, you will have to evaluate and weigh carefully what you are reading (as you saw in chapters 13 and 14). You will also need to make notes of what you read. This chapter gives suggestions for reading and taking notes. Bibliographical notes appear in chapters 18 and 20, together with instructions for preparing bibliographies.

Reading

Reading is one of the most profitable of all intellectual activities. In reading, ideas and facts go from one mind to another through the printed page or online sources. However, not all books have the same effect on the reader. Francis Bacon, English philosopher and writer of the sixteenth century, said that some books should be tasted, others swallowed; only a few might be chewed and digested.[1] Some books are light reading and can be finished in one evening. Most of those needed for research are heavy and must be chewed and digested. Research reading—beyond the early exploratory reading—takes time and thought. The search for information and concepts demands concentration, determination, and time—much time.

Research reading demands the understanding of (1) words—look up the ones you do not know in a dictionary, either in print or online; (2) phrases and

1. "Of Studies," in *Harvard Classics*, ed. Charles W. Eliot (New York, NY: Colliers, 1909), 3:128.

sentences; (3) paragraphs—try summarizing the contents of each paragraph in one sentence; (4) the chapter—summarize each in a maximum of three sentences; and (5) the book—summarize it in one paragraph. Making these summaries, mentally or on paper, fixes the content in your mind.

Research reading begins with finding information about the author, possibly on the back cover or the dust jacket of the book. It continues with the title page and its verso, where there is information regarding the publisher and date of publication. After carefully examining the table of contents, you should examine the introduction, where you should find information about the author's purpose, the recognized limitations of the work, and the audience for whom it is intended. Next, read, or at least browse, the concluding chapter, in which the author summarizes and draws conclusions. Only after all this work are you prepared to read the body of the book. By then, you may have decided to put the book aside as not useful to the study.

Some suggestions for successful reading:

1. Read in an appropriate place. You will need good light and ventilation. You need a place to write or type, for you will be taking notes. Find a quiet place without distractions. Be prepared with pencils, cards, and other materials—not least of which may be your computer—so you do not need to interrupt your study.
2. Read when you are most apt to be awake and alert. Some people do best in the morning; others at night. Find your own best time and use it well.
3. Alternate periods of study with moments of relaxation and physical exercise. Although some people can sit for hours, most tend to lose their power of concentration after an hour or so. Some scholars say they like to study hard for about fifty minutes and then get up for a drink and five minutes of exercise before returning to their desks. If you cannot sit still that long, build up your resistance by five minutes at a time. Start by forcing yourself to sit and concentrate for fifteen minutes. Eventually you will be able to endure an hour. To work efficiently, keep your body in top condition with proper rest, diet, and exercise.
4. Take notes of what you read. The intellectual exercise of putting information on paper or into your computer helps your brain absorb the materials you read. Only if you assimilate your reading can you organize, analyze, and synthesize it.
5. Do not wait until you feel like reading or studying. Make yourself a schedule and stick to it. Do not let yourself be distracted by other matters, interesting as they may be.

Taking Good Notes

Notes come in two varieties: content and bibliographical. The first help you remember what you have read. The second help you remember where you found it. We will deal with bibliographical notes at the end of the chapter. You will find information on the format of notes (footnotes or endnotes) and bibliographies in chapters 18 and 21-23.

Content notes are taken to remember what we read from those sources we have already identified as the most helpful; they must be complete and painstakingly accurate. Time spent taking proper notes is time saved in the total process. There is no efficient way to do good research without taking good notes, either manually or on a computer.

The specific method or medium for taking notes must work for you, and it must enable you to achieve efficient retrieval of the information needed when you are writing the paper. Short-term projects do not need elaborate systems for accomplishing this objective. The guiding principle should be simplicity, using skills already in place. However, long-term projects such as a thesis or dissertation deserve careful planning early in the process. Then the time investment required by a learning curve for new skills or technology applications can be amortized with a net savings in time and accuracy over the life of the project. Keep in mind that function is primary, technology is secondary.

A Method for Manual Note Taking

The most accessible and time-tested method of research note taking engages the technology of the handheld pen or pencil on a manufactured writing surface such as paper. The advantages of this method and medium include (1) a minimal learning curve (uses prior skills, i.e., handwriting); (2) flexible working contexts (electrical plug-in not needed); and (3) the cognitive reinforcement of learning that naturally occurs when both hand and eye are engaged in information recording. The only major disadvantages include the problems of readability, acquiring the needed physical materials, and note cards not being searchable like notes taken on a computer. However, reviewing the same cards over and over, looking for something, has a positive learning value.

The most effective "old-fashioned" method of note taking uses note cards or slips of paper. These slips or cards are easy to organize; they can be arranged and rearranged to suit changes in outline or approach. Cards may be added or deleted without affecting the total scheme. Finally, when put in order, they almost write the paper by themselves.

Note Cards

All the cards should be of the same size, usually 3 by 5 or 4 by 6 inches. Typing paper cut in four equal parts may also be used. Some researchers prefer a larger card, but the small one is a reminder of a basic rule of note taking: only one item on a card. Since bibliography cards are used at the same time as note cards, it helps to use a different color or type of paper or even a slightly different size so the two kinds of cards are not confused.

Filing System

Before beginning to read and take notes, prepare one card—a little larger, stiffer, and of a different color than the note cards—for each of the sections of the paper, as envisioned in the tentative outline. These index cards are labeled to serve as dividers for a simple filing system. Rubber bands or elastics may be used to keep each packet of notes together, or a small box may be used as a file cabinet. As you read, you will certainly add and modify headings.

As you do your reading, take notes as needed. At the end of your reading session, put your notes in the appropriate section of your file. This system is simple, yet effective.

Parts of the Note Card

Each note card has three indispensable parts: (1) heading, (2) text, and (3) source. Notes may be written in ink or pencil; the first looks messy when corrections are made, but pencil lead tends to dim with time and use. Some library research rooms allow only the use of pencils; in that case, pencil will have to do.

Heading

The headings on the cards correspond to sections of the paper. A paper on the history of Nestorianism in China would include a section on Rabban Sauma. One heading would be RABBAN SAUMA. There would also be several subheadings under the main heading: biographical data, relation with Rabban Mark, travels in Europe, return to Mongolia, and so on. Sub-subheadings may also be used. As you review your cards, especially if you change your outline, you may need to revise your headings. For starters, however, give the information a place where it can belong.

Headings on the note cards may be written in a different color; however, changing pens every few minutes may be a nuisance. Whatever the color, write clearly. The heading must always be located in the same place on the note card. The upper right corner is quite handy.

Text

The text of a note card may be a direct quotation, a summary of what has been read, or the researcher's reaction to the reading.

Direct quotations. For a direct quotation, the card must say exactly what the source said. No spelling or punctuation differences are allowed. Even if there is an evident error, it must be copied. But immediately following the error, place the bracketed word [*sic*], which is the Latin for "thus" and means that, right or wrong, this was what appeared in the source. If you omit anything the author wrote, use ellipsis marks. For an omission . . . within a sentence, three double-spaced dots are used. If the omission includes a break between sentences, four dots are used. . . . If the quoted sentences or phrases are from two different paragraphs, ellipsis marks are not permitted; you must record two quotations. If a quotation comes from two pages (80, 81), mark the page break // on your note, so that if you use only part of the quotation, you can tell whether it is from page 80 or 81. Put quotation marks around all quoted material.

Summaries. It is not always necessary to copy an author's actual words. A summary or synthesis may be sufficient. However, when you do this, be careful not to change the sense or thrust of the author's thought. Make sure that summary cards tell you they are summaries, not quotations.

Comments. Another kind of card contains comments. I can easily forget my reactions to a certain reading, so I need to jot down my comments and impressions. These may be notes on the reading, ideas about possible sources, or suggested modifications to any part of the paper. They may be doubts or questions, sometimes only tangentially related to the topic. However, I need to write them down and give them a heading—possibly the item that triggered them—so that later I can retrieve my brilliant idea. A date on the comment card can help me reconstruct my intellectual pilgrimage. I initial these cards to identify them as comments or queries.

Source. Each note card must record the source from which the material was quoted or summarized. The page(s) and the author's last name usually are enough, except when you are using two books by the same author or items whose authors have the same last name. In the first case, an abbreviated form of the title must be used: Bruce, *Acts*, 24. In the second case, an initial with the surname is enough: L. Smith, 78.

While you are making these careful notes on content, do not forget to gather all the needed bibliographic information. Rather than making bib cards, make an alphabetical listing of all your sources. This will become your bibliography. If you are using Turabian footnote/bibliography style (chapter 21), you will follow this model to the end! Save yourself trouble later by respecting the format provided. Other bibliography formats are presented in chapters 22 and 23.

Useful Advice

The most useful note card is the short one that contains only one idea, one reference, or one precise piece of information. It is written on only one side of the card or slip.

The note system just described is efficient precisely because any card or slip may be moved without disturbing the whole. When there is only one idea on a card, moving it is simple. If two ideas are copied on one card, organization may later demand they be separated—which will require recopying. When only one idea is written on each card, there will be many cards, but the ease of organization makes up for having to deal with many cards. Model note cards are shown in the next section.

When to quote and when to summarize? When dealing with ideas, you can summarize, but always take care not to distort the meaning or emphasis of the original. When an author expresses an idea with lucidity or in picturesque words, better than any other way to express that idea, you probably should quote. In any case, when in doubt, copy the actual quotation. Later you can decide whether to quote or to summarize. You will be happy to have the full information when you are writing your paper late the night before the paper is due.

The system of taking notes described in this chapter may be new to some students—and even to some professors who guide research. There is little doubt that it works well. The first attempt may take some time, but the ease and precision gained should make the time spent worthwhile. By using this system conscientiously, you will avoid returning to the source once you have done your reading.

Finish all your reading on a given topic (or section of your topic) and sort your notes before sitting down to write. This will give you a full picture of your topic. It will also allow you to write seamless prose, blending different authors into their correct position in your writing.

Here are ten tips for better note taking on paper:

1. Use cards or slips of paper of uniform size. There are computer programs that allow for four cards on a regular sheet of paper. Make heading cards for each section of the paper and keep slips organized, in a box or using rubber bands.
2. Write clearly (or type) on one side only.
3. Put only one idea, one thought, one piece of information on each card to facilitate the organization of the paper.
4. Make short notes (remember number 3), but if you do need a second card, clearly indicate that it is the second card of a set.
5. Put a heading and a subheading (and even a sub-subheading) on each card.
6. Indicate clearly (yet in abbreviated form) the source of information.

7. Indicate clearly whether you have quoted or summarized. Be consistent in your system.
8. Summarize as often as possible; quote only when the author's words are impossible to improve on.
9. When quoting, copy material exactly as it appears. Use ellipsis marks for omission. Use [*sic*] to show that an error has been copied from the original material.
10. Make your notes so clear and understandable that anyone else could take over your incomplete work.

Sample Note Cards

These samples illustrate what has been explained. Use your own creativity—always within an organized system—to produce useful note cards for your paper.

```
Codices—Earliest Christian—Egypt

    The existence of Christian codices in Egypt "was histor-
ically plausible if not downright necessary." There are no
historical or technical arguments against their existence.

Tiede, 7
```

```
R. Sauma—Report on Mongols

    Asked by cardinals in Rome about his religion, Sauma said:
"Know ye, O our Fathers, that many of our Fathers have gone
into the countries of the Mongols, and Turks, and Chinese and
have taught them the Gospel, and at the present time there
are many Mongols who are Christians. For many of the sons of
the Mongol kings and queens have been baptized and confess
Christ. And they have established churches in their military
campus and they pay honour to the Christians, and there are
many among them who are believers."

Budge, 174
```

Computer Note Taking

In many higher education settings, the computer is the technology of choice for writing assignments. For skilled computer users, this technology potentially saves time and ensures accuracy and readability. Whether I take a laptop to the library or bring the books to my desktop computer, I can easily type up the notes I need.

Several computer-based approaches have emerged, fitting different types of computer and learning preferences. In order to be effective, whatever approach you choose, you still need to account for the informational elements described above in the section on manual note taking.

Using a Word Processor

The advantages of using the same word processor for note taking that you are using for writing the paper include (1) readability, (2) a minimal learning curve, (3) keyword searching of the notes, and (4) easy transfer of information from the notes to the paper (copy/paste). The problem is sorting the information to fit an outline in a way comparable to sorting cards.

Let me share instructions for a hybrid system that works well for a visual person like me.

1. Make your page margins as small as the printer will allow; then subdivide your page (either letter or A4) into 4 or 6 pages. Number your subpages in a small font (bottom center).
2. Take notes as described in the manual system. Be sure to put in appropriate headings and subheadings. Do not forget to write down the source. If you have a two-page note, be sure to indicate the number of the first page on the second one so you can put them together (something like "follows 35").
3. Use two files simultaneously—one for bibliography, one for content notes. Make an alphabetical listing of bib entries on one; take notes on the other file. Save often. Also back up your data on a flash drive or external hard drive; a computer crash could be disastrous. May I reiterate this last sentence?
4. Print out your note cards, cut the pages up, and sort as you would manually. You will be able to see what you are doing and arrange and rearrange your piles.
5. When you write your paper (input it into the computer), using your piles of notes, have three files open. One has the bibliography (from which you will take the sources for your footnotes); another holds the notes

from the source; the third, the developing paper. When you come to a quotation, simply paste it in place from the note file, without retyping it. Make sure you are careful in transferring information, so that the format is not damaged. Cut and paste bibliographical information from the bib file (remembering, of course, to change bibliography form into footnote form).

Using a Database or Spreadsheet

A couple of electronic tools usually bundled with a word processor can work much the same but add the sorting feature. Examples include software that comes with Microsoft Office, such as the database Access or the spreadsheet software Excel. With these tools, you will be able to efficiently (1) label and sort the entries, (2) search the entries for keywords, and (3) copy and paste entries into the paper. If the original source is in electronic form, it is even possible to copy and paste text into the database.

Access has advantages over Excel. The memo field can contain more material, and there is less risk of loss of data should the computer suddenly quit. Sorting is also less prone to error than with Excel.

However, Excel is easier to set up and use, and it has an auto-fill feature that is nice. For short projects, Excel is more than adequate, though for longer projects, such as a dissertation, Access is more stable, less prone to accidental corruption, and has significant advantages in terms of space for content and sorting options.

Another class of database that can be used for keeping track of notes is the bibliographic manager—for example, Zotero, Citavi, EndNote, EasyBib, Mendeley, and RefWorks. While their primary function is to format footnotes and bibliographies integrated into papers, each has the capacity to include extensive note taking. The advantage of these programs is that the notes are kept with the source from which they are taken. These can be searched in any number of ways, including keyword. Citavi has an additional feature, labeled as a knowledge base, that allows the notes to be integrated into an outline. However, these programs have a steep learning curve, so unless you anticipate writing a thesis or dissertation, you must thoroughly enjoy computer-based challenges to want to use them. One analogy with regard to these tools is that they are like a large moving van—invaluable for hauling large loads long distances but rather awkward for short hauls of small loads around town. The other disadvantage is that, except for Citavi, notes cannot be sorted to fit an outline.

Other Computer Tools

Other online tools that have potential for research note taking have recently become available. I have not used them in a major project, but they do deserve a mention.

One class of tools makes it possible to mark up .pdf files, using highlighting and sticky notes. Because many periodical databases now provide .pdf files of the articles, and because scanning equipment is becoming less expensive and easier to use, it is feasible to have a scanned copy of all the sources you need for a paper. This digitally emulates making photocopies and writing on the copies.

The second class of tools is a graphical hypertext interface for filing, tagging, sorting, and linking information. These include programs such as *Microsoft Office OneNote* and the open source online program *Evernote*. Those who are conversant in social media may find these tools intuitive, while others could find them to have a significant learning curve.

Just last week, a former student told me that he now takes photos of his materials with his iPhone. He then tags them and sends them to his computer. Having already done a PhD dissertation, he recognizes the value of safely committing his reading to notes in his computer. Perhaps I will need to learn this skill.

Registering Bibliographical Data

In the "olden days" we used to make bib cards that looked like the note cards. Now, I recommend making a bibliographical list of all items—books, journal articles, websites, recordings, whatever.

Your library's online catalog, WorldCat, and most online databases will allow you to copy and paste bibliographic information for each book or article or to download it into a bibliographic management program such as Zotero, Citavi, EndNote, or RefWorks. There may be some formatting discrepancies with what we suggest here regarding citation styles (APA or Turabian), but you will save yourself considerable time—and avoid misspelling some names or words! Learn how this feature works and use this practical tool.

Make this list in alphabetical order and include the elements noted below for the required style. The examples below follow Turabian style. For APA style see chapter 23. For Turabian author-date style, see chapter 22. Following the style accurately and fully at this point will make the inclusion of this entry in the final paper much more efficient. Please note the periods, or full stops, after each element. When you are preparing this list, do not press return until the entry is complete. Then you can alphabetize it with your computer. If you wish to make notes about this item, you may do so without pressing "enter" before the note.

Format the bib paragraph as "hanging"—that means the first line will reach the left margin, but subsequent lines will all be indented.

Books

Several items must be considered: author, title, edition, and publication data. In addition, there are special rules for multivolume works and series. If you do this step thoroughly at this point, you will have an easier time preparing the bibliography in the final paper. For your convenience, this information will be repeated in chapter 18 so it is handy when you are writing footnotes and the final bibliography.

Author

Normally, the order of the author or editor statement is surname, comma, given names (or name and initial), period (or full stop). Honorific or academic titles are not used.

When a book has more than one author, all names are given. However, only the first is inverted (surname first). Subsequent authors appear with given name first and surname last. Commas separate the names. In a reference note, an item with three or more authors appears "Smith and others"; all names appear in the bibliography. Fortunately, books that have many authors usually have a principal author or editor. Only that one needs listing.

Stanley, Andy. *Deep and Wide: Creating Churches Unchurched People Love to Attend*. Grand Rapids, MI: Zondervan, 2016.

McClymond, Michael J., and Gerald R. McDermott. *The Theology of Jonathan Edwards*. New York, NY: Oxford University Press, 2012.

Editor in place of author

Bauer, Bruce, and Wagner Kuhn, eds. *Biblical Principles for Missiological Issues in Africa*. Berrien Springs, MI: Andrews University, Department of World Mission, 2015.

Corporate Author

When the item has been prepared by a committee or a corporate entity, that name is used in place of an author's name:

United Nations. *Yearbook of the United Nations*. New York, NY: Department of Public Information, United Nations, 1992.

No Author Given

If no author or editor is given, the bibliographical entry begins with the title of the book:

The Illustrated Bible Dictionary. 3 vols. Wheaton, IL: Tyndale, 1980.

Title

The title comes one space after the period (full stop) following the author's name. The title of a book, pamphlet, or journal must appear in italics. If there is a subtitle, it appears after a colon and is also in italics. Titles in English have first and last and all important words capitalized—usually all but conjunctions, prepositions, and articles. Titles in German have capitals on the first word and on all the nouns. French, Spanish, and Latin titles have capitals only on the first word. Titles of books in non-Latin scripts may be transliterated; a translation into English should appear in brackets, not underlined but capitalized in sentence style immediately following the title.

Schweitzer, Albert. *Das Abendmahlsproblem auf Grund der wissenschaftlichen Forschung des 19. Jahrhunderts und der historischen Berichte*. Tübingen, Germany: J. C. B. Mohr (Paul Siebeck), 1929.

Stam, Juan B. Apocalipsis y profecía: *Las señales de los tiempos y el tercer milenio*. Buenos Aires, Argentina: Kairós, 1998.

Tak, Myung-hwan. *Hankuk ui Shinheung Jonggyo* [New religions in Korea]. Seoul: Song Chong Sa, 1972.

Edition

If the item is of any edition other than the first, this must be indicated. Printings do not count, because a book is changed only when a new edition is made. Give the number of the edition or the exact wording (such as Amer. ed.). Note the period and one space between title and edition. A period comes after the edition, before the place of publication.

Ferguson, Everett. *Backgrounds of Early Christianity*. 3rd ed. Grand Rapids, MI: Eerdmans, 2009.

Multivolume Works

If the source is made up of several volumes, this information is given after the title. For bibliographical entries of multivolume works with individual titles, see examples in chapter 21.

Balz, Horst, and Gerhard Schneider, eds. *Exegetical Dictionary of the New Testament.* 3 vols. Grand Rapids, MI: Eerdmans, 1990-1993.

Series

The series to which a book belongs follows the title and is not in italics. The series statement ends with a period. A volume within the series is recorded as it appears on the title page.

Overholt, Thomas W. *Prophecy in Cross-Cultural Perspective.* SBL Sources for Biblical Study, 17. Atlanta, GA: Scholars, 1986.

Facts of Publication

Place of publication

To make things easy for those whose geographical knowledge is limited, include the city and the country (or the city and the state in the US). If two or more places are given, use only the first. Abbreviations may be used, but always consistently. For cities in the United States, use consistently *only* one option; we suggest postal codes. (For those not used to the United States system, see these options in appendix E). If there is no place of publication, either in the book or in the library catalog, use n.p. for "no place" (capitalized N.p. following a period).

Healdsburg College. *Eleventh Annual Calendar.* N.p.: Healdsburg College, 1894.

Publisher

The publisher is separated from the place of publication by a colon and one space. Certain parts of the publisher's name, such as "limited" and "incorporated," are always omitted. An abbreviated form may be used if done consistently (as is done in this book): Zondervan instead of Zondervan Publishing House. However, university publishers cannot be abbreviated: Chicago University Press. If no publisher information is found, either in the book or in the library catalog, use n.p. for "no publisher." To avoid misunderstanding, use InterVarsity Press and Moody Press in their full forms, because they are separate entities from other organizations with the same name.

Avondale School for Christian Workers. *Twelfth Annual Announcement.* Cooranbong, Australia: n.p., 1908.

Gould, Paul M. *Cultural Apologetics: Renewing the Christian Voice, Conscience, and Imagination in a Disenchanted World.* Grand Rapids, MI: Zondervan, 2019.

Gregor, Brian, and Jens Zimmermann, eds. *Bonhoeffer and Continental Thought: Cruciform Philosophy*. Bloomington, IN: Indiana University Press, 2009.

Date of publication

The date of publication is separated from the publisher by a comma and one space. If there is no date, either in the book or in any catalog, use n.d. for "no date." The date given should be that of the edition, not of the printing. For reprint editions, give as much information as you have, in the following form.

Magil, Joseph. *The Englishman's Hebrew-English Old Testament: Genesis-2 Samuel*. New York, NY: Hebrew Publishing, 1905; reprint, Grand Rapids, MI: Zondervan, 1976.

If a multivolume source has different dates of publication, the beginning and end dates are given in a full bibliographical entry. If the work has not been completed, give only the beginning date: 1964-.

Charlesworth, James H., ed. *The Old Testament Pseudepigrapha*. 2 vols. Garden City, NY: Doubleday, 1983-1985.

When the material used is only a part of the multivolume set, this may be indicated as follows:

Robertson, A. T., and Wesley Perschbacher. *Word Pictures in the New Testament*. Rev. ed. 6 vols. Grand Rapids, MI: Kregel, 2004. 6:137-180.

Ebooks

The bib record for ebooks follows the same patterns as for books, except for one additional element, the name of the online database or URL where you are reading it.

Comba, Emilio. *History of the Waldenses of Italy, From Their Origin to the Reformation*. London: Truslove & Shirley, 1889. HathiTrust.

Torrey, R. A. *How to Succeed in the Christian Life*. New York, NY: Revell, 1906. http://commons.ptsem.edu/id/howtosucceedinch00torr.

Walters, James. *Loving Your Neighbour in an Age of Religious Conflict: A New Agenda for Interfaith Relations*. London: Jessica Kingsley, 2019. ProQuest Ebook Central.

Magazines and Journals

Magazines tend to be general in nature, addressed to a lay population. Examples are *Moody Monthly, National Geographic, Time, Christianity Today,* and *Adventist Review.* The bibliographical entry below shows the correct form for magazine articles. Even if the magazine has volumes, these are not included. If the date includes a number, it is appropriate to use the Library style or European style: 9 November 2012. The traditional American style would be November 9, 2012. Notice the extra comma. Whichever form you use, do so consistently and with the approval of your professor.

Bass, Dorothy, "Receiving the Day the Lord Has Made." *Christianity Today*, 6 March 2000, 63-67.

Monroe, Sylvester. "Does the Rev. Jesse Jackson Still Matter?" *Ebony*, November 2006, 170-180.

Journals are academic and generally focused on one discipline. *Missiology, Journal of Biblical Literature, Theology Today,* and *Review of Religious Studies* are considered journals. For journals, the bibliographical entry must include the volume number.

Costas, Orlando E. "The Mission of Ministry." *Missiology* 14 (1986): 463-471.

The year of the journal is added in parentheses to make finding the item easier. If paging is continuous throughout the volume, the year is enough. If each issue starts with page 1, a month or season must be included: 15 (Spring 1991): 35. Note the space between the colon and the page(s) in a journal reference. When no month or season is given, the number of the issue follows the volume:

Merling, David. "The Search for Noah's Ark." *College and University Dialogue* 11, no. 3 (1999): 5-8.

Additional Materials

The entry for a chapter written by one author in a book edited by another is tricky. Note the *total* number of pages *before* the facts of publication. According to Turabian, this kind of entry should read as follows:

Larson, Donald N. "The Viable Missionary: Learner, Trader, Story Teller." In *Perspectives on the World Christian Movement: A Reader*, ed. Ralph D. Winter and Steven C. Hawthorne, 444-451. Pasadena, CA: William Carey Library, 1992.

Signed articles in specialized dictionaries or encyclopedias also deserve special attention:

Jepsen, Alfred. "אמן." In *Theological Dictionary of the Old Testament*. Edited by G. Johannes Botterweck and Helmer Ringren. Translated by John T. Willis. Grand Rapids, MI: Eerdmans, 1980-2006. 1:292-323.

Given the use of dissertations as research sources, an example should be included:

Gane, Roy Edwin. "Ritual Dynamic Structure: Systems Theory and Ritual Syntax Applied to Selected Ancient Israelite, Babylonian, and Hittite Festival Days." University of California, Berkeley, CA, 1992.

Following these instructions, you will be able to prepare a good bib list. Of course, the examples given in this section correspond to normal entries. More examples, especially of problem bibliographical entries, are found in chapter 21. Turabian 9 author-date style appears in chapter 22. APA notes and reference list entries are in chapter 23.

This chapter has discussed reading and taking notes. These notes will be the building blocks of the paper. They will also supply the information you need for preparing footnotes and bibliographies, which are presented in detail in chapter 20.

chapter sixteen

RESEARCH WRITING

Your research is now complete. You have consulted all relevant sources. Your notes, organized according to the final outline, are ready to be transformed into a written report. The time to write has come. You have already put in about two-thirds of the total time needed to complete the paper; writing and rewriting will take another third. For many, this last third is the hardest. That's one reason why you will meet a lot of ABDs—"All but dissertation" doctoral students. Of course, if you do not write the report, your well-done research will pass unnoticed. Therefore, you need to write a clear, concise, readable report.

This chapter describes research English, makes suggestions on how to write coherent and interesting paragraphs, and instructs on the use of transitional and introductory phrases. It also outlines the stages of the writing process and lists helps for the novice writer.

Research English

English research writing uses simple, concise, and clear language. Other words to describe it are concrete, impersonal, objective, formal, dignified, factual, and unbiased. Helen Sword wrote, "All stylish academic writers hold three ideals in common: communication, craft, and creativity. *Communication* implies respect for one's audience; *craft*, respect for language; *creativity*, respect for academic endeavor."[1]

Impersonal language minimizes the importance of "me" and "I." Generally speaking, the first-person singular does not appear in research writing. A modern trend does allow for its use, especially in the introduction and conclusion; even then, the emphasis must not be on the writer but on the research topic.

1. Helen Sword, *Stylish Academic Writing* (Cambridge, MA: Harvard University Press, 2012), 173.

Some writers refer to themselves as "the writer" or "the researcher" to avoid use of the first-person pronoun. Others use the first-person plural, "we." Neither of these is desirable. While the passive voice ("the cake was eaten by the boy") can be employed to avoid the first-person pronoun, its use makes sentences heavy. As often as possible, use the active voice. Keep your writing alive. Write naturally, directly. While minimizing yourself, avoid the impersonal passive as much as you can. For example, instead of saying in the introduction, "I decided to limit this paper . . . ," write "The natural limits of the topic determined the shape of the paper." Be sure to consult the preferences of your school and adviser on the matter of impersonal language.

A paper or thesis is not the place to use fancy words, metaphors, and similes. Imaginative phrases and comparisons, as well as superlatives ("best," "finest," "largest"), are to be shunned. Idiomatic expressions are out of place. Exclamation marks do not fit.

Research language is modest and tentative. Instead of definite and dogmatic words such as "never," "all," or "none," use "some," "somewhat," or "often." Even when you have evidence for what you write, do not overstate your case.

A well-written research paper will not contain as many adverbs and adjectives as nouns and verbs. Adverbs such as "marvelously" do not fit. In research language, no one is going to be "an outstanding success." But neither should research language be boring. Instead of a general noun such as "man," use a more specific one: "youth," "gentleman," or "scholar." Instead of a verb such as "go," use "amble," "stride," "ride," or "fly." To find these more specific and colorful synonyms, use a dictionary or thesaurus; the ones that come with Microsoft Word and WordPerfect are most helpful.

Research language is standard, not colloquial; it never uses slang. The contracted forms of the negative ("can't," "won't," "didn't") are out of place. The full form should be used. Of the following four levels of English, the proper research language is the standard:

FORMAL	STANDARD	COLLOQUIAL	SLANG
Superlative	Excellent	First-rate	Cool
Exasperating	Irritating	Aggravating	Burns me up
Deranged	Irrational	Crazy	Nuts

The greatest temptation of theology students is to use sermonic instead of research language. The language of the pulpit is not the language of the thesis. Phrases such as "souls won to the truth" should be replaced with something understandable to the general public: "people baptized into the church."

Another aspect of writing that demands attention is inclusive language. The times require sensitivity to gender issues. Without making syntactical errors ("everyone did their homework") or excessive recourse to "he or she" (or worse, "he/she"), write in ways that include both genders and do not stereotype sex roles. "Mankind" becomes "humanity"; singular "he" is changed into plural "they" or alternates with "she."

Excellent writing takes time and effort. Mediocre writing is faster and easier, but it rarely merits the professor's approval, a reader's interest, or your own satisfaction.

The Paragraph: Smallest Unit of the Paper

The smallest unit of the paper, the paragraph, is somewhat like a link in a chain. And, as in the case of the chain, the paper is only as strong as its weakest paragraph. Therefore, time spent learning how to write strong paragraphs is time well spent.

A paragraph should be all about one topic. Its length is determined by how much has to be said about the matter. If it is too long, it probably includes ideas that do not belong to the topic. Rule of thumb: if your paragraph fills more than one computer screen, it is suspect. Here, short is better than long. But a paragraph cannot be extremely short either—one sentence is never a true paragraph—because it cannot cover the topic thoroughly.

Many types of effective and interesting paragraphs can be designed. However, certain elements are found in all paragraphs that communicate well and please the reader. Specific elements discussed in this section are unity and coherence. A sampling of paragraphs is also presented.

Paragraph Unity

A good paragraph puts in one place all the material that belongs together and keeps it apart from other items that do not belong. Every well-constructed paragraph has one unifying thought. All the items included are somehow related to that thought. This precludes inclusion of extraneous ideas and comments.

One device that fosters paragraph unity is the topic sentence. This sentence, which states the main idea of the paragraph, may come at any point in the paragraph. Its purpose is not only to give the chief idea of the paragraph, but also to provide an anchor, so to speak, for the rest of the sentences in the paragraph.

It does so by providing a center to which the rest of the paragraph can relate. Examples of topic sentences are found in the majority of paragraphs in this book, including this paragraph.

Paragraph Coherence

A strong paragraph hangs together; it coheres. Paragraph coherence is concerned with the order in which the information is presented and with the clear and logical relationship of one statement to the next in the development of ideas. A coherent paragraph conveys information clearly and effectively.

In the following paragraph from Ralph Waldo Emerson's "Self-Reliance," coherence depends on the repeated references to the hypothetical man being described and on the movement from the small, personal, and material to the intangible and universal.

> The civilized man has built a coach, but has lost the use of his feet. He is supported on crutches, but lacks so much support of muscle. He has a fine Geneva watch, but he fails of the skill to tell the hour by the sun. A Greenwich nautical almanac he has, and so being sure of the information when he wants it, the man in the street does not know a star in the sky. The solstice he does not observe; the equinox he knows as little, and the whole bright calendar of the year is without a dial in his mind.[2]

Sample Expository Paragraphs

The following paragraphs are built around definition, enumeration or classification, comparison, and cause and effect. Other types, such as reiteration, question and answer, and analogy, could also be cited.

Definition

> The term *leitourgia* in classical Greek described the performance of a special honorific service for the state, such as, for instance, outfitting a warship or providing a choir for a theatrical performance at a major ceremony. The honor dimension was important to the term. By the second century B.C. the word was used in popular language for priestly service in the worship of the gods. In the Septuagint it was used for the Hebrew *sharath* to designate participation in the divine worship, either as an officiant or as a worshiper. While in the New Testament the more common

2. Ralph Waldo Emmerson, "Self-Reliance," in *The Collected Works of Ralph Waldo Emerson* (Cambridge, MA: Belknap Press of Harvard University Press, 1979), 2:48.

term for serving is *diakonia*, by Hippolytus' time *leitourgia* and *munus* were the accepted terms for the performance of Christian worship, especially the Eucharist. These words conveyed the idea of the prestige of the one who could officiate in the church service.[3]

Enumeration or Classification

Women [in the nineteenth century] were not accorded what the twentieth century considers basic human rights. Politically, women were virtual nonentities. Their contributions were confined largely to the domestic realm. They could not secure employment in the occupation of their choice, and higher education was practically closed to them. In addition, they were not only denied the right to vote; they were, socially and individually, perceived as being under the jurisdiction of men. Once married, a woman lost all claim to any property she had previously owned; it was transferred to her husband. She had legal claims neither to her own body nor to her children in the event of divorce.[4]

Comparison/Contrast

In the evangelical Christian community, the issue of headship/submission/equality lies at the heart of the fundamental differences between the two major proactive groups in the ordination debate. The Council on Biblical Manhood and Womanhood, representing those who oppose women's ordination, ultimately bases its biblical argument on the premise that the divine plan in creation affirmed equality of the sexes in spiritual status but included role distinctions involving the headship of man over woman. . . . Those holding this position have been referred to as "patriarchalists," "hierarchalists," or (their preferred self-designation) "complementarians." The second group, Christians for Biblical Equality, representing evangelicals who support women's ordination, argue that the divine plan at Creation affirmed full equality of the sexes without any male headship or female submission. . . . Those holding this view have been referred to as "Christian feminists" or (their preferred self-designation) "egalitarians."[5]

---

3. Daniel Augsburger, "Clerical Authority and Ordination," in *Women in Ministry: Biblical and Historical Perspectives*, ed. Nancy J. Vyhmeister (Berrien Springs, MI: Andrews University Press, 1998), 83. (Hereafter referred to as *WIM*.)

4. Alicia Worley, "Ellen White and Women's Rights," *WIM*, 357.

5. Richard M. Davidson, "Headship, Submission, and Equality in Scripture," *WIM*, 259.

Cause and Effect

> Even in the religious arena, [nineteenth-century] women were limited. Most churches did not ordain women and either prohibited or frowned upon women speaking in public. Because a large sector of society perceived the church as responsible for the denigration of women, many elements in the women's movement became hostile to it. For example, powerful crusader Elizabeth Gage called the church the bulwark of women's slavery. For her, no entity was more offensive than organized religion. For this reason, freedom from religious orthodoxy became crucial to feminist leadership.[6]

These samples illustrate good writing. They also show different ways of constructing paragraphs.

Transitions and Introductions

Student writers often have trouble finding an appropriate word to make the transition from one idea or sentence to another. A further difficulty is finding words to introduce quotations. This section suggests some terms for both purposes.

Transitional Words

Following is a list of transitional words and phrases that may be useful in relating sentences and ideas from one to another.[7] Using these words can further improve your research writing style.

- accordingly
- again
- also
- and
- at the same time
- besides
- but
- consequently
- finally
- first (second, etc.)
- further
- hence
- however
- in addition
- in like manner
- last
- likewise
- meanwhile
- moreover
- next
- nor
- on the other hand

6. Worley, 357.

7. Kate L. Turabian, *Student's Guide for Writing College Papers*, 3rd ed. (Chicago, IL: University of Chicago Press, 1976), 71.

on the whole	then	to sum up
or	therefore	too
similarly	thus	
so	to conclude	

To summarize, words and phrases such as these can be used effectively to smooth transitions and *thus* make for easier reading. *However*, be sure you are certain what the word means and choose the one that best fits your writing. *Finally*, use a variety of these transition words. Thus and likewise can be used too many times in a project.

Introducing Quotations

Quotations are the words and ideas of another author. We borrow them to enhance a position or strengthen an argument. These quotations need to be introduced. Readers are jolted when a quotation comes out of the blue and upset when they have to look at the footnote to find who said such a thing. However, frequently introducing quotations with the phrase "So-and-so wrote that" bores the reader. Here is a list of verbs that can be used to introduce quotations:

accepts	denies	recommends
adds	describes	reports
admits	discusses	reveals
affirms	expresses	states
agrees	indicates	stipulates
argues	labels	submits
asks	objects	suggests
believes	opposes	thinks
combats	points out	verifies
confirms	points to	writes
declares	portrays	
defends	recalls	

In introducing quotations, tense usage is important. To refer to an event of the past, use the past: "John Wesley argued that . . ." or "Manalo defended . . ." When referring to stated views and beliefs of present or past writers, the present tense may be used. The idea still stands. In a discussion of the theological understanding of Bultmann, it is correct to say, "Bultmann admits . . . but points out that . . ." One could even write, "Luther accepts that . . . and confirms . . . ," even when Luther has been dead for centuries. However, you should avoid changing back and forth between past and present. The simplest solution to the tense dilemma is to consistently use the past tense for whatever happened or was written in the past. Whatever the choice, consistency is mandatory; the rationale for using one verb tense over another should be clear.

Formal quotations may be preceded by a colon or a comma. The setting will determine your choice. Quotations must remain identical to the source, with only the possibility of changing the case of the initial letter. For example, Paul wrote to the Corinthians, "Pursue love" (1 Cor 14:1). The quotation remains intact.

A quotation may also be woven into your sentence. In that case the initial cap will change to a lower case. The syntax of your sentence is the one that counts. For example, if your sentence began "Paul wrote to the Corinthians that," you would need to change the quotation. I could write: Paul wrote to the Corinthians that they should pursue love (1 Cor 14:1). You had to change the person (you to they) and the tense (pursue to should pursue). What Paul wrote is now part of what you are saying. This is a paraphrase, but it still needs a reference. As you make quotations fit smoothly into your writing, be especially careful with the person and the tense. Above all, be faithful to your source; use brackets to show any addition or modification.

Quoting Bible texts presents unique problems. We often hear: "First Samuel 3:10 says" (at least the sentence begins with a written-out number!). Obviously, the passage cannot speak. We need to look for another way to quote it. "In 1 Samuel 3:10 we read" would be appropriate. Or I could write, "The story reads: 'Now the LORD came and stood there' (1 Sam 3:10)." In the Pauline letters, it is appropriate to write: "Paul wrote." When quoting from Chronicles, I would have to speak of the Chronicler or the author of Chronicles. Note that American usage calls for double quotation marks around what is quoted. If what I quote contains something in quotation marks, those marks will become single quotation marks within my quotation.

The quotation of longer passages has its own rules. According to Turabian, when you quote five or more lines, in which there are at least two separate sentences, you have a "block quotation." APA mandates a block quotation for forty or more words. In a block quotation, you will indent the quotation, at least from the left, and you will single space. This chapter gives you several examples. Naturally, you still need to introduce the quotation.

Be careful to include all the necessary quotation marks and footnotes (or endnotes) to avoid being labeled a plagiarist. Even if you paraphrase, give the reference. The origin of a borrowed phrase or idea must be acknowledged by a footnote.

The Writing Process

Writing a paper is a process to be achieved in stages: writing, correcting, and rewriting. Two drafts and a final copy may be enough to produce a good paper; often three or four drafts are needed. If your native language is not English, or if the subject is complex, writing and rewriting become even more necessary. Some students may need to find editorial assistance, since ghost-writing papers is not part of the professor's job description.

First Draft: Write and Rewrite

Writing cannot be done effectively in small segments of time. Set aside enough time to write one complete section of the paper. If you have to stop and start too many times, you will waste time rereading what you have written to "get the feel of things" again.

In bygone days, teachers recommended a first hand-written draft, to be typed later. Today computers make keyboarding the first draft a good idea. You can edit and "cut and paste" to your heart's content, all the while working from a rough draft. If you are computer illiterate, now is the time to learn the computer skills needed for scholarship. If you must write your first draft by hand, leave an empty space between every line so you can make legible corrections.

Write one section at a time, following the order of outline given by your notes. The wording of the notes suggests the wording for the paper. When you come to a quotation, you may paraphrase it, copy it from your hand-written note card, or cut and paste from your computer notes to your paper (numbered notes, digital or physical, make this easy). Remember to reference the source of the quotation, citation, or allusion.

How you write will depend on how you have taken notes. If you are writing by hand, you will put the footnote number in the text and make a list of the footnotes on a separate sheet of paper. You may also use the computer, with three files: one contains the notes, another contains the alphabetical list of bibliographical entries, the third contains the developing text. Finally, you can use one of the bibliographic management programs that make automatic footnotes directly from the bibliographical entries you have entered into it.[8] Modernizing your work style will spare you sweat and tears.

Once the first writing is completed, allow the draft to rest for a day or so. Then reread and rewrite, making the necessary corrections. A word to

---

8. Examples of popular bibliographic management programs include Zotero, Citavi, EndNote, EasyBib, Mendeley, and RefWorks. See Chapter 15.

the wise: experience tells me that I see mistakes more easily on a printed page than on a computer screen. Rewriting includes deleting, adding, rearranging, checking spelling and punctuation, completing footnotes, and general editorial work.

Second Draft: Rewrite and Type

After you have corrected the first draft, even you may have trouble reading through the red marks you made. Rewrite, retype, or—better by far—enter the corrections in the document already in your word processor. This becomes the second draft.

Now is a good time to read the whole paper again, this time aloud to yourself or someone else. Another person often finds problems you cannot see. Many students find spouses to be excellent critics of their literary work. Students who do not write well in English may need an editor to make corrections.

Whether you input your paper on the computer or hire someone to do it, you are responsible for any mistakes, in both spelling and format. Advertisements around schools tout "low prices" for computer work. Saving money on this work is not wise. You need a computer operator who knows the required format and gives you a perfectly typed paper. Remember, you are responsible for the contents, language, and presentation of your paper. This being so, you probably should acquire the computer skills to do your own work.

Revising

In the revision process, the writer needs to look for incorrect spellings, bad punctuation, unclear sentences, and anything else that mars the reading. The following is a list of specific areas that may cause problems. Pay special attention to them.

1. Flow of ideas: There should be a natural continuity from one idea and one sentence to the next.
2. Coherence: There should be cohesion (a "sticking together") of ideas and sentences. In order to have coherence, there must be some organizing principle.
3. Bridges: There should be natural bridges from one topic to another; over these the reader may walk from one part of the paper to the next. There should be no abrupt transitions or changes of thought.
4. Logic of organization: There must be a reasonable explanation for the way the ideas and topics are organized. The ideas must also be expressed in logical sentences.

5. Weak spots or omissions: There should be no places where it appears there has been insufficient research or something has been left out. If you discover such a spot, go back to the library and look for something to enrich the poor portion of the paper.
6. Awkward sentences: There is usually a better way to say something. If the sentence does not sound right, change it. The best possible syntax and grammar should be used.
7. Unnecessary words: There should be no more words than needed. Such words as "pretty," "rather," and "very" are useless and must be eliminated. The best way to say something is the simplest and shortest way.

These seven items provide a good basis for examining and revising the paper. Obviously, this kind of rewriting takes time. But high marks and the satisfaction of having done excellent work will repay your effort.

Help for the Novice Writer

The following books from the University of Chicago Guides to Writing, Editing, and Publishing series provide a wealth of material to help you write better:

Booth, Wayne C., Gregory G. Colomb, Joseph M. Williams, Joseph Bizup, and William T. FitzGerald. *The Craft of Research.* 4th ed. Chicago, IL: University of Chicago Press, 2016.

Chicago Manual of Style. 17th ed. Chicago, IL: University of Chicago Press, 2017.

Turabian, Kate L. *A Manual for Writers of Research Papers, Theses, and Dissertations.* 9th ed. Revised by Wayne C. Booth, Gregory G. Colomb, Joseph M. Williams, Joseph Bizup, William T. FitzGerald, and the University of Chicago Press Editorial Staff. 9th ed. Chicago, IL: University of Chicago Press, 2018.

These books on writing could help you too:

Birkenstein, Cathy, and Gerald Graff. *They Say / I Say: The Moves that Matter in Academic Writing*, 4th ed. New York, NY: W. W. Norton, 2018.

Hacker, Diana, and Nancy Sommers. *A Writer's Reference.* 9th ed. Boston, MA: Bedford/St. Martins, 2018.

Hudson, Robert. *A Christian Writer's Manual of Style.* 4th ed. Grand Rapids, MI: Zondervan, 2016.

Pinker, Steven. *The Sense of Style: The Thinking Person's Guide to Writing in the 21st Century*. New York, NY: Viking, 2014.

Strunk, William, Jr., E. B. White, and Frank McCourt. *The Elements of Style*. 4th ed. New York, NY: Pearson Longman, 2018.

Sword, Helen. *Stylish Academic Writing*. Cambridge, MA: Harvard University Press, 2012.

This chapter described English research writing style. Chapter 20 will deal with the format required for research papers and dissertations.

chapter seventeen

ORGANIZING THE PAPER

Organizational decisions take place from the moment you choose a topic until that last change just before you hand the paper in. You must deal with macro-organization as well as micro-organization. This chapter speaks to both issues. The larger picture deals with the organization of the parts of the paper, especially the body of the report. Micro-organization deals with smaller items, including the visible organization of headings and enumerations.

Parts of the Paper

A well-written research paper should have five main parts: preliminary pages, introduction, body, summary and conclusions, and bibliography. If needed, appendixes may be added.

The principal parts of the paper—introduction, body, and conclusion—must harmonize. That is, they must integrate into one whole. The introduction sets the stage, preparing the reader to understand the purpose, nature, and direction of the research. The main body of the text gives a clear report of the findings. The conclusion summarizes and evaluates the results of the investigation. The bibliography documents what has been presented.

To achieve the overall harmony of the paper, take your proposal seriously. Then begin writing with the first content chapter (chapter 1 in a paper, chapter 2 in a dissertation), leaving the introduction for later. Write the rest of the body, chapter after chapter. Then summarize and draw conclusions. After all that, you will be ready to smooth the proposal into an introduction. Then prepare the bibliography and appendixes before going to the preliminary pages, which include the table of contents.

Preliminary Pages

In a class paper at the graduate level, the preliminary pages include the title page, the table of contents, and, if needed, lists of figures, tables, and illustrations. A thesis may include a dedication and/or acknowledgment. In a short class paper, the preliminary pages are not numbered; the beginning of the introduction is page 1. In a thesis or dissertation, the preliminary pages are numbered from the title page (no number typed here!) with lowercase Roman numerals at the bottom center of the page. These details may vary at different educational institutions. Described here is a generally accepted traditional model or format.

Title Page

The title page includes the name of the institution where the paper is being presented, the title of the paper, the name of the class or program for which the paper is written, the name of the writer, and the date. The professor's name is not included. A thesis or dissertation also requires an approval sheet (see chapter 20). A model title page also appears in chapter 20.

Table of Contents

The table of contents lists everything that comes after it, starting with lists of abbreviations and illustrations and continuing through the bibliography. Chapter titles, as well as headings and subheadings to the third level, are listed. An example of the format of a table of contents is given in chapter 20. Use Arabic numbers for your chapters.

List of Illustrations

If two or more tables, figures, or illustrations are used, these should be listed. The format to follow is shown in the list of illustrations for this book. If there are only a few of each, the list of tables and figures may be on the same page, as part of a list of illustrations.

List of Abbreviations

To avoid writing out the titles of books and journals you use repeatedly, you may insert a list of abbreviations just before the introduction and then use only the abbreviations in the work itself. Some schools require that the abbreviated sources be spelled out the first time they are used even if they are in a list; others consider that the abbreviation list takes the place of the first reference. Know what your school requires. Include in this list only items used in the paper or dissertation. This list does not take the place of a bibliography. Abbreviations of titles of books and journals should be italicized. Other abbreviations, such as PW for Pauly-Wissowa,

Real Encyclopädie der classischen Altertumswissenschaft, are not italicized. Websites that give access to online lists of acceptable abbreviations appear in appendix C.

Introduction

A carefully written proposal is the basis for a clear and effective introduction, which should contain the same parts suggested for the proposal (see chapter 12). The introduction is a reader's guide to the paper. It tells the reader what problem was studied, how the researcher found the answers, and perhaps what the solution to the problem would be.

Whereas the proposal may simply list the items included (statement of the problem, purpose of the research, significance of the research, definition of terms, limitations and delimitations, procedure, and an outline), the introduction polishes the writing and smooths the transition from one section to the next. It often adds a paragraph or more on the background of the problem. Additionally, the future tense of the proposal becomes past tense, since the research has now been completed.

The length of the introduction varies. An introduction to a class paper may be only one page long. An introduction to a thesis may contain twenty or more pages. What is important is that all parts are included and the paper is correctly introduced.

Page 1 of the introduction is the first page of the paper. In class papers the title, INTRODUCTION, is given chapter standing (on the 13th line or 2 inches from the top edge of the page), but not a chapter number. In a thesis or dissertation, the introduction usually is chapter 1.

Main Body of the Paper

In this part of the paper you report the findings of the research. The body is the longest part of the paper. It is divided into chapters (or major sections in a short paper), each with its own divisions and subdivisions. Since the organization of the main body of the paper is so important, this topic will be covered in a separate section.

Summary and Conclusions

As the title indicates, this part of the paper summarizes the findings and draws conclusions. No new evidence is brought in. The presentation of data has been done in the main body. The summary should be brief—only as long as needed to bring the issue into focus. The conclusions are then drawn from the summary. Remember that many paper/dissertation readers never read more than the introduction and summary/conclusions. Everything you want readers to know about your research must be in those two places.

Take the time needed to craft your concluding section with care. The conclusion or conclusions must fit the problem or research question declared in the introduction of the paper. It would make no sense to ask one question and answer another. Conclusions presented may be firm or tentative. Sometimes the research only "suggests" a solution to a problem. At times the research may turn up areas that need to be investigated and could be a topic for further study. It is proper to note such instances in the conclusions.

The status of the summary and conclusions must match that of the introduction. If the introduction was given a chapter number, the summary and conclusions must be considered a chapter. If the introduction was not a chapter, the summary and conclusion will not be a chapter either.

Appendixes

A paper may have one or more appendixes. These are added sections that contain materials not indispensable for reading and understanding the paper, but useful for gaining deeper insight or for validating and documenting what has been stated. Use lowercase (appendix) to refer to them in the text of the paper. Appendixes may include raw numerical data, statistical information, photocopied materials, or whatever else the researcher needs to present. Appendixes are much more common in dissertations than in papers. When there are several appendixes, as in this book, each has a title and is listed in the table of contents.

Bibliography

The bibliography documents and gives weight to the research. It tells the reader how serious the study was. It also leads readers to sources for further study on the topic.

In research papers, the bibliography, as well as the reference list in APA, follow the appendixes. Instructions on preparing bibliographies appear in chapter 18. Model bibliographies are those in chapter 20 and at the end of this book.

A general overview of the organization of the paper may suffice. But organizing the body of a paper demands special attention. The next section deals with this specifically.

Organizing the Body of the Paper

There are no firm and exact rules regarding how the body of a paper should be organized. Whatever system you choose must be clear and logical—to you and to your adviser, as well as to your readers. Ask your adviser and your peers for a critique of your suggested outline. Be able to defend your organization by answering this question: Why does it make sense to start where you do and follow the thought path you do? Reread the section on "Organization" in chapter 10.

Each chapter must be a self-contained unit. That is, everything on one topic should be in the same chapter. Everything in one section should be related to the same matter; no extraneous material should be allowed. The same topic should not be discussed in several sections. Naturally, there may be references from one section to another, but good organization demands dividing the topic into independent units, tied to each other in some logical manner, but not repeating the same information.

The outline approved by the professor or adviser when the proposal was presented was a good starting point; it served as the skeleton for your paper in its initial stages. However, after reading and studying, you may need to change that outline. Remember to talk to your adviser before you write on the basis of a new outline.

Two sample outlines, each styled differently, were given in chapter 12. One important rule of outlining is that a section that is subdivided must have at least two subsections. You cannot cut an apple into one piece! Likewise, you cannot have a section A (or 1 or a) without a corresponding section B (or 2 or b). Another rule is to make the titles of subsections parallel to each other, in form and content.

Since there is no one accepted method of organizing a paper, this section presents a sampling of possibilities. Again, consultation with the advising professor is indispensable.

Historical topics lend themselves to a chronological method. What happened first is narrated first. The biography of Hudson Taylor, missionary to China, can be divided into sections: childhood, youth, early mission, death of his wife, founding of the China Inland Mission, and so on.

The spatial (geographical) method might be used in reporting the research on an ancient city. The New Testament city of Ephesus could be described part by part: the port, the theater, the library, the Temple of Diana, the marketplace, and so forth.

A comparative method could be used in comparing the Buddhist and Hindu beliefs concerning death. First, each would be described fully; then they would be compared.

For some studies a cause-to-effect method is appropriate. A study of the rapid growth of Christianity in Korea could use this method. The different factors leading to this phenomenon would be studied, one by one. Then the effect (the growth of the Christian church) would be delineated.

Some topics do well with an unfolding method. Here one idea needs to be clearly explained so that it can lead to another. For example, an understanding of the ceremonies of the Israelite tabernacle would need to be established before progressing to an analysis of the way the author of Hebrews deals with these ceremonies.

A practical theology project or thesis normally has a theoretical basis and a practical application. That means the work is organized into two main parts. The theoretical foundation may be divided into biblical, theological, and sociological parts. The practical part may well be chronological—what happened first, and what was next. DMin projects often use this form (see chapter 8).

The starting point for research need not be the same in every case. One may begin from the specifics and arrive at general conclusions—inductive reasoning. Another may begin with general facts and arrive at specific conclusions—deductive reasoning. What is important is that the research process is so designed and executed as to make sense to the readers and to the professor.

Someone has suggested that writing a research report is like building a temple. One must lay the foundation, then erect each pillar. Finally, the roof is placed on the structure. As happens with all parables, this one too falls short. However, it does illustrate the need for balance and careful building so that a clear and convincing result may be achieved. It also suggests that each research paper is a unique construction and, to some extent, a work of art.

Specific guidelines for the organization of literary and bibliographic research are scarce. Specific schemes for organizing biblical-theological-pastoral research must be designed by the student, preferably in collaboration with the professor or committee for whom the paper or thesis is written.

Practical Helps for Organizing the Paper

The final organization of the topic takes place once all the research is finished. The task is difficult and important. This section gives practical suggestions for dividing up the topic and arranging its sections, and for planning the visible organization of the written report.

Organizing the Notes

When you use note cards, you have an advantage as long as each note card or slip has its heading and subheading. The notes can easily be separated into piles. Use a table—or the floor—and separate the slips by headings and subheadings and sub-subheadings, if there are any. Then look through each pile and read each note. Organize each pile into a logical sequence. If there are notes that do not belong, take them out; put them where they do belong or discard them. Do not be surprised if the tentative outline no longer seems to fit. Once all the cards are distributed, a better outline may suggest itself.

When all the small piles are organized within themselves and put in a logical sequence with the other small piles that belong with them in a larger topic, the order and organization of each section or chapter of the paper are easy to see. Put an elastic or rubber band around each section to keep it separate and organized (if yours is a long paper, try using a shoe box). Then confirm your decisions regarding the sequence of chapters.

Now read the note cards in sequence, trying to feel (or see or hear) how these bits of information fall into place. If you are not satisfied with the way the cards fit together, re-sort your cards. It may take several sortings to organize the cards—and your paper. But the time will be well spent, for you will write with greater ease and speed for having gone through this process.

When you use a computer program, such as Access or Excel, to record your notes, you will need to sort the notes. I suggest using extra columns with a numbering or letter system so the notes can be automatically sorted using the sort feature in the program. The numbers/letters from the tentative outline prepared at the time of the proposal provide a reasonable beginning place, with one column for each level in the outline, plus one additional column to order notes within the level. This way the first sort can be done quickly in a few seconds. However, if you need to resort them, then you will need to change the numbers/letters to match the new order.

Visible Organization in the Written Report

Using different levels of headings and enumerations helps to visibly organize the contents of a paper. How to do it is discussed in the following paragraphs.

Headings

Throughout this book different kinds or levels of headings have been used. These headings show how a topic is divided and subdivided and what belongs with what. The headings and subheadings represent the different parts of the outline. Once more, a heading must have two subheadings or none.

A first-level heading indicates a main division of the chapter. In this chapter, "Practical Helps for Organizing the Paper" is a first-level heading. It is centered and bolded.

The second-level heading indicates a subdivision of that main division. In this chapter "Visible Organization in the Written Report" is a second-level heading. It is centered but not bolded. Its "twin" is "Organizing the Notes." The graphic presentation shows it is a part of "Practical Helps for Organizing the Paper."

The third-level heading indicates a part of the second-level subdivision. In this chapter "Headings" and "Enumerations" are third-level headings. These headings are placed flush with the left margin and bolded. In the three kinds of headings already listed, the first, last, and principal words are capitalized.

The fourth-level heading indicates a division of a third-level heading. It is flush with the left margin, but not bolded. Only the first word is capitalized. "Within the paragraph" is an example of a fourth-level heading in this chapter.

The fifth-level heading, the smallest organizational subdivision in a paper, shows that what follows is a part of a fourth-level heading. This heading is reserved for a small segment of the paper, often only a paragraph. A fifth-level heading is part of the paragraph; it is indented (like the paragraph), bolded, and followed by a period, or full stop. Only its first word is capitalized. Below are examples, "With short sentences" and "With longer sentences."

If the organization of a paper does not need so many levels of headings, you may choose to use only three, for example, those that are bolded. However, you cannot use one scheme (complete sequence) in one chapter and the incomplete scheme (bold only) in another chapter. Consistency is required.

Use the same type font and size for headings and text: for example, Times New Roman, 12 points. The difference is in the location (flush left or centered) and the bolding.

Notice the extra empty line between the text above and the next subtitle, whichever level it is. This is a visual aid to organization—for you and for your readers.

Enumerations

Enumerations help to visibly organize materials in the written report. They can be used within a paragraph and within a sentence. Instructions follow.

Within the paragraph

Follow the model provided below. Indent the Arabic number, but allow the following lines to reach the left margin. You may have trouble with Word thinking it knows more than you do! It will make these into hanging indent paragraphs. Disable that automatic feature!

1. The number is typed after the same indentation as the paragraph and followed by a period or full stop, after which there is one empty space.

2. Double spacing is used as in the rest of the paper.
3. A period or full stop follows each item. There may be several sentences after each number.
4. If double-digit numbers are used, the indentation must be modified so that all the periods are aligned.

Within the sentence

An enumeration within a sentence may use letters or numbers, set in parentheses. Numbers usually represent a larger division; letters, a smaller one. The items are set off by commas unless they have punctuation within them, in which case they are set off by semicolons. For example:

> He gave three reasons for his resignation: (1) age, (2) gradually failing eyesight, and (3) desire to live under less pressure.
>
> His failing eyesight is due to (a) age, now 65 years; (b) a congenital, worsening disease; (c) stress, caused by the responsibilities of the job.

This chapter has explained the general organization of the paper and given suggestions, both theoretical and practical, for organizing the material in the research report. The actual writing skills are covered in chapter 16. How to reference your borrowed materials is the topic of chapter 18.

chapter eighteen

DOCUMENTATION

When you get ready for an international trip, you need documentation. You have a passport to *prove* your citizenship. In it there are visas that *confirm* your permission to enter certain countries. Your airplane ticket *verifies* that there is a seat on that plane for you. A vaccination certificate *validates* that you are ready to face a certain tropical illness. Your hotel reservation *proves* that you will have a bed.

In research, documentation has similar functions. Documentation *verifies* that you searched and found sources to *validate* what you are saying. Documentation *proves* that you competently searched for and found pertinent information. Documentation *confirms* your integrity so as to avoid any appearance of plagiarism.

According to Turabian, research documentation comes in three principal forms: reference notes, content notes, and bibliographical entries. You have met them in previous chapters, but here we will take some extra time to ensure that you know how to prepare and present them.

Reference Notes

Reference notes may be footnotes (at the bottom of the page) or endnotes (either at the end of the chapter or the end of the book). Reference notes may also be parenthetical, as is done in Turabian author-date style and APA style.

Student researchers are often in doubt concerning whether they should cite a given item. Once they have decided they should, they wonder how to do it. This chapter elucidates both aspects of the note. A comparison of notes and bibliographical entries appears in chapter 21 for traditional Turabian users, of parenthetical Turabian author-date style in chapter 22, and of parenthetic notes and reference lists in chapter 23 for APA users.

Endnotes are considered appropriate for short papers and are always numbered consecutively throughout the chapter or paper. Footnotes are normally required in theses and dissertations; they can be numbered consecutively throughout the chapter (as in this book) or page by page.

Why Reference Notes?

Noted educator from Stanford University Philip H. Rhinelander poked fun at some abuses of reference notes. My favorites are:

1. The *hidden ball* footnote says, in effect, "If I snow you with enough references you won't bother to ask what I'm trying to say."
2. The *false modesty* footnote: "I don't want to parade my learning, but I have read a lot of books."
3. The *I-know-more-than-you-do* footnote: "Use a lot of foreign languages in these. It's terribly learned—and besides, there's a good chance the reader won't be able to translate them anyway."
4. The *I'm-no-fool* footnote: "Yes, I've read Professor Z's book too."[1]

Rhinelander must have read many student papers, because before he was done with his list, he had catalogued fifteen equally laughter-invoking examples. Of course, these abuses are not appropriate to research and should be avoided.

There are, however, legitimate uses for notes that show where information was obtained. They serve a triple purpose: (1) to indicate that there is authority behind statements made, in order to strengthen the researcher's assertions; (2) to help the scholar who is looking for information on the topic, in order to easily find the material referred to; (3) to admit honestly one's intellectual indebtedness to another author (see chapter 10).

When Reference Notes?

Content notes are used at the discretion of the writer—anytime the addition of a note would enrich or enhance the elaboration of ideas. Reference notes, however, are mandatory and are used whenever materials from another author are cited or quoted.

A reference note is used to indicate the source of a quotation—whether it be three words or three lines. It is also used to show the source of an idea, even though that idea may be expressed in the researcher's own words. Failure to use

1. Philip H. Rhinelander, "Furtive and Frivolous Functions of Footnotes," quoted from the *Edpress Newsletter*, in *Phi Delta Kappan* 44, no. 9 (June 1963): 438.

quotation marks for quoted materials or to give due credit to a source by using a reference note is considered a major flaw in research. Plagiarism, as such illegitimate copying is called, is a dishonest use of another's property—intellectual thievery. (On this see chapter 10.) Therefore, a writer must give references for all quoted or cited words or ideas, and remember to use quotation marks for every borrowed phrase or sentence.

No reference notes are needed when the ideas and words in the paper are yours or are common knowledge. If you present a paper with no footnotes, your reader would surmise that you did everything by yourself, that you are not indebted to anyone. Such a paper would contain only your opinions or be superficial, consisting exclusively of general knowledge; it would not qualify as research. Facts that everyone knows—such as AD 79 for the eruption of Mount Vesuvius—need no footnotes. For an idea or a piece of information to qualify as common knowledge, it must appear in several places. However, if eighteen authors say one thing, and two say something different, you will want to note the dissenters in a footnote.

Format of the Reference Note

Since the purpose of a reference note is to permit a reader to find the original source, you must provide sufficient information to make locating it easy. Using a uniform format helps the reader and impresses your professor.

In the text, the reference note appears only as a superscript Arabic number at the end of the quotation, citation, or allusion. If you are using the up-to-date version of Word, for example, how the note appears at the bottom of the page or end of the chapter is more or less automatic. However, you are responsible for making sure that the local rules are followed. For example, the last two editions of Turabian have indicated a note format like the one used in this book. If this is required, it involves highlighting the number in the footnote, unclicking the superscript in the font toolbar, and adding the period. This may seem a bit tedious, but I am unaware of any shortcuts. Further information on formatting appears in chapter 20.

In reference notes, abbreviations are commonly used. Be sure to use them consistently. In current Turabian usage, the abbreviation for page or pages is omitted. In indicating pages, 2-4 means pages 2 through 4, including page 3; using 2, 4 means only pages 2 and 4. The publication data are in parentheses, and the only period, or full stop, is the final one.

In many sources, the hyphen between page numbers may appear as an "en dash." Considering the difficulty of creating such an item, we suggest you simply use a hyphen between numbers: pages 4-6 or chapters 20-23.

Full Reference Notes

The following are examples of full reference notes, used the first time an item is mentioned. They are the basic models: a book, a journal article, a magazine article, a chapter in a multiauthored book, and a thesis. Use the bibliographical information you gathered and typed into a list as the basis for your footnotes. See examples of more kinds of footnotes in chapter 21.

Book

As promised in chapter 15, this information is repeated for your convenience as you write the footnotes.

Author's name in normal order, title in italics with first and last and all important words capitalized, publication data in parentheses, page (or pages) at the end of the note. For every city you must give the state or the country. The name of the state is now usually the two-letter postal abbreviation (IL). Follow whatever system your school indicates. Another choice shows in my use of Baker for Baker Book House. If I use a short form for one publisher, I must use the short form of all other publishers: Zondervan, Hendrickson, Orbis. However, do not shorten the name of university presses (University of Chicago Press, Princeton University Press) or of presses that otherwise would be confused with something else, for example, InterVarsity Press and Moody Press. This is necessary to preserve the identity of the publisher.

1. Grant R. Osborne, *The Hermeneutical Spiral: A Comprehensive Introduction to Biblical Interpretation* (Downers Grove, IL: InterVarsity Press, 2010), 25.

Journal article

Author, title of article in quotation marks (in English, commas go inside the quotation marks), title of journal in italics, no comma before or after volume number, date of issue in parentheses, colon, one space, page number. If paging is continuous in each volume (as in this example), the year is enough. If paging is not continuous, month or season should be given.

2. Jorge Torreblanca, "Una definición de tema central en el Pentateuco," *TeoBíblica* 1 (2015): 27-48.

(Special notes on this entry: In Spanish and French, only proper names are capitalized in the title; use a Spanish keyboard so that you do not miss accents and the ñ. In German, almost every word is capitalized. You may need to use Hebrew and Greek words. Computers have keyboards for many languages. Take advantage of the progress, which makes writing the Greek word by hand unnecessary.)

Magazine article

Do not give volume number for a popular magazine; the date is enough. The date may be expressed in Library or European style, as here, or in the traditional American style: April 24, 2000 (note the extra comma). Use one style or the other, but do so consistently.

3. Loren Wilkinson, "Saving Celtic Christianity," *Christianity Today*, 24 April 2000, 80.

Chapter in a multiauthor book

Note the "in," showing that the material to which you refer is part of a book. Note also the editor after the title of the book. Here "ed." means "edited by"; it is not pluralized. Since this is a note, you can use "et al." for the three other editors. In the bibliography, you need to give all the names.

4. Dana L. Robert, "Adoniram Judson Gordon, 1836-1895," in *Mission Legacies: Biographical Studies of Leaders of the Modern Missionary Movement*, ed. Gerald Anderson et al. (Maryknoll, NY: Orbis, 1994), 23.

Dissertation

A dissertation is not considered a published book; its title is presented in quotation marks. The specific degree, the university, and date are in parentheses.

5. Trust Ndlovu, "The Church as an Agent of Reconciliation in the Thought of Desmond Tutu" (PhD diss., Andrews University, 1999), 57.

Second or Later References

If reference is made to the same source more than once, consecutively, the references immediately following use "ibid." (for the Latin *ibidem*, "in the same place"). If the same page is quoted, Ibid. is enough. If a different page is used, the note will read: Ibid., 3. Here the word is capped at the beginning of a note; otherwise it is in lowercase. Some schools may ask for the author's surname and a short form of the title to be repeated.

If reference is made to the same source more than once, but not consecutively, the second time the information is abbreviated. Each school tends to choose its own way: only the author's surname is given, together with the page number, or the author's surname is followed by an abbreviated title and page number. However, if there are two authors by the same surname, distinction must be made by using at least an initial. If more than one work of an author is used, the shortened form of the title is mandatory to distinguish one work from another.

If the abbreviation for the title is announced in a list at the beginning of the paper or, as here, in the first appearance of the source, that abbreviation will be sufficient for all uses in the paper.

6. Laird R. Harris, Gleason L. Archer, and Bruce K. Waltke, *Theological Wordbook of the Old Testament* (*TWOT*), 2 vols. (Chicago, IL: Moody Press, 1980), 1:103.

7. *TWOT,* 1:157.

If two or more items by one author appear following each other in the same note, the second time the author's name used to be replaced by the word "idem" (not italicized), Latin for "the same." Today we repeat the author's surname. For example:

8. Turabian, *A Manual*, 46; Turabian, *Student's Guide*, 68.

Today, we use ibid. only for the same author and same source. Rather than using idem, we repeat the author's surname.

9. Richard N. Soulen, *Handbook of Biblical Criticism* (Atlanta, GA: John Knox, 1976), 24.

10. Ibid.

11. William D. Mounce, *Basics of Biblical Greek Grammar*, 4th ed. (Grand Rapids, MI: Zondervan, 2019), 201.

12. Soulen, 28.

13. William D. Mounce, *The Morphology of Biblical Greek* (Grand Rapids, MI: Zondervan, 1994), 302.

14. Walter C. Kaiser Jr., "What Commentaries Can (and Can't) Do," *Christianity Today*, 2 October 1981, 26.

15. Mounce, *Basics*, 52.

16. Otto Kaiser, "David und Jonathan: Tradition, Redaktion und Geschichte in I Sam 16-20: Ein Versuch," *Ephemerides Theologicae Lovanienses* 66 (1990): 291.

In APA, there is no difference between first and second reference.

Bible References

In a research paper on a nonbiblical topic, the biblical references probably will appear as footnotes or endnotes. In papers dealing with ministry, biblical studies, or theology, Bible references are commonly placed in parentheses directly in the text. However, if there are more than three references, they are normally placed in a footnote.

In English it used to be accepted practice that no version was indicated when one used the King James Version (KJV). Today all versions must be indicated. This is done usually in a footnote the first time the Bible is used (see next examples).

17. Unless otherwise indicated, all Bible references in this paper are from the *New American Standard Bible* (NASB) (La Habra, CA: Lockman Foundation, 1973).

18. All Greek references are from *The Greek New Testament*, 5th rev. ed. (Stuttgart, Germany: United Bible Societies), 2014.

Although you could use several versions of the Bible in one paper, this practice is frowned on. When you write a serious research paper, choose one version of the Bible and use it throughout. Jumping from one version to another, choosing the wording that suits your purposes, suggests that you are trying to make the Bible say what you want it to say.

In modern usage, the abbreviations of the books of the Bible are not followed by periods. A list of appropriate abbreviations appears in appendix B.

Content Notes

Content notes, used in both Turabian and APA styles, provide information that could disrupt or unnecessarily complicate the text. The content note may point out a contrast or discrepancy, give further explanations, or indicate sources for further study. These notes are more usual in theses and dissertations than in short research papers. They are also more varied in style than reference notes. Since many readers do not read footnotes, the text should make sense without the content notes. When a content note quotes or cites, it must give the source.

Doctoral dissertations often have extensive content notes—almost as many pages of notes as of text. Given the variety of structure and form of content notes, what is asked is that they be clear, logical, and as short as possible. Usually these notes are only read by the professor and a few specialists. Make sure the basic material you want read is in the text.

To make the reading of content notes easier, put the reference, in correct format, after the added information. Here are two examples:

1. J. I. Packer identifies different explanations of what Christ's death achieved. The first focuses on the subjective effect of the cross on humans, while the second focuses on the "satisfaction" for human sins ("What Did the Cross Achieve?," *Tyndale Bulletin* 25 [1974]: 19-25).

Or:

2. J. I. Packer identifies different explanations of what Christ's death achieved. The first focuses on the subjective effect of the cross on humans, while the second focuses on the "satisfaction" for human sins. "What Did the Cross Achieve?," *Tyndale Bulletin* 25 (1974): 19-25.

Notice that in the first case, the reference, or publication data, appears in parentheses, with no period after the last word of the comment. This mandates that any parentheses in the reference become square brackets. In the second case, a period follows the comment, and the reference is presented in regular format without parentheses.

As long as the reference follows the comments, either format is acceptable. However, only one style may be used in any one paper. Your school may have a style for the format of these notes.

Bibliographical Entries

Since bibliographical entries are part of the required research documentation, we will mention them here. However, you already met them in chapter 15. You will see them again in chapters 21 through 23.

A well-done bibliography, nicely presented in alphabetical order, will impress your professor and your readers. Take the time to do it well.

Include all items that you have quoted or alluded to. Also include any item that you have perused and that somehow has affected your thinking. That said, do not put in filler items just to make a longer bibliography. That's hardly honest!

This chapter has given the rationale for the use of reference and content notes and the basic guidelines for their format. It touched on bibliographical entries that you will see in detail in chapter 21, which presents examples of reference notes (footnotes) and bibliographical entries for different—and difficult—types of materials. Chapter 22 does the same in the Turabian author-date style. Chapter 23 gives all the details for using the APA system.

chapter nineteen

STATISTICS, TABLES, AND GRAPHS[1]

For many the word "statistics" brings to mind numbers and more numbers, devoid of all relation to reality, unintelligible to most mortals. Others may imagine vast computers that perform complicated operations, impossible to do by hand and head. This leads to attitudes that range from admiration to skepticism. Statistics are an instrument in the hands of politicians, business people, bankers, and others who must manage large quantities of information. They may also be a tool used by a researcher to turn small bits of information into interesting and reasonable conclusions.

Although many people shy away from statistics, in daily life they are used more often than one realizes. For example, Christian Schwarz says that "the factor with the strongest correlation to the overall quality and growth of a church is the readiness to accept help from the outside."[2] This is statistical language, and Schwarz used statistical methods to reach this conclusion. Or when Win Arn notes that one year after a Billy Graham crusade, of 100 converts, only 15 percent were active in the church, and 82 percent of those had a friend or relative in the church before joining, he is using statistics.[3] Even if you don't use statistics in your papers, you should be able to read and understand statistical information.

---

1. Thanks to Edward Maiorov, professor of mathematics and statistics, River Plate Adventist University, Argentina, for his help with the chapter on statistics.

2. Christian A. Schwarz, *Natural Church Development: A Guide to Eight Essential Qualities of Healthy Churches*, 3rd ed. (Carol Stream, IL: ChurchSmart Resources, 1998), 23.

3. Win Arn and Charles Arn, *The Master's Plan for Discipling* (Pasadena, CA: Church Growth, 1982), 134-135.

Some Basics of Statistics

Chapter 4 described sampling, one of the techniques of statistics. Here we consider basic ideas such as grouping of data, measures of central tendency, measures of dispersion, distribution, and correlation.

The first and essential idea of statistics is that of the list or inventory. History tells of the listing of population and economic data for planning wars or levying taxes. Egyptians and Assyrians recorded systematic and periodic censuses. The Bible records a census of men twenty years old or older (Num 1:18) and another of male Levites one month of age or older (Num 3:15).

Grouping of Data

Numerical data may be organized from large to small, or vice versa, in ascending or descending order. *N* (in italics) is shorthand for the number of persons or entries.

Suppose that the ages of the 50 members of a church are the following: 12, 12, 14, 14, 14, 15, 15, 16, 16, 18, 18, 18, 18, 20, 20, 20, 22, 22, 23, 23, 23, 25, 25, 25, 25, 27, 27, 27, 30, 30, 30, 32, 32, 32, 32, 32, 32, 32, 32, 36, 41, 41, 46, 46, 50, 55, 55, 65, 69, 69. Putting these numbers in order shows the distribution of ages in the membership.

The same information is given below in a frequency chart (where frequency shows how many persons are of a certain age). This step of statistical calculations is not part of the final report and is done only in a rough draft.

AGE	FREQUENCY	AGE	FREQUENCY
12	2	30	3
14	3	32	8
15	2	36	1
16	2	41	2
18	4	46	2
20	3	50	1
22	2	55	2
23	3	65	1
25	4	69	2
27	3		

Especially when *N* is very large, the data are grouped by intervals. Generally there should be no fewer than five intervals and no more than twelve.

The number of intervals will depend on the size of N. The same information as presented above is now grouped by intervals.

AGE	FREQUENCY
10-19	13
20-29	15
30-39	12
40-49	4
50-59	3
60-69	3

This kind of statistical treatment may be used by a pastor to divide the church members by age groups: youth, adults, and seniors. Limits must be set for each group: youth, 12-19; adults, 20-59; seniors, 60 and above.

Graphic Representation of a Frequency Distribution

The frequency distribution may be graphically shown by a histogram, a frequency polygon, or a frequency curve. Each graph has its special use.

Histogram

The histogram represents a frequency distribution. The width of its bars (or rectangles) is determined by the intervals. The height of the bars is given by the frequency. The scale need not be exactly the same for both dimensions. The histogram should be a little wider than it is high.

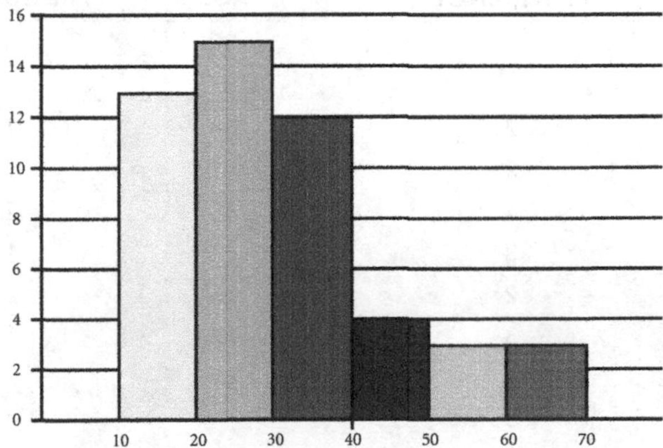

Fig. 1. Members of Church X, by ages

Frequency Polygon

Figure 2 shows the same data as the histogram. The points that shape the frequency polygon are given on the horizontal axis by the midpoint of each interval. On the vertical axis the points simply represent the frequency. The line is brought to the horizontal axis at the midpoint of the intervals before and after those used in the graph.

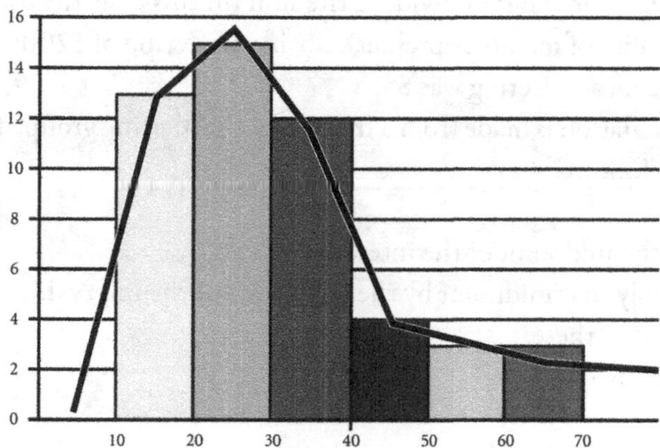

Fig 2. Members of Church X, by ages

Frequency Curve

When N is very large (for example, if the church had 1,500 members), more intervals are used, and the polygon becomes a curve. If the imaginary church of the previous examples had a similar age distribution, but a much larger membership, the graphical representation would be approximately that of figure 3.

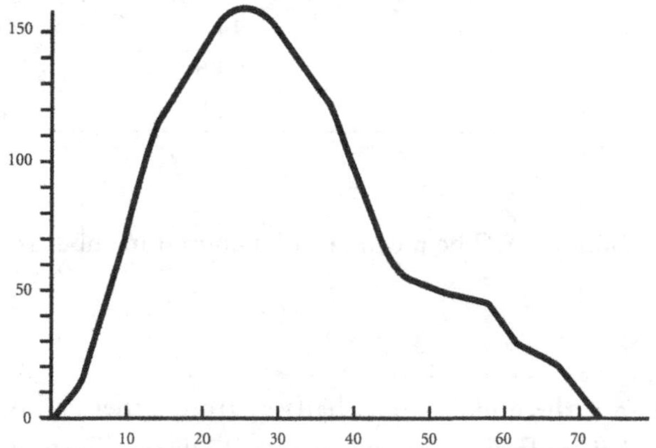

Fig. 3. Members of Church Z, by ages

Measures of Central Tendency

One might ask, how much mission offering does a member give each week? There are three ways to calculate the "average offering." These are called "measures of central tendency."

Average or Arithmetic Mean (m)

The mean is the result of dividing the sum (in this case, the total offering) by *N* (the number of members present). So, if an offering of $200 was given by 40 people, the mean offering was $5.

If the calculation is made from a frequency chart, using grouped data, these steps must be followed:

1. Find the midpoint of the interval.
2. Multiply that midpoint by the frequency of the interval.
3. Add all of these.
4. Divide by *N*.

Using the example of the fifty-member church, let us calculate the mean age of a church member. This step is merely a rough draft and not part of the final report; it needs no figure number.

AGE	FREQUENCY	MIDPOINT	FREQUENCY X MIDPOINT
10-19	13	14.5	13 x 14.5 = 188.5
20-29	15	24.5	15 x 24.5 = 367.5
30-39	12	34.5	12 x 34.5 = 414
40-49	4	44.5	4 x 44.5 = 178
50-59	3	54.5	3 x 54.5 = 163.5
60-69	3	64.5	3 x 64.5 = 193.5
			TOTAL = 1505.0

1505/50 = 30.1 years. The mean age of a church member is a little more than 30 years.

Median

The median is the middle value, halfway from either end of the listing. Consider the mission offerings for one quarter (13 weeks). To find the median, the sums must be placed in order: 534, 560, 580, 590, 595, 598, **600**, 602, 605,

610, 612, 620, 630. The median is 600 pesos, because there are six numbers (values) larger than 600, and six that are smaller.

If the number of values were even, one would have to average the two middle values to determine the median. For example: If the number of persons baptized after studying with six Bible instructors were 20, 22, 24, 30, 32, 38, the median would be halfway between 24 and 30, the two central values. Thus the median would be 27. The arithmetic mean is 27.7 candidates per instructor.

It is possible to obtain a median from grouped data. But if you need to do it, see a statistician.

Mode

The mode is the value that appears most often, the one with the greatest frequency. In the imaginary church of fifty members, the mode is 32 years of age. This age was given 8 times.

Mean, Median, and Mode

The mean, or mathematical average, is the most commonly used of the three. However, it is easily affected by extremes. For example, if the salary of five persons were $12,600; $4,500; $4,400; $4,300; and $4,200 a year, the average salary would be $6,000. This would not give a true picture of wages earned because only one of the five is earning that much. The median would be $4,400 and would give a more accurate picture of the five persons' earnings.

The mode is the least precise of these measures, but it is the easiest to calculate. A book seller is far more interested in the mode than the mean or median. He wants to know which is the most popular book in his store so he can order more copies. To find out, he needs to count only the number of each book sold.

Each of these measurements has its place. However, when you read or present statistics, be careful to note which of the three is being used.

Measures of Dispersion

These measures look not so much at what happens at the middle of the listing as at what happens at the ends. Measures of dispersion focus on differences rather than similarities.

Two church classes have five members each. The ages of the members of Class A are 60, 63, 21, 15, 11. The ages in Class B are 34, 40, 28, 30, 38. The mean (average) age in both classes is 34 years. But in Class A there are two seniors, one young adult, and two adolescents. Class B is more homogeneous as far as age is concerned. One could say that the ages of the members of Class A are more varied or more diverse.

Range

Range is the simplest measure of diversity. It is the difference between the highest and lowest values. In Class A, the range is 63-11 = 52; in Class B, the range is 40-28 = 12. The wide range shows that in Class A there is more variance in age than in class B.

Standard Deviation

$$S=\sqrt{\left(\frac{\Sigma d^2}{N}\right)}$$

Although the range is easier to figure, this measure is not precise. A more precise measure is the standard deviation, or S, which is the square root of the mean of the square of the variances from the arithmetic mean. The formula is:

CLASS A			CLASS B		
Age	x - m = d	d²	Age	x - m = d	d²
63	63 - 34 = 29	841	40	40 - 34 = 6	36
50	60 - 34 = 26	676	38	38 - 34 = 4	16
21	21 - 34 = -13	169	34	34 - 34 = 0	0
15	15 - 34 = -19	361	30	30 - 34 = -4	16
11	11 - 34 = -23	529	28	28 - 34 = -6	36

$\Sigma d^2=2576$ $\Sigma d^2=104$

$S=\sqrt{\left(\frac{2576}{5}\right)}=\sqrt{515.22}=22.69$ $S=\sqrt{\left(\frac{104}{5}\right)}=\sqrt{20.8}=4.56$

The symbol for sum is Σ; d is the difference between a value and its arithmetic mean (x - m). The standard deviation is more easily computed when the numbers are arranged in a table form.

The steps for calculation of standard deviation (S)are:

1. Find the arithmetic mean.
2. Find the variance, subtracting each value from the mean.

3. Square the value of the variance.
4. Add the square of the variances.
5. Divide by N.
6. Obtain the square root.

The larger the S (standard deviation), the greater the range or the variance, and the smaller the homogeneity.

Distribution

Graphic representations have already been used to give a picture of how values are distributed. Figures 2 and 3 show how the church members' ages are distributed. A frequency polygon shows the distribution of a small N (fig. 2), whereas the frequency curve represents a large N (fig. 3).

The distribution of values may be normal or skewed. These concepts are explored in the following section.

Normal Distribution

If we measure the height of a large number of people, we will find that these measurements form a symmetrical frequency polygon. There are about the same number of very tall individuals as very short ones. The majority are somewhere in the middle. The same happens with the measurement of a large number of leaves from the same tree, or the shoe size of men 25 years old in a given place. The larger the number, the more bell-shaped is the curve, similar to the one in figure 4. Theoretically, in a total population, the distribution of tall and short people should form a perfect curve, such as that in figure 5.

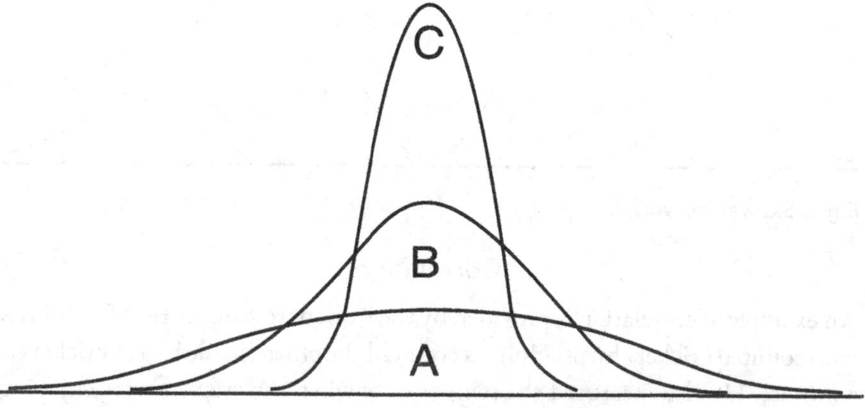

Fig. 4. Normal curves

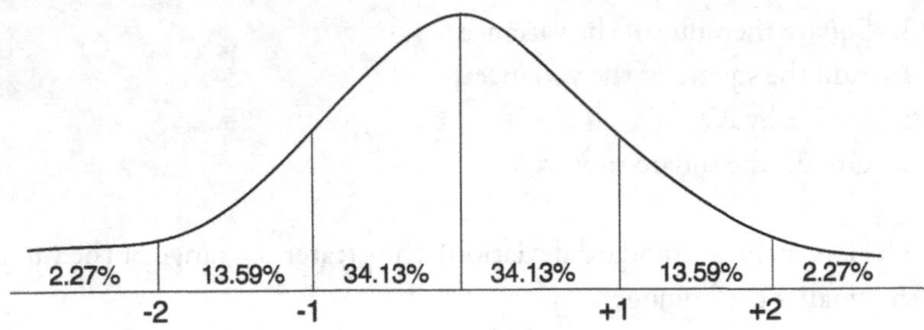

Fig 5. Percentage of area in each standard deviation

In one standard deviation (to either side of the mean), we find about 34 percent of the cases. Approximately another 14 percent fall in the second standard deviation, whereas only some 2 percent fall in the third standard deviation. As an example of this, let us use the measurement of IQs, where the arithmetic mean is 100 and the standard deviation is 15. These figures tell us that approximately 68 percent of the population may be expected to have an IQ between 85 and 115. Only about 2 percent will have an IQ of more than 130 or less than 70.

Skewed Distribution

If a population had a larger percentage than expected of higher extreme IQs or lower extreme IQs, the distribution—and hence the curve—would be skewed, similar to the ones in figure 6. Curve *A* shows a population with more high IQs than normal, while curve *B* shows more low IQs than expected. A skewed curve shows a distribution of characteristics different from what would normally be expected.

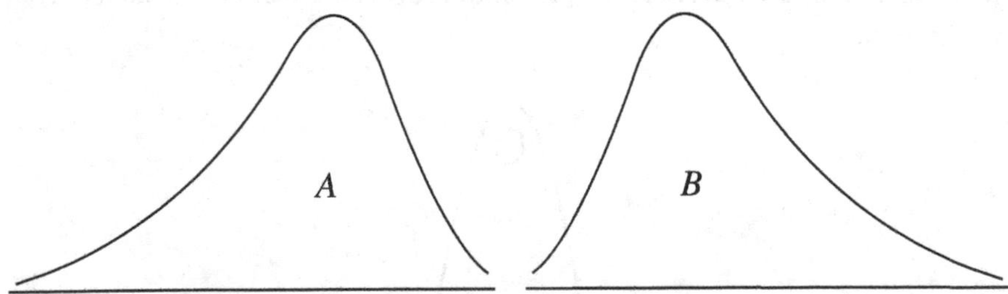

Fig. 6 Skewed curves

Correlation

An example of correlation is provided by the work of researcher Bert E. Holmes, who counted cricket chirps. Holmes counted the chirps made by 115 crickets in a minute. He also measured the temperature when the crickets were chirping. He discovered that when he counted the chirps for 15 seconds and added 37 to that number, the result was quite close to the Fahrenheit temperature—as long as it was not too cold or too hot, that is, between 45 and 80 degrees—at the time of counting.[4]

Without discussing whether the higher temperature caused more chirps or more chirps caused higher temperatures, we can state that there is a positive correlation between the temperature and the number of cricket chirps per second. The more temperature, the more chirps. In fact, Holmes found this positive correlation to be very high: 0.9919. A perfect positive correlation is +1.00, expressed r = +1.00.

In 1975 Mike Scofield studied the relation between the size of a church and the quantity of offerings that entered the treasury per member during the year. He found that when the church grew, the mean per capita offering diminished.[5] This is an example of negative correlation: more members, smaller offerings from each. A perfect negative correlation is expressed as r = -1.00.

When the correlation coefficient (r) is close to 1.00 (either plus or minus), correlation is said to be high (positive or negative). When the correlation coefficient is close to 0, correlation is low or nonexistent. In fact, a very low coefficient (positive or negative) might sometimes be considered a product of chance.

Used in a regression equation, the correlation coefficient may be employed for predictions. Given the value of one variable, the other may be predicted. Thus, without reading the thermometer, one could tell the temperature by the number of cricket chirps. After years of correlating the scores on entrance tests with students' academic performance, researchers can predict how well students will do. On this basis many universities require a certain score on these examinations.

The correlation coefficient becomes more meaningful as more pairs are studied. If a researcher announced that the correlation between long sermons and member satisfaction is r = -0.80, we would know that the longer the sermon, the shorter the satisfaction. But if the researcher told us that only four people were consulted, we would not pay too much attention. However, if 100 members were consulted, even if the r = -0.60, we would give credence to the report.

Once again: correlation does not mean causality. The crowing of roosters does not make the sun come out; neither does sunrise make roosters crow. But both do happen at approximately the same time. If a high correlation between two items is consistently reported many times, it becomes difficult to doubt a cause-and-effect relationship. Smoking and cancer, notably lung cancer, is a

4. Bert E. Holmes, "Vocal Thermometers," *Scientific Monthly* 25 (September 1927): 261-267.

5. Quoted in Gottfried Oosterwal, *Patterns of SDA Church Growth in America* (Berrien Springs, MI: Andrews University Press, 1976), 83-87.

good example. In this case, tobacco manufacturers admitted correlation but tried to deny causality.

The calculation of r is complicated. If you undertake a correlation study, get help from a statistician. Statistical calculators can do the calculations, but the design of the research requires professional help.

Statistical Graphs and Tables

Statistical information is sometimes included in the text of a research report, often in tables and graphs. Tables contain rows of numbers. Graphs represent the numbers by lines and spaces; they are visually more interesting. Tables and graphs allow much information to be given in an organized manner in little space. The rules governing the presentation of tables and graphs in research writing are explained on the following pages.[6]

Tables

All tables must have a number and a title. These are placed above the table, flush left, bold, in sentence-style capitalization, without a terminal period (see the examples). They must also be listed in a list of tables, which comes after the table of contents in the preliminary pages. If there are only a few tables, as in this book, these may be listed together with the illustrations.

If a table is too large to fit across one page, it may be placed lengthwise on a following page. If it is too large to fit either way, it may be prepared on a larger page that is then folded to fit into the paper. A smaller font or photographic reduction may also be used to make a table small enough to fit on a page.

Reference should be made to the table in the text. This draws the reader's attention to the location and the contents of the tables and graphs. A reader should be able to get a clear idea of the results of the research without having to examine every table and graph, even when all details are not in the text. The following example is taken from a description of pastors in South America.[7]

> Table 1 shows the contact of pastors with well-educated people. From the pastors' report, it appears that for the entire division the largest group (155, 45.9 percent) has some contact with educated people, and that the next largest group (112, 33.1 percent) reports little contact with them.

---

6. On graphs and tables, see Turabian, *A Manual for Writers of Research Papers, Theses, and Dissertations*, 86-101, 370-382.

7. The tables in this section are taken from my dissertation. Nancy J. Vyhmeister, "Implications of Selected

A comparison between the Spanish-speaking and Portuguese-speaking respondents shows that although a larger group of Portuguese-speaking pastors (38, 23.0 percent) said they have much contact with educated people, more Spanish-speaking pastors than Portuguese-speaking pastors reported some interaction with educated people (Sp.: 94, 54.3 percent; Port.: 61, 37.0 percent).[8]

Tables should be placed as soon as possible after they are mentioned in the text. However, they should not break a paragraph. If a table needs to be on a separate page, it should still appear as soon as possible after the reference to it.

TABLE 1. Reported contact of pastors with well-educated persons

PASTOR'S CONTACT	SPANISH-SPEAKING PASTORS		PORTUGUESE-SPEAKING PASTORS		SOUTH AMERICAN DIVISION	
	N	%	*N*	%	*N*	%
No answer	1	0.6	1	0.6	2	0.6
Much	20	11.6	38	23.0	58	17.2
Some	94	54.3	61	37.0	155	45.9
Little	54	31.2	58	35.2	112	33.1
None	4	2.3	7	4.2	11	3.2
	173	100.0	165	100.0	338	100.0

While they are not identical, all three tables are acceptable variations in style. Vertical lines (not allowed in some schools) are used in table 2. Do not mix different styles in one paper. The titles of the left-hand column are typed flush left. The titles of the other columns are centered over the numbers. Numbers are right aligned. The three dots represent nil or zero. The vertical spacing and the font size vary to fit the space available; the vertical spacing should be between one and two lines. The font may be small, but it must still be readable.

Use the table feature of your word processor. Once the table is complete, with all the information, decide which lines you will keep and which you will erase. Some schools have rules about the appearance of tables. Be sure to inquire.

Curricular Determinants for Seventh-day Adventist Graduate Theological Education in the South American Division, (EdD diss, Andrews University, 1978), https://digitalcommons.andrews.edu/dissertations/757/.

8. This text and the table it refers to are from the research for my dissertation. The table is an item I did not include, so there is no page.

TABLE 2. Time spent weekly in sermon preparation as reported by presidents, departmental directors, and pastors

WEEKLY	PRESIDENTS		DEPARTMENTAL DIRECTORS		PASTORS			
					Graduates		Nongrads	
	N	%	N	%	N	%	N	%
No answer	1	2.8	2	3.3	2	0.9	...	...
No time	...	...	...	...	...	...	2	7.1
0-2 hours	16	44.4	24	40.0	13	6.2	13	46.4
3-5 hours	13	36.1	26	43.3	91	42.7	10	5.8
6-9 hours	6	16.7	4	6.7	76	35.7	2	7.1
10-14 hrs.	...	...	4	6.7	29	13.6	1	3.6
Over 15 h.	...	...	...	...	2	0.9	...	...
Totals	36	100.0	60	100.0	213	100.0	28	100.0

When the information portrayed in the table comes from one's own research, no source is needed. Table 3 shows how to handle the reference to other sources.

TABLE 3. Ages of population in countries of South American Division*

COUNTRIES IN THE SOUTH AMERICAN DIVISION	5-19 %	20-29 %	30-44 %	45-59 %	60-74 %
Argentina	34	17	22	16	11
Bolivia	44	19	20	11	6
Brazil	39	21	22	12	6
Chile	33	21	24	14	8
Ecuador	43	21	20	11	5
Paraguay	42	21	22	10	5
Perú	41	21	20	12	6
Uruguay	29	17	22	18	14

*Source: *1991 Demographic Yearbook* (New York, NY: United Nations, 1992), 164-167.

Neatness and clarity are hallmarks of well-made tables. Sufficient white space around them sets them off. Normally, three empty lines precede and follow each table and graph. Your program or department will decide for you which variation you must use—they may even mandate another form.

Graphs

A simple, attractive, carefully presented graph stands out in a paper. A table may present more information, but a graph is a more effective communicator. The limitations of graphs are evident: (1) they do not show as much data as a table; (2) they represent approximate values; (3) they take time and some artistic talent to create.

Several computer programs create wonderful graphics that are informative and appealing. You can choose which you will use. Be sure only to use black and patterns using black instead of color. (Theses get copied in black and white.) The most common are bar, line, and circular graphs.

All figures must have a number and a title. These are placed below the figure, flush left, in sentence-style capitalization, without a terminal period/full stop (see the examples).

Bar Graphs

These may be simple, compound, or double (sometimes triple).

Simple bars

The bars may be drawn vertically or horizontally; here they are vertical. Care must be taken to achieve a pleasing appearance while maintaining maximum clarity.

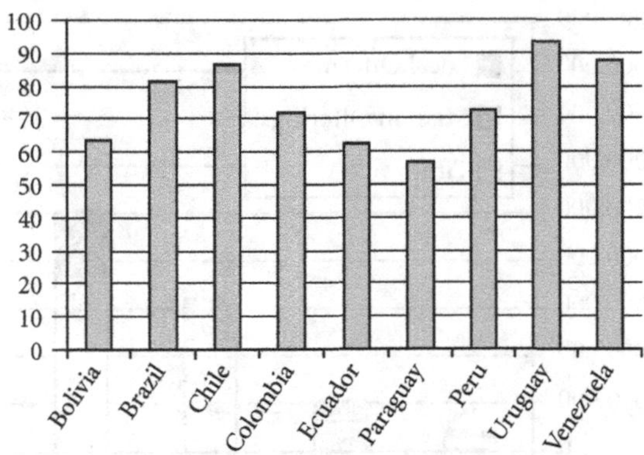

Fig. 7. Percentage of urban population in South American countries

Source: United Nations, *Demographic Yearbook, 2003* (New York, NY: United Nations, 2004), table 6, Urban and total population by sex, 1994-2003.

Compound bar graphs

Figure 8 is a compound bar graph showing the same information given in table 3. It is visually more interesting, but not as precise.

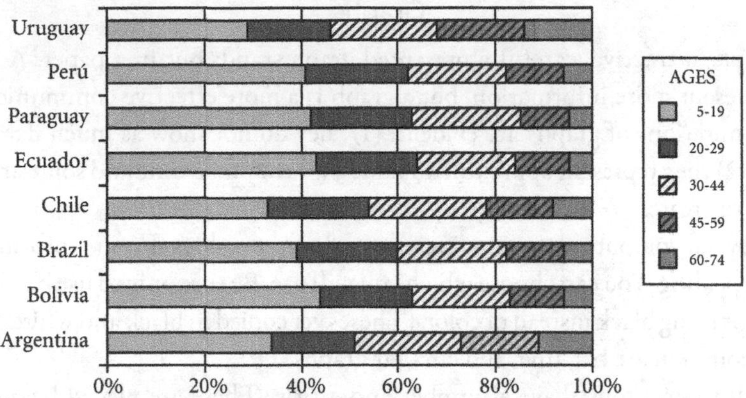

Fig. 8. Age distribution in countries of the South American Division

Source: *1991 Demographic Yearbook* (New York, NY: United Nations, 1992), 164-167.

Figure 9, another compound bar graph, compares the tithes and offerings in the Seventh-day Adventist Church worldwide from the years 1960 to 2000. It is visually attractive, but does not give specific sums for each kind of offering. This type of visual aid is useful in the oral presentation of research. If the graph is shown in colors using an overhead or slide projector, it can be particularly eye-catching. Unfortunately, color generally is not used in graphs in a thesis or dissertation.

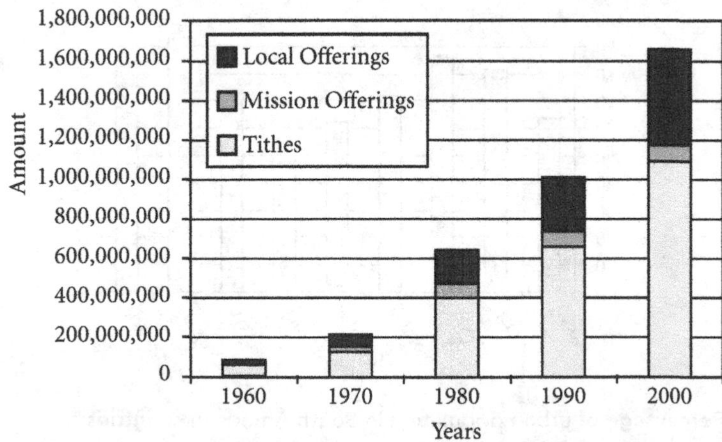

Fig. 9. A comparison of tithes, mission offerings, and local offerings from 1960 to 2000

Source: *Annual Statistical Report* (Silver Spring, MD: General Conference of Seventh-day Adventists, 2005), 4.

With compound bar graphs, one must be especially careful to make the colors (in the original) or the crosshatching sufficiently distinct. The distinctions can be lost in printing. Obviously, all figures will need to be done over more than once until they are clear.

Double bar graphs

Double bar graphs are used to compare at least two variables. Figure 10 shows the languages spoken by students of the Adventist University of Africa at the university's three extension centers in 2006. The three-dimensional bars are interesting but fail to show the exact number of students who speak each language. If numbers are important in your research, use a table.

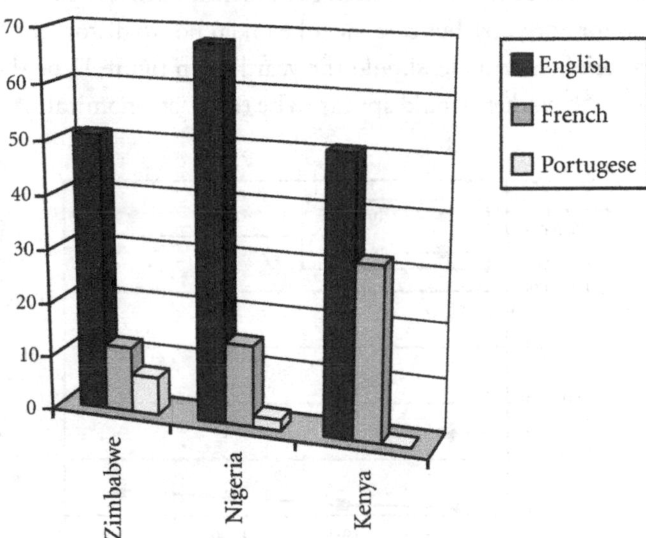

Fig. 10. Languages spoken by students in the three extension campuses of the Adventist University of Africa in 2006

Line Graphs

A line graph usually portrays change over time. The horizontal axis represents time; the vertical, another variable, which in figure 11 is the number of workers sent out of their home division by the Adventist Church between 1901 and 2000. Here a computer-generated graphic displays a visually interesting figure.

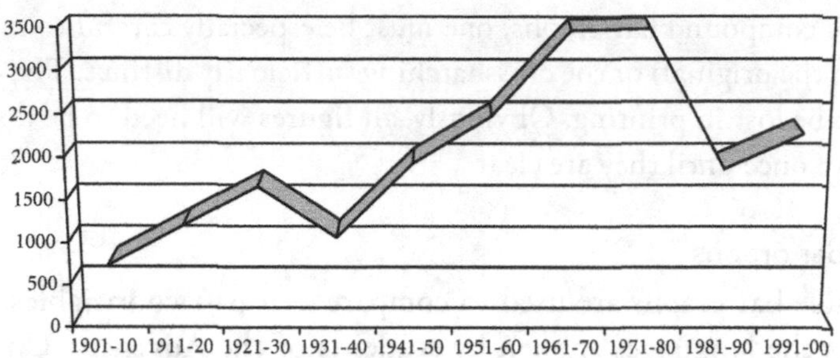

Fig. 11. Adventist workers sent from one world division of the Seventh-day Adventist Church to another, by decades.

Source: General Conference of Seventh-day Adventists, *Annual Statistical Report*, 1992 and 2001.

The scale on each axis does not need to be identical (that is, the same for one missionary as for one year), but care must be taken not to distort the impact of the information. For example, should the year line in figure 11 be shorter, the increase of church workers would appear to be truly astronomical.

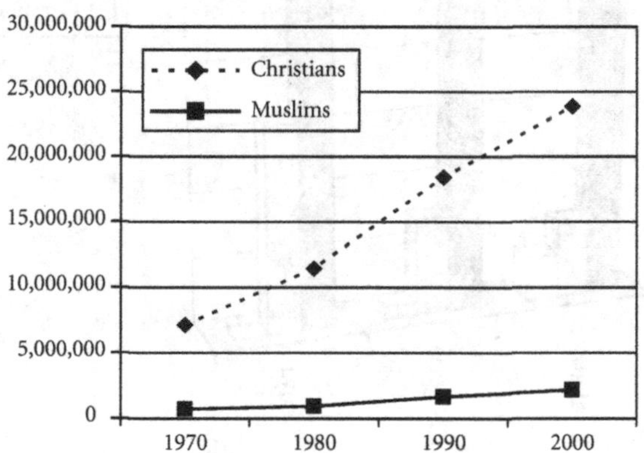

Fig. 12. A comparison of the growth of Christianity and Islam in Kenya, 1970-2000

Source: *World Christian Encyclopedia*, 2nd ed., vol. 1 (Oxford: Oxford University Press, 2001), s.v. "Kenya"; *World Christian Encyclopedia* (Nairobi: Oxford University Press, 1982), s.v. "Kenya." (S.v. stands for the Latin *sub verbo*; take it to mean "see under.")

Line graphs sometimes compare one phenomenon to another over time. The lines must be different to avoid confusion. Figure 12 shows a comparison of the growth of Christianity and Islam in Kenya between 1970 and 2000.

Circular Graphs

Also called pie charts, circular graphs represent the total divided into its parts.

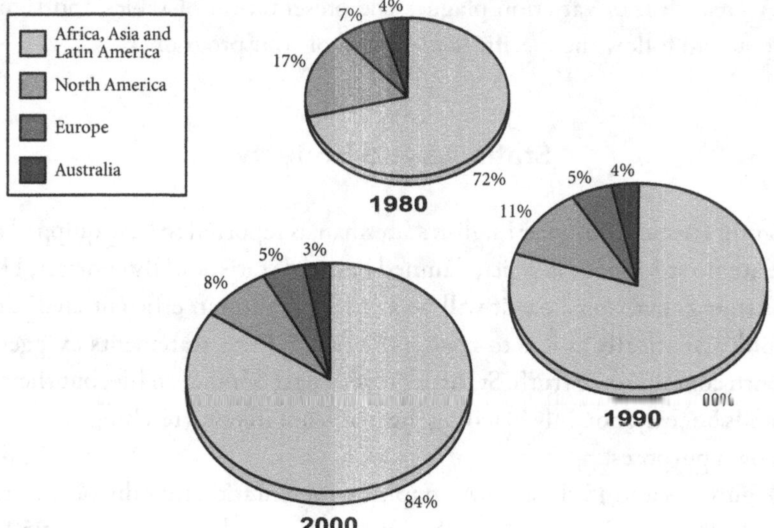

Fig. 13. Membership of the Seventh-day Adventist Church on different continents, 1980-2000

Source: General Conference of Seventh-day Adventists, *Annual Statistical Report*, 1980, 1990, 2000.

The figures usually are expressed in percentages, although actual figures may also be given. Figure 13 shows examples of pie graphs. These were made with Excel.

If you have no access to a computer program that makes circular graphs, you can construct your own with a percentage protractor. It gives you percentages rather than degrees of the circle. You can also calculate the areas of your circular graphs. Remember that 180 degrees is the same as 50 percent; 90 degrees is equivalent to 25 percent, and so on.

Divide the circle to represent the percentages. Then label each section with the percentage of the whole and the exact number. Make the different sections stand out by using different crosshatchings.

As with other graphs, the pie charts are eye-catching. However, they do not convey precise information as a table would. You must decide whether you need precision or visual appeal.

Experts produce figures in a matter of minutes using Microsoft Excel or some other computer program. Unless you are a whiz at computer graphics, you may want to ask someone to make the figures for you. You can also stay with old-fashioned tables—simpler to make, easy to understand, but not quite as exciting as computer-prepared charts and figures.

A great deal of variation plagues the presentation of tables and figures. Make sure to follow the specific instructions of your program.

Statistics and Honesty

Benjamin Disraeli, the great English statesman, is reported to have quipped that there are three kinds of lies: lies, damned lies, and statistics.[9] By contrast, H. G. Wells stated that "some day it will be as necessary for an efficient civilization to think statistically as it is to read and write."[10] Both statements exaggerate, but both contain some truth. Statistics form a part of modern life, but their use demands honesty, not only in telling the truth, but in not stretching facts to suit one's own purposes.

Figures 14 and 15 show how a graphic representation may distort information. The first one shows the growth of the world population between 1950 and 2000. The second modifies proportions, giving a distorted impression of reality.

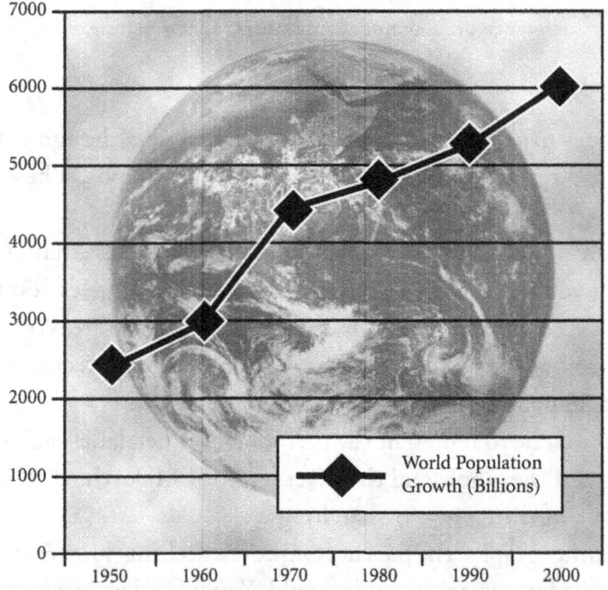

Fig. 14. Growth of world population, 1950-2000

Sources: *United Nations Statistical Yearbook* (New York, NY: United Nations, 1997), 95; and *Time Almanac 2000* (New York, NY: Time, 2000), 153.

9. D. Huff, *How to Lie with Statistics* (New York, NY: Norton, 1954), 1.

10. Huff, *How to Lie with Statistics*, 1.

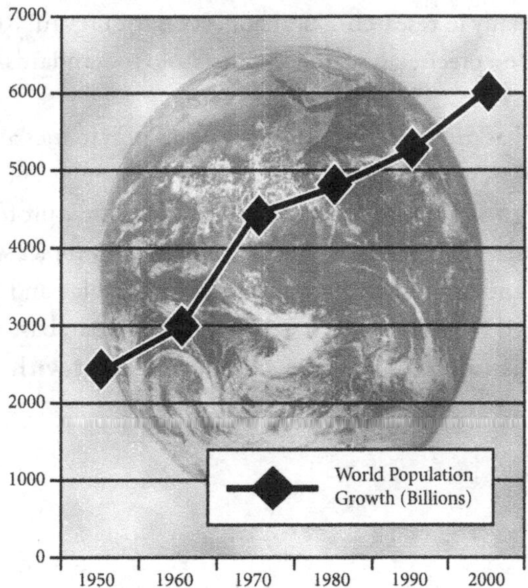

Fig. 15. A distorted view of the growth of world population, 1950-2000

In figure 15 the proportions on axis Y have been changed. The growth appears more accelerated, but the distorted image of Earth gives away that change. With no Earth to show the distorted proportions, the visual impact could fool the observer into panic over world overpopulation.

Percentages may also be used to convey erroneous information. A physician could state that only three of his patients had died, while someone could argue that the same physician had lost 75 percent of those he had cared for. Both could be telling a half truth. If there were four patients, three would be 75 percent. A percentage figure should be given along with the total number (*N*) on which it is based.

The base number for calculating percentages is important, as may be seen from the following example: If the manager reduces an employee's salary by 20 percent, and the original salary was $100, the employee would now be getting $80. If on this amount the boss gives his employee a 20 percent raise, the unlucky fellow would be getting only $96 (20 times 80 divided by 100 equals 16). What happened? The first calculation was made on the basis of 100; the second on the basis of 80.

When reading statistical reports, do not accept every piece of data without considering the total picture. All too often distortion for convenience is used by authors. It is necessary to apply critical thinking to the numbers you read.

Many ways of lying with statistics could be mentioned. None of them is appropriate, especially in research. Total honesty must prevail! Research reports must be accurate and precise. Researchers must hold to standards that are ethical and honest.

This chapter has presented some basic notions of statistics and instructions for preparing and presenting different kinds of tables and graphs. Further help in statistical design should be procured from a qualified professional on the subject. The calculation of statistics has become much simpler with the advent of the computer and appropriate software. In fact, tables and graphs may be computer generated from raw data or calculations in a database or spreadsheet. For this type of assistance, look for a computer expert with the right kind of experience.

Part Four

Presenting the Research

It matters little that you have carefully researched and written your topic unless you also present your paper in a way that is careful, clear, and correct. And by all means, follow the rules of your institution.

For that reason, the last three chapters will cover matters of format, both for the paper in general and for the details of footnotes and bibliographies. Because two forms of Turabian and one APA form are used in theological research, we will show the three ways. Of these three chapters (21-23), you may only need to read the chapter that corresponds with the citation format of your paper.

chapter twenty

FORMATTING THE PAPER

So far, this book on writing research papers has discussed the research process, shown how to make notes and bibliographies, explained ways of organizing the paper, and described English research language. Now it turns to the matter of format, since a paper, thesis, or dissertation must (1) demonstrate careful research, (2) show logical organization, and (3) be presented in perfect format.

There are different systems for formatting a paper. Of necessity, an arbitrary choice of one system rather than another must be made. If your school has a formatting manual, it is expected that you will follow it. Because the Turabian style is widely used for academic writing in the field of religion and theology, this book follows *A Manual for Writers*, 9th edition, both for references and for the main text.

This chapter gives basic guidelines for formatting the page and specific instructions for preparing different parts of the paper. The instructions assume that you are using a computer or word processor, probably Microsoft Word or WordPerfect, of which any version will work. "Tips on Format," in appendix D, gives format instructions.

Page Format

Set up the page format before you start typing. You will save yourself untold grief. Measurements are given in inches, but you can use the centimeter equivalent if you prefer (calculate 2.54 cm for each inch). Your word-processing program can work with either inches or centimeters.

Body Text

Here are the basic settings for the body text. The page should be letter size (unless you live where A4 is the norm and accepted by your school), and orientation should be portrait. Set the margins at 1 inch (this is default and does not need changing). Theses and dissertations that will be bound require 1.5 inches on the left. Set the line spacing for double spacing. Set the justification on left. Make sure you set the tabs you will need. The basic one is at the usual 0.5 inches from the left margin.

Choose a font that looks like printing (Garamond or Times New Roman). Some schools have a rule against a sans serif type such as Arial. That may be because sans serif type is more difficult to read. Sans serifs slow you down, which is why they work for advertising. Be sure you learn the instructions for your school. Fancy fonts are out. Usually you can choose the size within these limits: no larger than 12 points and no smaller than 10 points.

Page Numbering

The easiest way is to put the page number at the bottom center of all pages. Use the same font as you use for the body of the text. Make sure your school approves!

The first page of the introduction is page 1 (Arabic numeral). The preliminary pages are numbered in lowercase Roman numerals at the bottom center of each page, beginning with the title page, but do not type the number on the title page.

Titles and Headings

The number of the chapter is typed centered at 2 inches from the top edge of the paper. The chapter title is typed centered, one double space below the number (some schools want a triple space). If the title is longer than 4.75 inches, it must be divided, with the longer part on the first line, the shorter part on the second line, and a double space between. If the title takes three lines, use single space and put the lines in an inverted pyramid shape—first line longest, last line shortest.

Place the first line of text three single line spaces (one double plus one single) below the chapter title. Major headings, such as INTRODUCTION or BIBLIOGRAPHY, are also typed at 2 inches from the top edge of the page, the same as chapter numbers.

Triple spaces are used before any heading, from level one through level five. (Review headings in chapter 17, under "Practical Helps for Organizing the

Paper.") To get the right spacing, you will have to do a hard return (the one that completes your paragraph), change from double to single space, do one hard return, and change back to double space. In Word, use Ctrl+1 for single space, Ctrl+2 for double space. Better yet, write yourself a macro or a style that will do this in one simple stroke.

Titles for appendixes appear on a special title page: APPENDIX A is centered on the page, with the title one double space below. These are the only two items on the page. The appendix material begins on the following page.

Preliminary Pages

A table of contents should follow the model provided. When the table is more than one page long, it begins with the phrase TABLE OF CONTENTS centered at 2 inches from the top of the page. If shorter than one page, the whole table of contents may be centered. The table of contents usually includes only the first three levels of subheadings in a chapter.

Chapter titles are in caps. A double space goes between chapter title and the first heading, which is done in caps and lowercase. Use Arabic numerals for chapter numbers to save yourself grief (if that is fine by your school); otherwise, you need to align the dots after Roman numerals of varying size.

Having set the correct margins for the table of contents, I set the tabs at the top of the page as follows: four left tabs (at 0.25, 0.50, 0.75, and 1.00), then a right tab with dot leaders at 5.25 and a right tab without leaders for the page number at 5.75. If you prefer, you can omit the dot leaders in your table of contents—as long as this is okay with your school.

Long headings must not run beyond the last dot before the page number; if they do not, use two lines for the heading. What has been said about the table of contents applies also to the lists of illustrations, tables, and figures.

If you have a title page and one page of table of contents, you need not number them. If you have more than that (a longer table of contents, lists, acknowledgments, etc.), they should be numbered with lowercase Roman numerals at the bottom center of each page.

Footnotes and Quotations

The appearance of a paper is easily marred by incorrectly placed notes and quotations. The suggestions given here should help you do it correctly.

Footnotes

Technology has made footnoting simple. You would not even want to hear about how it used to be done! Instructions here fit Microsoft Word and WordPerfect. To avoid an irregular gap between the last line of text and the separator line, place notes "below the text." You do this in Word by opening the References tab, little box at the lower right corner of the footnotes section. If your school requires footnote numbers to start with 1 on each page, you can change this in the same place. However, do so only at the end of your work, just before turning your paper in. Having footnotes in numerical sequence while you do revising and editing is helpful.

The word-processing program will pick up the indents from the page setup for the body text. You should have no problems if you set up the page first. If the footnote does not look like those on the sample pages, you may have to fiddle until you get exactly what you want.

When you need to insert a footnote, simply place your cursor at the end of the phrase or sentence, after the punctuation marks, and insert a footnote. Your word processor takes it from there. Word has a bad habit: sometimes it puts the last footnote of the page on the following page. Get around this by shortening the text by one or two lines (putting those lines on the next page) so all footnotes for the page are where they belong. If you have a long footnote, it may continue on the next page. What we do not want is the footnote number in the text and the footnote not beginning on that page.

While the superscript number at the beginning of the footnote is the traditional way and Word uses only that form, you can make the footnotes look like they do in this book. Your school may require them. Try these websites, both accessed April 18, 2019:

> http://word.mvps.org/FAQs/MacrosVBA/UnSuperscptFnotes.htm.
> https://support.office.com/en-ie/article/video-change-footnote-font-size-and-formatting-1368deda-70b6-44a7-82d6-8df4dc52e04e.

Or convince your school to allow you to use the superscript footnote numbers as done automatically in Word.

Quotations

Short quotations—one sentence or less—are easily worked into the paragraph. Double quotation marks are mandatory for such quotations. In American usage, single quotation marks are used only for a quotation within a quotation. Closing quotation marks are placed outside the comma or the period after the last word of the quotation.

Longer quotations—usually two sentences or five or more lines—are typed as "block quotations." (Forty words in APA.) These quotations are single spaced and indented from the left margin as much as the regular paragraph. For both Microsoft Word and WordPerfect you can set up a paragraph style to make the quotation look like the one in the sample pages. When you complete a paragraph in body text with a hard return, click on the style you have created to make the block quotation look like it is supposed to look.

No quotation marks are used for block quotations. When the quotation starts at the beginning of the original paragraph, there is an additional indentation. If the quotation comes from the middle of the paragraph, there is no indentation within the block quote. To emphasize a quotation, even if it is not five lines long, you may set it off in a block quotation.

To show emphasis, italicize words or phrases in a quotation. Do so sparingly lest you overdo your point. Always make clear to your reader what was italicized by the author and what you italicized. Normally you will indicate this in the footnote, where you will give the reference and the phrase "italics mine" or "emphasis added" in parentheses after the page number: "Jones, 37 (italics mine)." If you put a word or phrase within the quotation, place your insertion in square brackets.

A quotation is followed by an appropriate reference, usually a footnote. However, a Bible quotation may have the reference in parentheses, followed by the period, as in (Jn 3:16). In the case of block quotations followed by a reference in parentheses, the period precedes the parentheses.

> I appeal to you therefore, brothers and sisters, by the mercies of God, to present your bodies as a living sacrifice, holy and acceptable to God, which is your spiritual worship. Do not be conformed to this world, but be transformed by the renewing of your minds, so that you may discern what is the will of God—what is good and acceptable and perfect. (Rom 12:1-2)

Tables, Figures, and Illustrations

Tables, figures, and illustrations may be used to enhance a paper, thesis, or dissertation. They should be well made, clear, and large enough to be easily read. Colored ink cannot be used because theses or dissertations are reproduced in black and white. Instead of color, use different kinds of lines, crosshatching, or various gradations of shading. The making of tables is described in chapter 19, which also includes a number of figures to be used as models. Each figure or table must have a number, a title, and a source, if it is not the result of the research being reported.

When the tables or figures are small enough to fit on the page, they may be placed between paragraphs, as close as possible to the text in which they are discussed. It is wise to make a reference to the figure or table in the text: "Figure 4 shows the outline of the walls of Jerusalem in the days of Hezekiah." Leave three empty lines (two double spaces) above and below so that tables and figures do not look crowded.

Larger tables and figures are often placed on separate pages, as soon as possible after the text that mentions them. Computer typing makes this kind of insertion mandatory. Neat appearance and ease of reading are the criteria for designing the pages on which tables and figures are included.

Titles of tables are placed above the table. Titles of figures are placed below the figure. Their format is similar: they begin at the left margin and have sentence capitalization. See chapter 19 for examples.

Spelling and Punctuation

Needless to say, spelling, punctuation, and other small details are important in a research paper. Professors judge by what their eyes see. You, the student, are responsible for all the details. Read your paper carefully and make the corrections as needed. When the paper is handed to the professor, it should be perfect. The professor should not be expected to correct spelling or point out typographical errors.

Spelling

Depending on your school, the spelling will be either British (Saviour, centre, etc.) or American (Savior, center, etc.). Both are correct, but most American schools prefer American spelling. Quotations keep their original spelling. Whichever spelling you and your adviser select must be used consistently.

The spelling of foreign words, whether in titles of books and journals or in the text, must be accurate. That means using all the accents and diacritical marks in the original. WordPerfect and Word include multinational characters such as ç, ø, ü, and é. Foreign words that do not appear in English dictionaries are italicized. An apparent contradiction is that you can insert a quotation in another language without italicizing. If you translate a word, give the English in brackets, as you do with any interpolation to a quotation. For non-Latin scripts, follow standard transliteration patterns, such as the ones for biblical languages in appendix A. (Note that a reference to parts of the paper does not capitalize the name of the part, chapter, appendix, or bibliography.)

Abbreviations appear in notes but not in the text. Use standard ones, as given in your dictionary, Turabian 9 (chapter 24), or the *Chicago Manual of Style* (chapter 10). One abbreviation unique to biblical studies is "v." for "verse" and "vv." for "verses." Abbreviations—except for the initials of an author (E. A. Jones)—have no space after the period included in them (e.g., Ph.D., but you could be more up to date by using PhD). Your school may permit AD and BC—as well as academic degrees—with no periods. Find out.

Word processors check the spelling for you, helping you to avoid spelling mistakes. However, this process is not infallible. I still chuckle when I see *periscope*, a computer autocorrect for *pericope* (a selection from a book). Word processors can also automatically divide words properly at line breaks, but unless your adviser encourages word division, you do not need to worry about it.

Punctuation

If you are unclear about the punctuation rules of the English language, review them. An English grammar is an important tool for writing research papers. Turabian 9 has a section on punctuation. Take the time to review it.

Besides putting periods and commas before the final quotation marks, English punctuation has other idiosyncrasies. In research language, an enumeration or series needs a comma before the word "and" or "or" (called the "serial comma"). For example: We like bananas, mangoes, and papaya. At the same time, the tendency to eliminate commas, except as needed for clarity, is evident. An author whose name includes "Jr." or a Roman numeral is written John Jones Jr.—without a comma. When you invert the name, as in a bibliography, you will use commas: Jones, John, Jr.

Lines, short and long, can also cause problems. A hyphen has no space on either side of it. The printed em dash must be typed as two hyphens, with no space on either side of them. For example: We saw someone—who it was, we have no idea—leaving the house. If your computer program turns the double hyphen into an em dash—so be it. However, use one or the other consistently. The en dash is shorter than the em dash and longer than the hyphen; it goes between numbers, as in Luke 2:4–6. You will find it (and the em dash) among the symbols that the word processor can insert in your paper. However, we suggest you simply use a hyphen. Underlining is no longer used for anything (use italics instead). Even in the bibliography, where we used to use 8 spaces of underlining to replace an author's name in multiple listings by the same author, we now use three em dashes.

Current usage puts only one space after the period, or full stop. In fact, all punctuation marks are followed by one space, with one exception. When a colon or a period is used to separate parts of books, there is no space after it.

For example: *TWOT*, 1:112 means volume 1, page 112; Irenaeus *Against Heresies* 2.2.3 refers to book 2, chapter 2, paragraph 3.

Other Details

Among these details is the use of numbers. In a scientific paper, Arabic numbers are always used in reporting statistics. For example, 23 percent of the 345 respondents (notice the use of "percent" rather than the symbol) said they preferred bananas. Numbers larger than one thousand have a comma: 4,567. Arabic numbers cannot be used at the beginning of a sentence; spell out the number in words. Use Arabic numbers for volumes of books or journals. Use Roman numerals only when transcribing a quotation that has them or as page numbers for the preliminary pages of your paper (lower case at the bottom of the page).

In a theological paper, you would spell out cardinal numbers up to one hundred. However, if you are citing statistics from your original research, such as describing a church and giving information on membership, you would not need to write out the numbers. Round numbers, such as "five thousand," are written. Fractions are written out: one-half. However, Bible references and page numbers, as well as dates, decimal numbers, percentages, and sums of money are never written out in words.

Ordinal numbers below ten are written out. Larger round numbers are also written out in the text: eighth, one-hundredth. In the documentation, however, they are given as numerals: 1st, 2nd, 3rd, 4th. You may use the superscript if you so desire: 1st, 2nd, 3rd, 4th. Be consistent, whichever you choose.

These important details are covered in English grammar books and specifically in Turabian's *Manual for Writers*. Use these works to produce an A-grade paper. However, always take into account your school's rules.

Sample Pages

The next few pages show examples in correct format of the proper appearance of different parts of a paper. Unfortunately, in this printed book these are not the originals on 8 1/2 by 11 inch paper. Use your imagination.

The two papers from which the following models were taken come from work done by two students who participated in my African research classes. Both are now professors—Peter (after completing a DMin) in Zambia and Melak (after completing a PhD in Old Testament) in Kenya. I praise God for a chance to help train trainers.

Chapters 21-23 show you proper referencing in three different formats. Make sure you use the proper one for your school.

ABSTRACT

REDISCOVERING THE THEOLOGY OF LAY MINISTRY:
GOD'S MASTER-PLAN FOR EQUIPPING THE LAITY
FOR EVANGELISM IN, ZAMBIA

by

Peter Chulu

Adviser: Werner Vyhmeister

ABSTRACT OF GRADUATE STUDENT RESEARCH

Project

Adventist University of Africa

Title: REDISCOVERING THE THEOLOGY OF LAY MINISTRY: GOD'S MASTER-PLAN FOR EQUIPPING THE LAITY FOR EVANGELISM IN ZAMBIA

Name of researcher: Peter Chulu

Name and degree of faculty adviser: Werner Vyhmeister, Ph.D.

Date completed: August 2009

The Seventh-day Adventist Church accepts the Gospel Commission of Matthew 28. Adventists further believe that the second advent of Christ is very near. Contrary to the implications of these two beliefs, the work of evangelization is centered on over-worked clergy. This has resulted in minimal church growth and un-entered communities even in areas where the church has existed for almost 50 years, such as Livingstone in Zambia.

In an effort to help alleviate the problem, a cost-effective, lay empowering program was developed to train lay members to launch personal and public evangelism. On the basis of the study of the Bible and other literature, a training program was developed to equip the laity for evangelism in the Livingstone Pastoral District.

Three sets of lessons were developed: Spiritual Gifts, Personal (Door to Door evangelism), and Organizing and Conducting Public Evangelistic Campaigns. These lessons were taught every weekend for two months—April to May 2006. A field school followed the classroom lessons. After the practices, Bible instructors operated in their residential areas, evangelizing their neighborhoods.

In the three churches of Livingstone, five series of evangelistic meetings were conducted by the laity. Lay Bible instructors made up some 1424 contacts from 2006 to 2008. An evangelistic mindset was created in members. Two congregations were formed and three were revived.

REDISCOVERING THE THEOLOGY OF LAY MINISTRY:
A MASTER_PLAN FOR EQUIPING LAITY FOR
EVANGELISM IN ZAMBIA

A project
Presented in partial fulfillment
Of the requirements for the degree
Master of Arts in Pastoral Theology

By

Peter Chulu

APPROVAL BY THE COMMITTEE

______________________________ ..   ______________________________
Adviser: Dean of the Seminary
Werner Vyhmeister, Ph.D.   Joel Musvosvi, Ph.D.

____
Reader:
Gheorghe Razmerita, Ph.D.

Extension Centre: Solusi University

Date: August 2009

Measurements on this page depend on the size of the committee and the length of the title. As well, make sure to follow the rules of your school.

Adventist International Institute

of Advanced Studies

WHOLE-BODY GESTURES WITH THE CONTEXT OF

WORSHIP IN THE BOOK OF PSALMS

A dissertation

presented in partial fulfillment

of the requirements for the degree

DOCTOR OF PHILOSOPHY IN RELIGION

by

Melak Alemayehu Tsegaw

September 2017

TABLE OF CONTENTS
[triple space:
two empty lines]

v

CHAPTER 2

A BRIEF SURVEY OF WHOLE-BODY GESTURES IN THE CULTIC WORSHIP OF THE OLD TESTAMENT

Cult is a "term used for public worship in general, especially the festivals, rituals and sacrifices in service to God or the gods."[3] Gerald Klingbeil provides a better delineation between the connected concepts of cult and ritual. He notes that cult "describes the entirety of religious actions, which in turn consists of a specific number of rituals comprising subrites and distinct symbols."[4] He further elaborates on how ritual functions by pointing to its basic elements, one of which is ritual action.[5] Though he does

---

[3]Arthur G. Patzia and Anthony J. Petrotta, *Pocket Dictionary of Biblical Studies* (2002), s.v. "cult." Patzia and Petrotta explain, "Popular usage employs the term as a derogatory designation for new religious movements, but scholars employ it as a descriptive term for worship of any kind." Because of this derogatory designation, Waltke prefers to use liturgy in place of cult to express the same concept. According to him, "cult or liturgy refers to the external expression of religion." Waltke, *Old Testament Theology*, 447-448. On the other hand, Sigmund Mowinckel seems to use the words cult and ritual interchangeably. "Cult or ritual may be defined as the socially established and regulated holy acts and words in which the encounter and communion of the deity with the congregation is established, developed, and brought to its ultimate goal." Sigmund Mowinckel, *The Psalms in Israel's Worship* (Nashville, TN: Abingdon, 1962), 15.

[4]Gerald Klingbeil, *Bridging the Gap: Ritual and Ritual Texts in the Bible* (Winona Lake, IN: Eisenbrauns, 2007), 8. See also Peterson, *Engaging With God : A Biblical Theology of Worship* (Grand Rapids, MI: Eerdmans, 1993), 30-36.

[5]Klingbeil illustrates ritual actions with the consecration ritual preceding the covenant-making between YHWH and Israel in Exod 19:14-19. The sanctifying of the people, the people washing their garments, the trembling of the people, the bringing out of the people to meet God, and the standing of the people are some of the ritual actions identified in the pericope. Klingbeil, *Bridging the Gap*, 181-189. The other ritual elements that Klingbeil considers to be at the heart of ritual are ritual objects, ritual participants, ritual time, and ritual space. Ibid., 181.

33

not separately analyze whole-body gestures such as dancing, walking, standing, sitting, bowing low, and prostrating one's self, when performed in the context of worshiping the deity, they fall into this category of ritual action.

Several cultic worship scenarios are recorded in the Old Testament. This chapter presents a brief survey of some of these accounts in which the whole-body gestures are mentioned. In fact, the motivation for the selection of the passages included in this survey is the explicit mention of whole-body gestures. The objective of this survey is to provide a general background to the specific study of the whole-body gestures within a worship context in the book of Psalms. However, it should be noted that this chapter is not an exhaustive list of references to all whole-body gestures in the context of worship in the OT nor does it aim at detailed exposition of the passages mentioned.

Admittedly, the aforementioned objective of this chapter presupposes a close connection between the book of Psalms and OT cultic worship. Though there are different views on the cultic setting of the book of Psalms,[6] "more interpreters would

---

[6]Hermann Gunkel played a prominent role in the study of the Psalms and the cult in the beginning of the twentieth century. See Hermann Gunkel, *The Psalms: A Form-Critical Introduction* (Philadelphia, PA: Fortress, 1967), 1-4. His student, Sigmund Mowinckel further developed the cultic setting of the psalms and asserted that the Psalms are originally cultic poems, composed for the use in cultic ritual. See Mowinckel, *The Psalms in Israel's Worship*, 1-8. However, as Jerome F. D. Creach noted, since the last quarter of the twentieth century, the study of the Psalms as a canonical book and its literary shape have pushed the topic of cult to the side. Despite this shift of focus, he argues that "the subject holds important theological treasures for those who are patient enough to explore it." Jerome F. D. Creach, "The Cultic Context of the Psalms," in *Interpreting the Psalms: Issues and Approaches*, ed. David Firth and Philip S. Johnston (Downers Grove, IL: InterVarsity Press, 2005), 119, 120. See the succinct summary of different views on the origin of the Psalms in S. Edward Tesh and Walter D. Zorn, *Psalms,* The College Press NIV Commentary (Joplin, MO: College Press, 1999), 24-40.

BIBLIOGRAPHY

Adams, Doug. "Communal Dance Forms and Consequences in Biblical Worship." In *Dance as Religious Studies*, edited by Doug Adams and Diane Apostolos-Cappadona, 35-47. New York, NY: Crossroads, 1990.

Adler, Joshua J. "The Historical Background of Psalm 24." *Jewish Bible Quarterly* 20, no. 4 (1992): 268-270, 279.

Allen, Leslie C. *Psalms 101-150*. Word Biblical Commentary 21. Dallas, TX: Word, 2002.

________. "ידה." *New International Dictionary of Old Testament Theology and Exegesis*. Edited by Willem A. VanGemeren. Grand Rapids, MI: Zondervan, 1997. 2:405-408.

________. "סבב." *New International Dictionary of Old Testament Theology and Exegesis*. Edited by Willem A. VanGemeren. Grand Rapids, MI: Zondervan, 1997. 3:219-220.

Allen, Ronald, and Gordon Borror. *Worship Rediscovering the Missing Jewel*. Portland, OR: Multnomah, 1982.

Alonso-Schokel, Luis. "The Poetic Structure of Psalm 42-43." *Journal for the Study of the Old Testament* 1 (1976): 4-11.

Alter, Robert. *The Book of Psalms: A Translation with Commentary*. New York: W. W. Norton, 2009.

Amsden, Patti. "A Brief History of Dance in Worship." In *Music and the Arts in Christian Worship*, edited by Robert E. Webber, 4:720-728. Nashville, TN: Star Song, 1994.

Amsler, S. "עמד." *Theological Lexicon of the Old Testament*. Edited by Ernst Jenni and Claus Westermann. Peabody, MA: Hendrickson, 1997. 2:921-924.

________. "קום." *Theological Lexicon of the Old Testament*. Edited by Ernst Jenni and Claus Westermann. Peabody, MA: Hendrickson, 1997. 3:1136-1141.

272

chapter twenty-one

TURABIAN 9, FOOTNOTE AND BIBLIOGRAPHY STYLE

Reference notes come from bibliographical entries. This chapter shows you how Turabian 9 wants both done. If your school and program use the Turabian 9 footnote and bibliography style, this is the way to do bibliographical entries and footnotes. For further information, consult Turabian 9[1] and the *Chicago Manual of Style*.[2]

If your school or program follows *SBL Handbook of Style*, which is similar to Turabian, yet different in some style features, please refer to that handbook.[3] If your required style is Turabian in-text, follow the instructions in the following chapter. If your school uses APA, please follow the *APA Manual*[4] and chapter 23.

In preparing notes and bibliographical entries that do not seem to fit into any category, follow the rules as closely as possible, using common sense to make modifications as needed. References should make it easy for a reader to locate any source.

One detail that frequently varies in the school style manuals regards how to report place names. In some schools, well-known cities not in the United States (London, Buenos Aires, Tokyo) do not need country of publication. A simpler way is to put the country or state on all cities.

---

1. Kate L. Turabian, *A Manual for Writers of Research Papers, Theses, and Dissertations*, 9th ed. (Chicago, IL: University of Chicago Press, 2018).

2. *Chicago Manual of Style*, 17th ed. (Chicago, IL: University of Chicago Press, 2017).

3. For ancient Near Eastern, biblical, and early Christian studies, you will find additional information in Billie Jean Collins, Bob Buller, and John Kutzko, eds., *The SBL Handbook of Style*, 2nd ed. (Atlanta, GA: SBL Press, 2014).

4. American Psychological Association, *Publication Manual of the American Psychological Association*, 7th ed. (Washington, DC: American Psychological Association, 2020).

Published Materials

Published materials include books (specialized and general), pamphlets, and periodicals (journals and magazines). Facts of publication must be given in full form in the first reference. Here we also show the format for second references.

Abbreviations can be used for often-repeated titles or series. If there are only a few, give the abbreviation in addition to the full reference the first time the item is mentioned; after that you may use the abbreviation. If you use many abbreviations, put a list of them in the paper or thesis, usually just before the introduction (appendix C refers you to where you can find lists of accepted abbreviations). Abbreviations may be used in the notes, but not in the bibliography. When the abbreviations stand for the title of a book or journal, they should be italicized.

The 2N examples show how a second reference can be shortened. Although the use of only the author's surname may be permissible, it is safer to use author and title. Just make sure your readers can find the reference and you always do your notes in the same way. The use of *ibid.* is now discouraged. When used, it must *only* be used for a reference immediately following one where you have given the full reference.

General Books

Under this heading, several issues are addressed. First, and most frequent, are those related to authorship. Next come examples of how to handle multivolume works. Finally, you will find entries showing how to deal with series, reprints, and secondary sources.

The examples presented in this chapter use the following abbreviations:

N (for Note) gives the format for a common, uncomplicated note or footnote. These carry numbers to identify them. The traditional form is to use a superscript number both in the text and at the beginning of the note. This is the easiest form because computers do it automatically. Another form is to use the superscript in the text and a plain number, followed by a dot, in the note. Make sure you follow the rules of your school.

B (for Bibliography) gives the format for a common, uncomplicated bibliographical entry.

BP (for Bibliography Partial) indicates the format to use when only a part of the source has been consulted.

BA (for Bibliography All) indicates the format to use for the whole source (in contrast with BP).

2N (for second reference to the same source) shows how you should footnote an item after the first time. Of course, these footnotes have numbers.

Authorship

One author

N 1. Mary Lederleitner, *Women in God's Mission* (Downers Grove, IL: InterVarsity Press,[5] 2018), 54.

B Lederleitner, Mary. *Women in God's Mission*. Downers Grove, IL: InterVarsity Press, 2018.

2N 9. Lederleitner, *Women in God's Mission*, 73.

Two or three authors

N 2. Jerome H. Neyrey and Eric Clark Stewart, *The Social World of the New Testament: Insights and Models* (Peabody, MA: Hendrickson, 2008), 134.

B Neyrey, Jerome H., and Eric Clark Stewart. *The Social World of the New Testament: Insights and Models*. Peabody, MA: Hendrickson, 2008.

2N 15. Neyrey and Stewart, *Social World of the NT*, 165.

More than three authors

Your school may allow the shortening of the author statement in the note, as does Turabian 9. The Latin form "*et al.*" may be used for "and others." All names should be in the bibliography. Make sure to check your school's rules.

N 3. Willem A. VanGemeren et al., *The Law, the Gospel, and the Modern Christian* (Grand Rapids, MI: Zondervan, 1993), 78.

B VanGemeren, Willem A., Greg L. Bahnsen, Walter C. Kaiser Jr., Wayne G. Strickland, and Douglas Moo. *The Law, the Gospel, and the Modern Christian*. Grand Rapids, MI: Zondervan, 1993.

2N 24. Van Gemeren et al., *Law, Gospel, and the Modern Christian*, 94.

---

5. Although most publishers' names are given without the word "publishers" or "press," because InterVarsity by itself has a different meaning, use "InterVarsity Press."

Corporate author

N 4. Southern Baptist Convention, Committee on Baptist Faith and Message, *The Baptist Faith and Message: A Statement Adopted by the Baptist Convention, June 14, 2000* (Nashville, TN: LifeWay Christian Resources, 2000), 29.

B Southern Baptist Convention. Committee on Baptist Faith and Message. *The Baptist Faith and Message: A Statement Adopted by the Baptist Convention, June 14, 2000*. Nashville, TN: LifeWay Christian Resources, 2000.

2N 17. Southern Baptist Convention, *Baptist Faith and Message*, 31.

No author, edition other than first, with translator

N 5. *Bhagavad-Gita as It Is*, abr. ed., trans. A. C. Bhaktivedanta Swami Prabhupada (New York, NY: Bhaktivedanta Book Trust, 1972), 74.

B *Bhagavad-Gita as It Is*. Abridged edition. Translated by A. C. Bhaktivedanta Swami Prabhupada. New York, NY: Bhaktivedanta Book Trust, 1972.

2N 21. *Bhagavad Gita as It Is*, 72.

Editor instead of author; joint publication

N 6. James C. VanderKam and William Adler, eds., *The Jewish Apocalyptic Heritage in Early Christianity* (Assen, Netherlands: Van Gorcum; Minneapolis, MN: Fortress, 1996), 35.

B VanderKam, James C., and William Adler, eds. *The Jewish Apocalyptic Heritage in Early Christianity*. Assen, Netherlands: Van Gorcum; Minneapolis, MN: Fortress, 1996.

2N 32. VanderKam and Adler, *Jewish Apocalyptic Heritage*, 38.

Component part by one author in a work edited by another

N 7. Blasious M. Ruguri, "Biblical Principles for Tribal Unity," in *Biblical Principles for Missiological Issues in Africa*, ed. Bruce Bauer and Wagner Kuhn (Berrien Springs, MI: Department of World Mission, Andrews University, 2015), 411.

B Ruguri, Blasious M. "Biblical Principles for Tribal Unity." In *Biblical Principles for Missiological Issues in Africa*, ed. Bruce Bauer and Wagner Kuhn, 409-431. Berrien Springs, MI: Department of World Mission, Andrews University, 2015.

2N 18. Ruguri, "Biblical Principles," 420.

Multivolume Works

Here are examples of several different types—from simple to complex:

N 8. Justo González, *A History of Christian Thought*, 3 vols. (Nashville, TN: Abingdon, 1970-1975), 1:176.

B González, Justo. *A History of Christian Thought*. 3 vols. Nashville, TN: Abingdon, 1970-1975.

2N 56. González, *History of Christian Thought*, 1:182.

Multivolume work—one author, different titles

N 9. Kenneth Scott Latourette, *A History of the Expansion of Christianity*, vol. 3, *Three Centuries of Advance* (Grand Rapids, MI: Zondervan, 1970), 17.

BA Latourette, Kenneth Scott. *A History of the Expansion of Christianity*. 7 vols. Grand Rapids, MI: Zondervan, 1970.

BP Latourette, Kenneth Scott. *A History of the Expansion of Christianity*. Vol. 3, *Three Centuries of Advance*. Grand Rapids, MI: Zondervan, 1970.

2N 26. Latourette, *History of the Expansion of Christianity*, 3:1.

or

2N 26. Latourette, *Three Centuries of Advance*, 25.

Multivolume work—several authors

N 10. Bruce W. Winter, gen. ed., *The Book of Acts in Its First Century Setting*, 6 vols. (Carlisle, UK: Paternoster, 1994), vol. 3, *The Book of Acts and Paul in Roman Custody*, by Brian Rapske, 38.

B Winter, Bruce W., gen. ed. *The Book of Acts in Its First Century Setting*. 6 vols. Carlisle, UK: Paternoster, 1994. Vol. 3, *The Book of Acts and Paul in Roman Custody*, by Brian Rapske.

If for some reason the author of the book you are citing or quoting is more important than the multivolume source, you may use the following format:

N 11. Brian Rapske, *The Book of Acts and Paul in Roman Custody*, vol. 3, *The Book of Acts in Its First Century Setting*, ed. Bruce W. Winter (Carlisle, UK: Paternoster, 1994), 38.

B Rapske, Brian. *The Book of Acts and Paul in Roman Custody*. Vol. 3, *The Book of Acts in Its First Century Setting*, ed. Bruce W. Winter. Carlisle, UK: Paternoster, 1994.

2N 19. Rapske, *Book of Acts and Paul*, 35.

Part of a Series

N 12. Wayne C. Booth, Gregory G. Colomb, and Joseph M. Williams, *The Craft of Research*, 4th ed., Chicago Guides to Writing, Editing, and Publishing (Chicago, IL: University of Chicago Press, 2016), 155.

B Booth, Wayne C., Gregory G. Colomb, and Joseph M. Williams. *The Craft of Research*. Chicago Guides to Writing, Editing, and Publishing. Chicago, IL: University of Chicago Press, 2016.

2N 27. Booth et al., *Craft of Research*, 158.

Reprint

N 13. John L. Nevius, *Life of John Livingston Nevius*, reprint of *John Livingston Nevius: For Forty Years a Missionary in China* (New York, NY: Revell, 1895; reprint, n.p.: TheClassics Us, 2013), 174, 175.

B Nevius, John L. *Life of John Livingston Nevius*, reprint of *John Livingston Nevius: For Forty Years a Missionary in China*. New York, NY: Revell, 1895; reprint, n.p.: TheClassics Us, 2013.[6]

2N 33. Nevius, *Life of John Nevius*, 182.

N 14. H. R. Reynolds, "Introduction to the Gospel of St. John," in *The Pulpit Commentary*, ed. H. O. M. Spense and Joseph S. Exell, 23 vols. (Grand Rapids, MI: Eerdmans, reprint 1977), 17:v.

B Reynolds, H. R. "Introduction to the Gospel of St. John." In *The Pulpit Commentary*, ed. H. O. M. Spense and Joseph S. Exell, 23 vols., 17:iv-clxi. Grand Rapids, MI: Eerdmans, reprint 1977.

2N 25. Reynolds, "Introduction to the Gospel of St. John," 10.

---

6. Note here that n.p. means "no place" given in the information.

Secondary Source

Use secondary source references sparingly. They are complicated. Also, your readers will be less impressed with your use of a secondary source than of a primary source.

N 15. William Sanday and Arthur C. Headlam, *A Critical and Exegetical Commentary on the Epistle to the Romans*, International Critical Commentary (Edinburgh: T&T Clark, 1895), 423, quoted in Eldon Epp, *Junia: The First Woman Apostle* (Minneapolis: Fortress, 2005), 71.

B Sanday, William, and Arthur C. Headlam. *A Critical and Exegetical Commentary on the Epistle to the Romans*. International Critical Commentary. Edinburgh: T&T Clark, 1895, 423. Quoted in Eldon Epp, *Junia: The First Woman Apostle*. Minneapolis: Fortress, 2005.

2N 38. Sanday and Headlam, in *Junia*, 66.

Periodicals

Magazines

N 16. Kevin J. Vanhoozer, "Core Exercises," *Christianity Today*, November 2018, 46.

B Vanhoozer, Kevin J. "Core Exercises." *Christianity Today*, November 2018.

2N 19. Vanhoozer, "Core Exercises," 47.

Journals

N 17. P. Gerard Damsteegt, "Decoding Ancient Waldensian Names: New Discoveries," *Andrews University Seminary Studies* (*AUSS*) 54, no. 2 (Fall 2016): 239.

B Damsteegt, P. Gerard. "Decoding Ancient Waldensian Names: New Discoveries." *Andrews University Seminary Studies* 54, no. 2 (Fall 2016): 237-258.

2N 42. Damsteegt, "Decoding Ancient Waldensian Names," 241.

Once you have written out the full name of a journal and noted the abbreviation in a table that follows the table of contents, you may use the abbreviation—except in the bibliography. Use Arabic numerals for volume numbers. When no month or season is given for a journal that begins each issue with page 1, give the number of the issue with the volume: *Newsletter* 4, no. 3 (1980): 9.

Specialized Books

Classical Authors and Church Fathers

Generally, it is enough to give the author, title, book, and section of a work of one of the classical authors or of a church father. Whatever the edition, these works, somewhat like the Bible, are always divided the same way. However, it is a courtesy to the reader to give the place where you found the words or ideas. Notice the absence of punctuation between author and title of the work. This is simply a convention to be respected.

N 18. Irenaeus *Against Heresies* 2.2.3.

or

N 18. Irenaeus *Against Heresies* 2.2.3, ANF 1:421.

BP Irenaeus *Against Heresies*. The Ante-Nicene Fathers. Grand Rapids, MI: Eerdmans, n.d., 1:315-567.

BA Roberts, Alexander, and James Donaldson, eds. *Against Heresies*. The Ante-Nicene Fathers. Grand Rapids, MI: Eerdmans, n.d.

2N 28. Irenaeus *Against Heresies* 2.2.5.

N 19. John Chrysostom *The Priesthood* 3.17 (Migne, Patrologia Graeca, vol. 48, col. 656).

BP Chrysostom, John. *The Priesthood*. Patrologia Graeca. Edited by Jean Paul Migne. Paris: Apud Garnier Fratres, 1862. Vol. 48, cols. 623-692.

BA Migne, Jean Paul, ed. *Patrologia Graeca*, 161 vols. Paris: Apud Garnier Fratres, 1862.

2N 36. Chrysostom *Priesthood* 3.21.

N 20. Josephus *Jewish War* 2.14.5.

B Josephus, Flavius. *The Works of Josephus*. Edited by William Whiston. 4 vols. New York, NY: Oakley, Mason & Co., 1869.

2N 24. Josephus *Jewish War* 2.13.4.

Rabbinical Works

The Mishnah, which is the basic authority of rabbinic halakah, is divided into 63 tractates, which in turn are divided into *perakim* and *mishnayyoth*. This division is analogous to that of the Bible into books, chapters, and verses. Refer to the Mishnah by name of tractate, number of *perek*, and number of *mishnah*:

N 21. Mishnah *Sanhedrin* 10:3.

B *The Mishnah.* Translated by Herbert Danby. London: Oxford University Press, 1933.

2N 42. M. *Sanhedrin* 10:5.

The Talmud is an expansion of the Mishnah and is arranged as a commentary on the Mishnah. It is divided into the same 63 tractates. References to the Babylonian Talmud are customarily made in terms of the folio number and the side (a or b) of the folio in the most ancient Hebrew version. Because this system is unique to the Babylonian Talmud and different from that used in the identification of the parts of the Mishnah or the Jerusalem Talmud, many times the word Talmud is omitted in the reference. Thus *Sanhedrin* 10:3 is a clear reference to the Mishnah, while *Sanhedrin* 97a is a reference to the Babylonian Talmud.

N 22. B. T. *Sanhedrin* 97a.

or

N 22. B. Talmud *Sanhedrin* 97a.

B *The Babylonian Talmud.* Edited by I. Epstein. London: Soncino, 1935.

The Jerusalem Talmud is referred to by the same system used for the Mishnah. Care must be taken to add the letter "J" to distinguish from the Mishnah.

N 23. J. *Berakoth* 3:5.

or

N 23. J. T. *Berakoth* 3:5.

Bible Commentaries and Concordances

References to commentaries can be complicated. Some have one author for the whole commentary; others have one author for each book in a series, which may or may not have numbered volumes. Some have several authors for each book. Yet others have no known authors, only an editor. These variations show in the references.

Commentaries—author given

N 24. John B. Polhill, *Acts*, New American Commentary (Nashville, TN: Broadman, 1992), 175.

B Polhill, John B. *Acts*. New American Commentary. Nashville, TN: Broadman, 1992.

2N 28. Polhill, *Acts*, 178.

N 25. Edward R. Campbell, *Ruth*, Anchor Bible, vol. 7 (Garden City, NY: Doubleday, 1975), 27.

B Campbell, Edward R. *Ruth*. Anchor Bible, vol. 7. Garden City, NY: Doubleday, 1975.

2N 34. Campbell, *Ruth*, 28.

N 26. F. Delitzsch, *Biblical Commentary on the Book of Job*, 2 vols., Biblical Commentary on the Old Testament (Grand Rapids, MI: Eerdmans, 1949), 2:115.

B Delitzsch, F. *Biblical Commentary on the Book of Job*. 2 vols. Biblical Commentary on the Old Testament. Grand Rapids, MI: Eerdmans, 1949.

2N 48. Delitzsch, *Job*, 1:99.

N 27. Fred B. Craddock, "The Letter to the Hebrews: Introduction, Commentary, and Reflections," *New Interpreter's Bible*, 12 vols. (Nashville, TN: Abingdon, 1998), 12:75.

B Craddock, Fred B. "The Letter to the Hebrews: Introduction, Commentary, and Reflections." *New Interpreter's Bible*. 12 vols. Nashville, TN: Abingdon, 1998. 12:3-173.

2N 39. Craddock, "Hebrews," 12:78.

N 28. G. Ernest Wright, "Exegesis of the Book of Deuteronomy," *Interpreter's Bible* (New York, NY: Abingdon, 1954), 2:331.

BP Wright, G. Ernest. "Exegesis of the Book of Deuteronomy." *Interpreter's Bible*. New York, NY: Abingdon, 1954. 2:331-540.

BA Buttrick, G. A., ed. *Interpreter's Bible*. 12 vols. New York, NY: Abingdon, 1954.

2N 45. Wright, "Deuteronomy," 2:350.

Commentaries—no author given

N 29. Edward Hastings, ed., *The Speaker's Bible*, 18 vols. (Grand Rapids, MI: Baker, 1971), 17:159.

To point out the exact phrase commented on, the following entry may be used:

N 30. "The Blood of Christ" [Heb 9:13-14], *The Speaker's Bible*, ed. Edward Hastings (Grand Rapids, MI: Baker, 1971), 17:159.

BP "The Blood of Christ" [Heb 9:13-14]. *The Speaker's Bible*. Edited by Edward Hastings. Grand Rapids, MI: Baker, 1971. 17:159.

BA Hastings, Edward, ed. *The Speaker's Bible*. 18 vols. Grand Rapids, MI: Baker, 1971.

2N 36. "Blood of Christ," *Speaker's Bible*, 17:160.

Concordances

N 31. Robert Young, *Analytical Concordance to the Bible*, 22nd Amer. ed. (Grand Rapids, MI: Eerdmans, n.d.), s.v. "soul."

B Young, Robert. *Analytical Concordance to the Bible*. 22nd American ed. Grand Rapids, MI: Eerdmans, n.d. S.v. "soul."

2N 42. Young, *Analytical Concordance*, s.v. "soul."

Here "s.v." stands for the Latin *sub verbo*; it means you will find the item under the word that follows.

Dictionaries and Encyclopedias

Dictionaries and encyclopedias come in many stripes. Some deal with modern languages (for example, Webster's and Larousse). Some deal with themes: *Theological Dictionary of the New Testament* and *The Anchor Bible Dictionary*. Most in the first category have unsigned articles, while most in the second have signed articles. These variations must be taken into account in notes and bibliographies.

Dictionaries and encyclopedias with unsigned articles

Reference to a modern-language dictionary appears in a footnote but not normally in the bibliography. While publication data are not considered important, the number of the edition or the year of the edition is important.

N 32. *Merriam-Webster's Collegiate Dictionary*, 11th ed., s.v. "sin."

2N 56. *Webster's Dictionary*, s.v. "sin."

For well-known dictionaries and encyclopedias, omit the place and publisher in the note and omit the whole entry from the bibliography.

N 33. *Columbia Encyclopedia*, 8th ed., s.v. "war."

2N 61. *Columbia Encyclopedia*, s.v. "war."

Specialized dictionaries and encyclopedias with unsigned articles do not need the place or publisher in the note, but they do need an edition or date. Note the format for the date rather than edition. This type of source goes in the bibliography, with complete publication data.

N 34. *Nelson's New Illustrated Bible Dictionary* (2000), s.v. "angel."

BP *Nelson's New Illustrated Bible Dictionary*. Rev. ed. Edited by Ronald F. Youngblood. Nashville, TN: Nelson, 2000. S.v. "angel."

BA *Nelson's New Illustrated Bible Dictionary*. Rev. ed. Edited by Ronald F. Youngblood. Nashville, TN: Nelson, 2000.

2N 40. *Nelson's New Illustrated Bible Dictionary*, s.v. "angel."

N 35. *Seventh-day Adventist Encyclopedia* (1996), s.v. "Kingsway College."

BP *Seventh-day Adventist Encyclopedia*. Revised ed. 2 vols. Hagerstown, MD: Review and Herald, 1996. S.v. "Kingsway College."

BA *Seventh-day Adventist Encyclopedia*. Revised ed. 2 vols. Hagerstown, MD: Review and Herald, 1996.

2N 47. *SDA Encyclopedia*, s.v. "Kingsway College."

Dictionaries and encyclopedias with signed articles

Full information must be given for this kind of source, both in the note and the bibliography. The only exception is the use of abbreviations when the item appears in a list of abbreviations at the beginning of the paper. The first example presupposes the existence of such a list.

N 36. Hayim Lapin, "Rabbi," *ABD*, 5:601.

or

N 36. Hayim Lapin, "Rabbi," *Anchor Bible Dictionary*, 6 vols., ed. David Noel Freedman (New York, NY: Doubleday, 1992), 5:601.

BP Lapin, Hayim. "Rabbi." *Anchor Bible Dictionary*. 6 vols. Edited by David Noel Freedman. New York, NY: Doubleday, 1992. 5:600-602.

BA Freedman, David Noel, ed. *Anchor Bible Dictionary*. 6 vols. New York, NY: Doubleday, 1992.

2N 58. Lapin, "Rabbi," 5:603.

The Greek or Hebrew title may be transliterated and italicized or typed in the original language. Handwritten script is not acceptable. An acceptable transliteration scheme is given in appendix A.

N 37. Rudolf Bultmann, "*Aidōs*," *Theological Dictionary of the New Testament* (Grand Rapids, MI: Eerdmans, 1964-1976), 1:169.

BP Bultmann, Rudolf. "*Aidōs*." *Theological Dictionary of the New Testament*. Grand Rapids, MI: Eerdmans, 1964-1976. 1:169.

2N 45. Bultmann, "*Aidōs*," 1:169.

BA Kittel, Gerhard, and Gerhard Friedrich, eds. *Theological Dictionary of the New Testament*. 10 vols. Translated by Geoffrey Bromiley. Grand Rapids, MI: Eerdmans, 1964-1976.

N 38. Aaron Demsky, "Education: In the Biblical Period," *EJ*, 6:384.

or

N 38. Aaron Demsky, "Education: In the Biblical Period," *Encyclopaedia Judaica* (Jerusalem: Encyclopaedia Judaica, 1972), 6:384.

BP Demsky, Aaron. "Education: In the Biblical Period." *Encyclopaedia Judaica*. Jerusalem: Encyclopaedia Judaica, 1972. 6:382-398.

BA *Encyclopaedia Judaica*. 16 vols. Jerusalem: Encyclopaedia Judaica, 1972.

2N 53. Demsky, "Education," *EJ* 6:384.

Collected Works of Individual Authors

A great deal of variation is observed in references to collected works of well-known authors. When in doubt, use common sense. Be consistent in whatever you do.

N 39. Karl Barth, *Church Dogmatics*, III/3 (Edinburgh: T&T Clark, 1960), 82.

BP Barth, Karl. *Church Dogmatics*. Edinburgh: T&T Clark, 1960. III/3.

2N Barth, *Church Dogmatics*, III/3, 83.

N 40. Martin Luther, *Sermon on the Sum of Christian Life*, *Luther's Works* (*LW*), Amer. ed. (Saint Louis, MO: Concordia, 1955-1976), 51:260.

BP Luther, Martin. *Sermon on the Sum of Christian Life*. *Luther's Works*. American ed. Saint Louis, MO: Concordia, 1955-1976. 51:259-287.

BA Luther, Martin. *Luther's Works*. American edition. 55 vols. Saint Louis, MO: Concordia, 1955-1976.

A second reference could read:

2N 41. Luther, *On the Sum of Christian Life*, *LW*, 51:259.

Book Reviews

N 42. Stephen Bauer, review of *Christian Ethics: Four Views*, ed. Steve Wilkins, *Andrews University Seminary Studies* 56, no. 2 (2018): 221.

B Bauer, Stephen. Review of *Christian Ethics: Four Views*, ed. Steve Wilkins. *Andrews University Seminary Studies* 56, no. 2 (2018): 220-224.

2N Bauer, review of *Christian Ethics*, 222.

Unpublished Materials

The search for information should not be limited to published materials. Theses and dissertations, interviews and voice recordings, as well as manuscripts—all of these academic or nonacademic unpublished materials can contribute worthwhile data to a research project.

Academic Sources

Theses and dissertations are the most commonly cited unpublished academic papers. Other miscellaneous academic papers may also be used.

Theses and Dissertations

N 43. Melak Alemayehu Tsegaw, "Whole-body Gestures with the Context of Worship in the Book of Psalms" (PhD dissertation, Adventist International Institute of Advanced Studies, 2017), 35.

B Tsegaw, Melak Alemayehu. "Whole-body Gestures with the Context of Worship in the Book of Psalms." PhD dissertation, Adventist International Institute of Advanced Studies, 2017.

2N 62. Tsegaw, "Whole-body Gestures," 37.

N 44. Jaimie Marie Eckert, "Biblical Narratives as a Methodology for Guided Worldview Shift in Islamic Contexts" (MA thesis, Middle East University, 2016), 18.

B Eckert, Jaimie Marie. "Biblical Narratives as a Methodology for Guided Worldview Shift in Islamic Contexts." MA thesis, Middle East University, 2016.

2N 68. Eckert, "Biblical Narratives," 19.

N 45. Paul Brent Dybdahl, "The Stairway to Heaven: A Critique of the Evangelical Gospel Presentation in North America" (PhD diss., Andrews University, 2004), 3, https://digitalcommons.andrews.edu/dissertations/44/

B Dybdahl, Paul Brent, "The Stairway to Heaven: A Critique of the Evangelical Gospel Presentation in North America." PhD diss., Andrews University, 2004. https://digitalcommons.andrews.edu/dissertations/44/.

2N 53. Dybdahl, "Stairway to Heaven," 3.

N 46. Maria V. Schrampfer, "I am Baptized, I am Deified: Baptism as *Theosis* in Martin Luther's Theology" (MA thesis, Saint Louis University, 2018), 3. ProQuest Dissertations & Theses Global.

B Schrampfer, Maria V. "I am Baptized, I am Deified: Baptism as *Theosis* in Martin Luther's Theology." MA thesis, Saint Louis University, 2018. ProQuest Dissertations & Theses Global.

2N 51. Schrampfer, "I am Baptized," 9.

Miscellaneous Academic Papers

Class papers

N 45. Teresa Reeve, "The 'Just Man' in the Writings of Philo," paper presented for THEO 611 Philo Seminar, University of Notre Dame, South Bend, IN, December 1997, 13.

B Reeve, Teresa. "The 'Just Man' in the Writings of Philo." A paper presented for THEO 611 Philo Seminar, University of Notre Dame, South Bend, IN, December 1997.

2N 52. Reeve, "Just Man," 12.

N 45. Wann Marbud Fanwar, "He Who Created the Heavens and the Earth: Contributions of Isaiah to Rev 14:7c," seminar paper for GSEM 920 Religious Studies Seminar, Andrews University, Berrien Springs, MI, May 1999, 19.

B Fanwar, Wann Marbud. "He Who Created the Heavens and the Earth: Contributions of Isaiah to Rev 14:7c." Seminar paper for GSEM 920 Religious Studies Seminar, Andrews University, Berrien Springs, MI, May 1999.

2N 66. Fanwar, "He Who Created," 21.

Syllabi

N 47. Nancy Vyhmeister, Course outline for GSEM 620, Thesis and Research Writing, Middle East University, Beirut, Lebanon, 2008, 3.

B Vyhmeister, Nancy. Course outline for GSEM 620, Thesis and Research Writing. Middle East University, Beirut, Lebanon, 2008.

2N 59. Vyhmeister, Course outline, 4.

Class notes

N 48. Paul Saghbini, "An Introduction to Literary Theories," Class notes, Literary Criticism and Theory, Middle East University, Beirut, Lebanon, January 24, 2019.

R Saghbini, Paul. "An Introduction to Literary Theories." Class notes, Literary Criticism and Theory, Middle East University, Beirut, Lebanon, January 24, 2019.

2N 60. Saghbini, "Introduction," January 24, 2019.

Miscellaneous Unpublished Sources

Footnotes and bibliographical entries for miscellaneous unpublished materials can be difficult. To make them useful, clarity and consistency are vital. A good dose of common sense is also essential. Examples for reports, speeches, manuscripts, letters, and interviews are provided. Make sure the second mention is clear.

Reports

N 49. Seventh-day Adventist Theological Seminary, Far East, "Financial Statement of Graduate Apartments," 31 August 1985, 4.

B Seventh-day Adventist Theological Seminary, Far East, Philippines. "Financial Statement of Graduate Apartments." 31 August 1985.

2N 68. SDA Seminary, "Financial Statement," 5.

N 50. Association of Theological Institutions in Eastern Africa, "1978/79 Bachelor of Divinity Degree Syllabus," 3.

B Association of Theological Institutions in Eastern Africa. "1978/79 Bachelor of Divinity Degree Syllabus."

2N 64. Assoc. Theological Institutions in East Africa, 4.

Speeches and Presentations

N 51. C. Mervyn Maxwell, "Which Sacrifice, Lord?" Seminary Chapel sermon, Andrews University, Berrien Springs, MI, 20 October 1976, 10, typewritten.

B Maxwell, C. Mervyn. "Which Sacrifice, Lord?" Seminary Chapel sermon. Andrews University, Berrien Springs, MI, 20 October 1976. Typewritten.

2N 71. Maxwell, "Which Sacrifice," 9.

N 52. Jon Paulien, "The 1260 Days in the Book of Revelation," paper presented at the *Fourth International Bible Conference* in Rome, Italy, June 11-21, 2018, 5.

B Paulien, Jon. "The 1260 Days in the Book of Revelation." Paper presented at the *Fourth International Bible Conference* in Rome, Italy, June 11-21, 2018.

2N 68. Paulien, "1260 Days in Revelation," 6.

Manuscripts

References to manuscripts must permit readers to know exactly what the item is and where it is found. The name of the collection and its location must be clear.

N 53. Peter L. Benoit, 1875 diary, Archives, University of Notre Dame, South Bend, IN.

B Benoit, Peter L. 1875 diary. Photocopy of typewritten transcript of Canon Benoit's diary of a trip to America, 6 January to 8 June 1875, including descriptions of Josephite missions among freed slaves. Archives, University of Notre Dame, South Bend, IN.

2N 59. Benoit, 1875 Diary.

N 54. Ellen G. White, Manuscript 154, 1902, Ellen G. White Research Center, Andrews University, Berrien Springs, MI (hereafter abbreviated EGWRC), 3.

B White, Ellen G. Manuscript 154, 1902. Ellen G. White Research Center, Andrews University, Berrien Springs, MI.

2N 67. EGWRC, 2.

Letters

A letter addressed to the author of the paper is assumed to be in the author's files. These are entered only in the notes. If the letter referred to is addressed to someone else, information should be given regarding its location. Quotations from letters should be as easy to verify as items from published sources.

N 55. Bryan Ball, editor of *The Essential Jesus*, to Nancy Vyhmeister, 13 March 2000.

2N 71. Ball to Vyhmeister. (If there are several letters, supply the date also.)

N 56. Ellen G. White to Dr. Patience Bourdeau, 8 June 1905, Letter 177, 1905, Ellen White Research Center, Newbold College, Bracknell, England.

B White, Ellen G., to Dr. Patience Bourdeau, 8 June 1905. Letter 177, 1905. Ellen White Research Center, Newbold College, Bracknell, England.

2N 79. White to Bourdeau.

Interviews

Use this kind of reference when you, as author, have a recorded version of the interview. You may attribute the information to an unnamed person, such as a "district pastor" or a "neighborhood health worker." You may also put the source into the text: "In a conversation with the author on January 2, 2019, pastor XX noted that . . ." Interviews with the author appear only in the notes.

N 57. George Knight, author and retired professor, interview by author, Loma Linda, CA, February 3, 2019.

Electronic Media

To show you how to footnote the multiple varieties of electronic media would be impossible. Here we show basics and urge you to use your educated imagination.

CD-ROMS

N 58. Ellen G. White, *Education*, Complete Published Ellen G. White Writings [CD ROM] (Silver Spring, MD: Ellen G. White Estate, 1999).

B White, Ellen G. *Education*. Complete Published Ellen G. White Writings [CD ROM]. Silver Spring, MD: Ellen G. White Estate, 1999.

2N 72. White, *Education*.

Video and Sound Recordings

Some information for this type of source may be lacking. Use whatever you can find. Follow the same organization as for other materials.

N 59. Lee Strobel, *The Case for a Creator*, 60-minute video (La Mirada, CA: Illustra Media, 2006), DVD.

B Strobel, Lee. *The Case for a Creator*. 60-minute video. La Mirada, CA: Illustra Media, 2006. DVD.

2N 62. Strobel, *Case for a Creator*.

N 60. Luis Landriscina, "Judío en el Vaticano," in *Mano a mano con el país*, vol. 5, Phillips 64232, 1985, audio cassette.

B Landriscina, Luis. "Judío en el Vaticano." In *Mano a mano con el país*, vol. 5. Phillips 64232, 1985. Audio cassette.

2N 75. Landriscina, "Judío en el Vaticano."

Websites

In these examples, notice that some do not have all the elements you would expect to find in a bibliography entry or footnote. Put in everything that is available and you think is reasonable. For more information, refer to *The Chicago Manual of Style*, 17th edition, sections 14.205 through 14.267 or Turabian 9, chapter 17.

Online journal articles with complete bibliographic information may be done as regular journals, although you should note the online site. If page numbers are missing, be sure to give the URL.

You may break the URL *after* a colon or a double slash or *before* a period or a single slash. Do not add a hyphen to indicate a break (some URLs contain hyphens).

Some additions to our traditional vocabulary (you don't need to be a computer specialist to use these!):

HTTP: Hyper Text Transfer Protocol, the protocol used by the World Wide Web to define how messages are formatted and transmitted.
HTTPS: Hyper Text Transfer Protocol Secure means the same as the previous, but adds that your message is secure.
URL: Uniform Resource Locator, a unique identifier used to locate a web address containing the information you want to find.
DOI: Digital Object Identifier system, a string of numbers, letters, and symbols used to permanently identify an article or document on the web.

The main novelty in this new edition is that you are no longer required to record the date you found the information. Your school, however, may still want your access date.

N 61. Shelly Whitman, "Women and Peace-Building in the Democratic Republic of Congo: An Assessment of Their Role in the Inter-Congolese Dialogue," *African Journal on Conflict Resolution* 6 (2006): 31, http://center.theparents circle.org /images /ebf709980d3642e8af0ecca3df18a051.pdf.

B Whitman, Shelly. "Women and Peace-Building in the Democratic Republic of Congo: An Assessment of Their Role in the Inter-Congolese Dialogue." *African Journal on Conflict Resolution* 6 (2006): 29-48. http://center .theparentscircle.org/images/ebf709980d3642e8af0ecca3df18a051.pdf.

2N 70. Whitman, "Women and Peace-Building," 33.

N 62. Prema Gaikwad and Blessing Obaya, "Wish to WISHCRAFT: A Peek into an Environmentally Friendly School," *International Forum* 21, no. 1 (June 2018): 137, https://internationalforum.aiias.edu/images/vol21no01 /8GaikwadObaya.pdf.

B Gaikwad, Prema, and Blessing Obaya. "Wish to WISHCRAFT: A Peek into an Environmentally Friendly School." *International Forum* 21, no. 1 (June 2018): 134-149. https://internationalforum.aiias.edu/images /vol21no01/8GaikwadObaya.pdf.

2N 73. Gaikwad and Obaya, "Wish to WISHCRAFT," 141.

N 63. UNICEF, *Female Genital Mutilation/Cutting: A Statistical Overview and Exploration of the Dynamics of Change* (New York, NY: United Nations Children's Fund, 2013), 3, https://data.unicef.org/wp-content/uploads /2015/12/FGMC_Brochure_Lo_res_1613.pdf.

B UNICEF, *Female Genital Mutilation/Cutting: A Statistical Overview and Exploration of the Dynamics of Change*. New York, NY: United Nations Children's Fund, 2013. https://data.unicef.org/wp-content/uploads /2015/12/FGMC_Brochure_Lo_res_1613.pdf.

2N 77. UNICEF, *Female Genital Mutilation*.

N 64. Willis J. Beecher, "Adonijah," *International Standard Bible Encyclopedia* (*ISBE*), 4 vols., ed. James Orr (Chicago, IL: Howard Severance, 1915), 1:57, https://www.christianresearcher.com/uploads /1/6/2/9/16298120/isbevol1.pdf.

B Beecher, Willis J. "Adonijah," *International Standard Bible Encyclopedia*, 4 vols., ed. James Orr. Chicago, IL: Howard Severance, 1915. 1:57. https://www .christianresearcher.com/uploads /1/6/2/9/16298120 /isbevol1.pdf.

2N 80. Beecher, "Adonijah," *ISBE* 1:57.

N 65. Augustine, "Of the Miracles Wrought by the True God Through the Ministry of the Holy Angels," in Augustine's *City of God*, chapter 12, Nicene and Post-Nicene Fathers, series 1, vol. 2, www.ccel.org/ccel/schaff/npnf102.iv.X.12.html.

B Augustine. "Of the Miracles Wrought by the True God Through the Ministry of the Holy Angels." In Augustine's *City of God*, chapter 12. Nicene and Post-Nicene Fathers. Series 1, vol. 2. www.ccel.org/ccel/schaff/npnf102.iv.X.12.html.

2N 83. Augustine, "Of the Miracles Wrought by the True God."

N 66. "Questions Muslims Ask," Jesus to Muslims, n.d. http://jesustomuslims.org/equip/questions-muslims-ask-christians.

B "Questions Muslims Ask." Jesus to Muslims. N.d. http://jesustomuslims.org/equip/questions-muslims-ask-christians.

2N 84. "Questions Muslims Ask."

N 67. "Free Spiritual Gifts Analysis" (Elkton, MD: Church Growth Institute, n.d.), www.churchgrowth.org/analysis/intro.php.

B "Free Spiritual Gifts Analysis." Elkton, MD: Church Growth Institute, n.d. www.churchgrowth.org/analysis/intro.php.

2N 70. "Free Spiritual Gifts Analysis."

Caveats for Website References

As we all know, websites come and go. When your professor gets around to checking your source, the website may be gone. Then what? First, save a copy—paper or electronic of the contents of the website. Second, put an access date in your own records. Then when professor Smith calls your research into question, you can say, "Well, it was there on May 15, 2019, and I will send you a copy of the contents I was reading then." Or immediately after the blue underlining appears, use CTRL+Z.

Since you will be copying the URL, you will have a bright blue, underlined address. Not to worry. Put your cursor just after the end of the blue, tap "backspace" and voilà—the blue and underlining will disappear.

Please follow your school's rules on details of format. If they want the date to be 15 May 2019, fine. If they want May 15, 2019, fine. Here's a good place to follow their rules.

For journal articles online that include a DOI—which are generally more stable than the URL—form the URL by appending the DOI rather than using the regular URL. Here is an example from Turabian 9, figure 16.1.

N Patricio Fernández, "Practical Reasoning: Where the Action Is," *Ethics* 126, no. 4 (July 2016): 872, https//doi.org/10.1086/685998.

B Fernández, Patricio. "Practical Reasoning: Where the Action Is." *Ethics* 126, no. 4 (July 2016): 869-900. https//doi.org/10.1086/685998.

2N Fernández, "Practical Reasoning," 873.

For electronic books you read on your computer, such as Kindle books, cite them as any other book, except that you add the words "Kindle edition." Today's Kindle books have page numbers; older ones may not. In such a case, note the chapter or section.

N Robert Pazmiño, *Doing Theological Research* (Eugene, OR: Wipf & Stock, 2009), Kindle edition, chapter 3.

B Pazmiño, Robert. *Doing Theological Research*. Eugene, OR: Wipf & Stock, 2009. Kindle edition.

chapter twenty-two

TURABIAN 9, AUTHOR-DATE STYLE

In this style, the author, date, and page are placed in parentheses in the text. Since the information given between the parentheses is limited, there must be a reference list with the text. And the information given between the parentheses must clearly lead to the appropriate item in the reference list.

The examples are of the same materials as appear in the two other chapters on notes and bibliography.

In preparing notes and reference list entries that do not seem to fit into any category, follow the rules as closely as possible, using common sense to make modifications as needed. When the reference is to several pages (28-32), we suggest using a hyphen. We believe that references should make it easy for a reader to locate any source.[1]

The examples presented in this chapter use the following abbreviations:

N (for Note) shows the format of a parenthetical note.
R (for Reference list) gives the format for a common, uncomplicated reference list entry.

Published Materials

When the author-date style, with the information in parentheses, is used, the reference list becomes even more important.

Abbreviations can be used for often-repeated titles or series. Make sure you give a list of abbreviations before the introduction. Appendix C refers you to

1. For further information on Turabian 9's author-date style, see Turabian 9, 223-289.

places where you can find lists of accepted abbreviations. Abbreviations may be used in the notes, but not in the reference list. When the abbreviations stand for the title of a book or journal, they should be italicized.

General Books

Under this heading, several issues are addressed. First, and most frequent, are those related to authorship. Next come examples of how to handle multivolume works. Finally, you will find entries showing how to deal with series, reprints, and secondary sources.

Authorship

One author

N (Lederleitner 2018, 54)

R Lederleitner, Mary. 2018. *Women in God's Mission*. Downers Grove, IL: InterVarsity Press.

Two or three authors

N (Neyrey and Stewart 2008, 134)

R Neyrey, Jerome H., and Eric Clark Stewart. 2008. *The Social World of the New Testament: Insights and Models*. Peabody, MA: Hendrickson.

Four or more authors

Your school may allow the shortening of the author statement in the note, as does Turabian 9. The Latin form "*et al.*" may be used for "and others." All names must be in the bibliographical entry. Make sure to check your school's rules.

N (VanGemeren et al. 1993, 78) or (VanGemeren and others 1993, 78)

R VanGemeren, Willem A., Greg L. Bahnsen, Walter C. Kaiser Jr., Wayne G. Strickland, and Douglas Moo. 1993. *The Law, the Gospel, and the Modern Christian*. Grand Rapids, MI: Zondervan.

Corporate author

N (Southern Baptist Convention 2000, 29)

R Southern Baptist Convention. Committee on Baptist Faith and Message. 2000. *The Baptist Faith and Message: A Statement Adopted by the Baptist Convention, June 14, 2000*. Nashville, TN: LifeWay Christian Resources.

No author, edition other than first, with translator

N (*Bhagavad-Gita as It Is* 1972, 74)

R *Bhagavad-Gita as It Is*. 1972. Abridged edition. Translated by A. C. Bhaktivedanta Swami Prabhupada. New York, NY: Bhaktivedanta Book Trust.

Editor instead of author; joint publication

N (VanderKam and Adler 1996, 35)

R VanderKam, James C., and William Adler, eds. 1996. *The Jewish Apocalyptic Heritage in Early Christianity*. Assen, Netherlands: Van Gorcum; Minneapolis, MN: Fortress.

Component part by one author in a work edited by another

N (Ruguri 2015, 411)

R Ruguri, Blasious M. 2015. "Biblical Principles for Tribal Unity." In *Biblical Principles for Missiological Issues in Africa*, edited by Bruce Bauer and Wagner Kuhn, 409-431. Berrien Springs, MI: Department of World Mission, Andrews University, 2015.

Multivolume Works

Here are examples of several different types—from simple to complex:

N (González 1970-1975, 1:176)

R González, Justo. 1970-1975. *A History of Christian Thought*. 3 vols. Nashville, TN: Abingdon.

Multivolume work—one author, different titles

N (Latourette 1970, 3:17)

R Latourette, Kenneth Scott. 1970. *A History of the Expansion of Christianity*. Vol. 3, *Three Centuries of Advance*. Grand Rapids, MI: Zondervan.

Multivolume work—several authors

N (Winter 1994, 3:38)

R Winter, Bruce W., ed. 1994. *The Book of Acts in Its First Century Setting*. 6 vols. Carlisle, UK: Paternoster, 1994. Vol. 3, *The Book of Acts and Paul in Roman Custody*, by Brian Rapske.

If for some reason the author of the book you are citing or quoting is more important than the multivolume source, you may use the following format:

N (Rapske 1994, 38)

R Rapske, Brian. 1994. *The Book of Acts and Paul in Roman Custody*. Vol. 3, *The Book of Acts in Its First Century Setting*, ed. Bruce W. Winter. Carlisle, UK: Paternoster.

Part of a series

N (Booth et al. 2016, 155)

R Booth, Wayne C., Gregory G. Colomb, Joseph M. Williams, Joseph Bizup, and William T. FitzGerald. 2016. *The Craft of Research*. Chicago Guides to Writing, Editing, and Publishing. Chicago, IL: University of Chicago Press.

Reprint

N (Nevius [1895] 2013, 174, 175)

R Nevius, John L. 1895. *Life of John Livingston Nevius*. Reprint of *John Livingston Nevius: For Forty Years a Missionary in China*. New York, NY: Revell. Reprint, n.p.: TheClassics.us, 2013.

N (Reynolds 1977, 17:v)

R Reynolds, H. R. 1977. "Introduction to the Gospel of St. John." In *The Pulpit Commentary*, ed. H. O. M. Spense and Joseph S. Excell, 17:iv-clxi. Reprint, Grand Rapids, MI: Eerdmans, 1977.

Secondary Source

Use secondary source references sparingly. They are complicated. Also, your readers will be less impressed with your use of a secondary source than of a primary source. Mention the original author and date in the text and cite the secondary source in the reference list.

N Sanday and Headlam, who wrote the *Critical and Exegetical Commentary on the Epistle to the Romans* in 1895 (quoted Epp 2005, 71), noted that . . .

R Epp, Eldon. 2005. *Junia: The First Woman Apostle*. Minneapolis, MN: Fortress, 2005.

Periodicals

Magazines

N (Vanhoozer 2018, 46)

R Vanhoozer, Kevin J. 2018. "Core Exercises." *Christianity Today*, November, 46-50.

Journals

N (Damsteegt 2016, 239)

R Damsteegt, P. Gerard. 2016. "Decoding Ancient Waldensian Names: New Discoveries." *Andrews University Seminary Studies* 54, no. 2 (Fall): 237-258.

Once you have written out the full name of a journal and noted the abbreviation, you may use the abbreviation—except in the reference list. Use Arabic numerals for volume numbers. When no month or season is given for a journal that begins each issue with page 1, give the number of the issue with the volume: *Newsletter* 4, no. 3 (1980): 9.

Specialized Books

The Bible

Bible references do not appear in the bibliography. References in the text are given in parentheses. The name of the Bible book usually is abbreviated, as suggested in appendix B.

If you are using only one Bible version, indicate that in the first Bible reference. If you are using several versions, indicate the versions in your notes. Include the abbreviated name of the versions in your list of abbreviations at the beginning of your paper.

N (John 3:16, NKJV)

N (Exod 20:8-11, NIV)

Classical Authors and Church Fathers

Generally, it is enough to give the author, title, book, and section of a work of one of the classical authors or of a church father. Whatever the edition, these works, somewhat like the Bible, are always divided the same way. These items often do not appear in the reference list.

N (Irenaeus, *Against Heresies* 2.2.3)

N (Chrysostom, *The Priesthood* 3.17)

N (Josephus, *Jewish War* 2.14.5)

Rabbinical Works

The Mishnah, which is the basic authority of rabbinic halakah, is divided into 63 tractates, which in turn are divided into *perakim* and *mishnayyoth*. This division is analogous to that of the Bible into books, chapters, and verses. Refer to the Mishnah by name of tractate, number of *perek*, and number of *mishnah*:

N (Mishnah *Sanhedrin* 10:3)

The Talmud is an expansion of the Mishnah and is arranged as a commentary on the Mishnah. It is divided into the same 63 tractates. References to the Babylonian Talmud are customarily made in terms of the folio number and the side (a or b) of the folio in the most ancient Hebrew version. Because this system is unique to the Babylonian Talmud and different from that used in the identification of the parts of the Mishnah or the Jerusalem Talmud, many times the word Talmud is omitted in the reference. Thus *Sanhedrin* 10:3 is a clear reference to the Mishnah, while *Sanhedrin* 97a is a reference to the Babylonian Talmud.

N (B. T. *Sanhedrin* 97a)

or

N (B. Talmud *Sanhedrin* 97a)

The Jerusalem Talmud is referred to by the same system used for the Mishnah. Care must be taken to add the letter "J" to distinguish from the Mishnah.

N (J. *Berakoth* 3:5)

or

N (J. T. *Berakoth* 3:5)

Bible Commentaries and Concordances

References to commentaries can be complicated. Some have one author for the whole commentary; others have one author for each book in a series, which may or may not have numbered volumes. Some have several authors for each book. Yet others have no known authors, only an editor. These variations show in the references.

Commentaries—author given

N (Polhill 1992, 175)

R Polhill, John B. 1992. *Acts*. New American Commentary. Nashville, TN: Broadman.

N (Campbell 1975, 27)

R Campbell, Edward R. 1975. *Ruth*. Anchor Bible, 7. Garden City, NY: Doubleday.

N (Delitzsch 1949, 2:115)

R Delitzsch, F. 1949. *Biblical Commentary on the Book of Job*. 2 vols. Biblical Commentary on the Old Testament. Grand Rapids, MI: Eerdmans.

N (Craddock 1998, 12:75)

R Craddock, Fred B. 1998. "The Letter to the Hebrews: Introduction, Commentary, and Reflections." *New Interpreter's Bible*. 12 vols. Nashville, TN: Abingdon. 12:3-173.

N (Wright 1954, 2:331)

R Wright, G. Ernest. 1954. "Exegesis of the Book of Deuteronomy." *Interpreter's Bible*. New York, NY: Abingdon. 2:331-540.

Commentaries—no author given

N (Hastings 1971, 17:159)

R Hastings, Edward, ed. 1971. *The Speaker's Bible*. 18 vols. Grand Rapids, MI: Baker.

Concordances

N (Young n.d., s.v. "soul")

R Young, Robert. N.d. *Analytical Concordance to the Bible.* 22nd American ed. Grand Rapids, MI: Eerdmans, s.v. "soul."

Dictionaries and Encyclopedias

Dictionaries and encyclopedias come in many stripes. Some deal with modern languages (for example, Webster's and Larousse). Some deal with themes: *Theological Dictionary of the New Testament* and *The Anchor Bible Dictionary.* Most of the first category have unsigned articles, while most of the second have signed articles. These variations must be taken into account in notes and reference lists.

Dictionaries and encyclopedias with unsigned articles

Reference to a modern-language dictionary appears in an entry but not normally in the reference list. While publication data are not considered important, the number of the edition or the year of edition is important.

N (*Merriam-Webster's Collegiate Dictionary*, 11th ed., s.v. "sin")

On well-known dictionaries and encyclopedias, omit the place and publisher in the note and omit the whole entry from the reference list.

N (*Columbia Encyclopedia*, 8th ed., s.v. "war")

Specialized dictionaries and encyclopedias with unsigned articles do not need the place or publisher in the note, but they do need an edition or date. Note the format for the date rather than edition. This type of source goes in the reference list, with complete publication data.

N (*Nelson's New Illustrated Bible Dictionary* 2000, s.v. "angel")

R *Nelson's New Illustrated Bible Dictionary.* 2000. Rev. ed. Edited by Ronald F. Youngblood. Nashville, TN: Nelson. S.v. "angel."

N (*SDA Encyclopedia* 1996, s.v. "Kingsway College")

R *Seventh-day Adventist Encyclopedia.* 1996. Rev. ed. 2 vols. Hagerstown, MD: Review and Herald. S.v. "Kingsway College."

Dictionaries and encyclopedias with signed articles

Full information must be given for this kind of source, both in the note and the reference list. The only exception is the use of abbreviations when the item appears in a list of abbreviations at the beginning of the paper. The first example presupposes the existence of such a list.

N (Lapin *ABD*, 5:601)

R Lapin, Hayim. 1992. "Rabbi." *Anchor Bible Dictionary*. 6 vols. Edited by David Noel Freedman. New York, NY: Doubleday. 5:600-602.

The Greek or Hebrew title may be transliterated and italicized or typed in the original language. Handwritten script is not acceptable. An acceptable transliteration scheme is given in appendix A.

N (Bultmann 1964-1976, 1:169)

R Bultmann, Rudolf. 1964-1976. "*Aidōs*." *Theological Dictionary of the New Testament*. 15 vols. Grand Rapids, MI: Eerdmans.

N (Demsky 1972, *EJ* 6:384)

Here it would be good to have the title, "Education: In the Biblical Period" in the text.

R Demsky, Aaron. 1972. "Education: In the Biblical Period." *Encyclopaedia Judaica*. Jerusalem: Encyclopaedia Judaica. 6:382-398.

Collected Works of Individual Authors

A great deal of variation is observed in references to collected works of well-known authors. When in doubt, use common sense. Be consistent in whatever you do.

N (Barth 1960, *Church Dogmatics*, III/3, 82)

R Barth, Karl. 1960. *Church Dogmatics*. Edinburgh: T&T Clark, III/3.

N (Luther, *Sermon on the Sum of Christian Life*, 51:260)

R Luther, Martin. 1955-1976. *Sermon on the Sum of Christian Life. Luther's Works.* American ed. Saint Louis, MO: Concordia. 51:259-287.

A second reference could read:

N (Luther, *Sermon on the Sum of Christian Life*, *LW* 51:259)

Book Reviews

N (Bauer 2018, 221)

R Bauer, Stephen. 2018. Review of *Christian Ethics: Four Views*, ed. Steve Wilkins. *Andrews University Seminary Studies* 56, no. 1:220-224.

Unpublished Materials

The search for information should not be limited to published materials. Theses and dissertations, interviews and voice recordings, as well as manuscripts—all of these academic or nonacademic unpublished materials can contribute worthwhile data to a research project.

Academic Sources

Theses and dissertations are the most commonly cited unpublished academic papers. Other miscellaneous academic papers may also be used. If the educational institution is in the United States, no location Is needed. If the institution is elsewhere in the world, use the place and country.

Theses and Dissertations

N (Tsegaw 2017, 35)

R Tsegaw, Melak Alemayehu. 2017. "Whole-body Gestures with the Context of Worship in the Book of Psalms." PhD diss., Adventist International Institute of Advanced Studies, Silang, Cavite, Philippines.

N (Eckert 2016, 18)

R Eckert, Jaimie Marie. 2016. "Biblical Narratives as a Methodology for Guided Worldview Shift in Islamic Contexts." Master's thesis, Middle East University, Beirut, Lebanon.

N (Dybdahl 2004, 3)

R Dybdahl, Paul Brent, "The Stairway to Heaven: A Critique of the Evangelical Gospel Presentation in North America." PhD diss., Andrews University, 2004. https://digitalcommons.andrews.edu/dissertations/44/.

N (Schrampfer 2018, 3)

R Schrampfer, Maria V. "I am Baptized, I am Deified: Baptism as *Theosis* in Martin Luther's Theology." MA thesis, Saint Louis University, 2018. ProQuest Dissertations & Theses Global.

Miscellaneous Academic Papers

Class papers

N (Reeve 1997, 13)

R Reeve, Teresa. 1997. "The 'Just Man' in the Writings of Philo." A paper presented for THEO 611 Philo Seminar, University of Notre Dame, South Bend, IN.

N (Fanwar 1999, 19)

R Fanwar, Wann Marbud. 1999. "He Who Created the Heavens and the Earth: Contributions of Isaiah to Rev 14:7c." Seminar paper for GSEM 920 Religious Studies Seminar, Andrews University, Berrien Springs, MI.

Syllabi

N (Vyhmeister 2008, 3)

R Vyhmeister, Nancy. 2008. Course outline for GSEM 620, Thesis and Research Writing, Middle East University, Beirut, Lebanon.

Class notes

N (Saghbini 2019, class notes)

R Saghbini, Paul. 2019. "An Introduction to Literary Theories." Class notes, Literary Criticism and Theory, Middle East University, Beirut, Lebanon, January 24, 2019.

Miscellaneous Unpublished Sources

Footnotes and bibliographical entries for miscellaneous unpublished materials can be difficult. To make them useful, clarity and consistency are vital. A good dose of common sense is also essential. Examples for reports, speeches, manuscripts, letters, and interviews are provided.

Reports

N (Financial Statement 1985, 4)

R Seventh-day Adventist Theological Seminary, Far East. 1985. "Financial Statement of Graduate Apartments." 31 August 1985.

N (Association of Theological Institutions in Eastern Africa 1978, 3)

R Association of Theological Institutions in Eastern Africa. 1978. "1978/79 Bachelor of Divinity Degree Syllabus."

Speeches and Presentations

N (Maxwell 1976, 10)

R Maxwell, C. Mervyn. 1976. "Which Sacrifice, Lord?" Seminary Chapel sermon. Andrews University, 20 October 1976. Typewritten.

N (Paulien 2018, 6)

R Paulien, Jon. 2018. "The 1260 Days in the Book of Revelation." Paper presented at the *Fourth International Bible Conference* in Rome, Italy, June 11-21, 2018.

Manuscripts

References to manuscripts must permit readers to know exactly what the item is and where it is found. The name of the collection and its location must be clear.

N (Benoit 1875)

R Benoit, Peter L. 1875. Photocopy of typewritten transcript of Canon Benoit's diary of a trip to America, 6 January to 8 June 1875, including descriptions of Josephite missions among freed slaves. Archives, University of Notre Dame, South Bend, IN.

N (White Manuscript 154, 1902)

R White, Ellen G. Manuscript 154. 1902. Ellen G. White Research Center, Andrews University, Berrien Springs, MI.

Letters

A letter addressed to the author of the paper is assumed to be in the author's files. If the letter referred to is addressed to someone else, information should be given regarding its location. Quotations from letters should be as easy to verify as those from published sources.

Letters—unless published, as is the second example—are only entered in the notes. Interviews with the author also appear only in the notes. It is often easier, therefore, to simply give the information in the text.

N In a 13 March 2000 letter from Brian Ball, co-editor of *The Essential Jesus*, to Nancy Vyhmeister, author of the chapter "The Jesus of History," concerning . . .

N (White to Bourdeau, 1905)

R White, Ellen G., to Dr. Patience Bourdeau. 8 June 1905. Letter 177, 1905. Ellen White Research Center, Newbold College, Bracknell, England.

Interviews

Use this kind of reference when you, as author, have a recorded version of the interview. You may attribute the information to an unnamed person, such as a "district pastor" or a "neighborhood health worker." You may also put the source into the text: "In a conversation with the author on January 2, 2019, pastor XX noted that . . ." There is no need for this information to be in the reference list.

N In a conversation with Professor George Knight (February 7, 2019), I was informed that . . .

Electronic Media

To show you how to make entries for the multiple varieties of electronic media would be impossible. Here we show basics and urge you to use your educated imagination.

CD-ROMS

N (White 1999)

R White, Ellen G. 1999. *Education*. Complete Published Ellen G. White Writings. Silver Spring, MD: Ellen G. White Estate. CD.

Video and Sound Recordings

Some information for this type of source may be lacking. Use whatever you can find. Follow the same organization as for other materials.

N (Strobel 2006, DVD)

R Strobel, Lee. *The Case for a Creator*. La Mirada, CA: Illustra Media. DVD.

N (Landriscina 1985, audio cassette)

R Landriscina, Luis. 1985. "Judío en el Vaticano." In *Mano a mano con el país*, vol. 5. Phillips 64232, audio cassette.

Websites

In these examples, notice that some do not have all the elements you would expect in a note or reference list. Put in everything that is available and you think is reasonable. For further information, check *The Chicago Manual of Style*, 17th edition, chapter 14.205 through 14.267 or Turabian 9, 15:4-5.

Online journal articles with complete bibliographic information may be done as regular journals, although you should note the online site. If page numbers are missing, be sure to give the URL.

You may break the URL *after* a colon or a double slash or *before* a period or a single slash. Do not add a hyphen to indicate a break (some URLs contain hyphens).

Some additions to our traditional vocabulary (you don't need to be a computer specialist to use these):

HTTP: Hyper Text Transfer Protocol, the protocol used by the World Wide Web to define how messages are formatted and transmitted.

HTTPS: Hyper Text Transfer Protocol Secure means the same as the previous, but adds that your message is secure.

URL: Uniform Resource Locator, a unique identifier used to locate a web address containing the information you want to find.

DOI: Digital Object Identifier system, a string of numbers, letters, and symbols used to permanently identify an article or document on the web. The main novelty is that you are no longer required to record the date when you found the information.

N (Whitman 2006, 31)

R Whitman, Shelly. 2006. "Women and Peace-Building in the Democratic Republic of Congo: An Assessment of Their Role in the Inter-Congolese Dialogue." *African Journal on Conflict Resolution* 6 (2006): 29-48. http://center.theparentscircle.org/images/ebf709980d3642e8af0ecca3df18a051.pdf.

N (Gaikwad and Obaya 2018)

R Gaikwad, Prema, and Blessing Obaya. 2018. "Wish to WISHCRAFT: A Peek into an Environmentally Friendly School." *International Forum* 21, no. 1 (June): 134-149. https://journals.aiias.edu/iforum/article/view/350.

N (UNICEF 2005)

R "Female Genital Mutilation/Cutting: A Statistical Exploration." 2005. New York, NY: UNICEF. www.unicef.org/publications/index_29994.html.

N (Beecher "Adonijah" 1915)

R Beecher, Willis J. 1915. "Adonijah," *International Standard Bible Encyclopedia*, 4 vols., ed. James Orr. Chicago, IL: Howard Severance, 1915. 1:57. https://www.christianresearcher.com/uploads/1/6/2/9/16298120 /isbevol1.pdf.

N Writing about the "Miracles Wrought by the True God," Augustine (*City of God*, chapter 12), noted that . . .

R Augustine, "Of the Miracles Wrought by the True God." In Augustine's *City of God*, chapter 12, Nicene and Post-Nicene Fathers, series 1, vol. 2. www.ccel.org/ccel/schaff/npnf102.iv.X.12.html.

N ("Questions Muslims Ask," n.d.)

R "Questions Muslims Ask." n.d. Jesus to Muslims. http://jesustomuslims.org/equip/questions-muslims-ask-christians.

N The "Free Spiritual Gifts Analysis" (n.d.) shows that . . .

R "Free Spiritual Gifts Analysis." n.d. Elkton, MD: Church Growth Institute. www.churchgrowth.org/analysis/intro.php.

Caveats for Website References

As we all know, websites come and go. When your professor gets around to checking your source, the website may be gone. Then what? First, save a copy—paper or electronic of the contents of the website. Second, put an access date in your own records. Then when professor Smith calls your research into question, you can say, "Well, it was there on May 15, 2018, and I will send you a copy of the contents I read then."

Since you will be copying the URL, you will have a bright blue, underlined address. Not to worry. Put your cursor just after the end of the blue, tap "backspace" and voilà—the blue and underlining will disappear. Or immediately after the blue underlining appears, use CTRL+Z.

Please follow your school's rules on details of format. If they want the date to be 15 May 2012, fine. If they want May 15, 2012, fine. Here's a good place to follow their rules.

For journal articles online that include a DOI—which are generally more stable than the URL—form the URL by appending the DOI rather than using the regular URL. Here is an example from Turabian 9, figure 16.1.

N (Fernández 2016, 872)

R Fernández, Patricio. 2016. "Practical Reasoning Where the Action Is." *Ethics* 126, no. 4 (July 2016): 872. https//doi.org/10.1086/685998.

Cite electronic books you read on your computer, such as Kindle books, as any other book, except that you add the words "Kindle edition." Today's Kindle books have page numbers; older ones may not. In such a case, note the chapter or section.

N (Pazmiño 2009, chapter 3)

R Pazmiño, Robert. 2009. *Doing Theological Research*. Eugene, OR: Wipf & Stock, 2009. Kindle edition.

chapter twenty-three

APA CITATION STYLE

Each discipline prefers its own citation style. While history and religion tend to use the Chicago style (Turabian), the social sciences typically adhere to the style known as APA (American Psychological Association), not to be confused with Turabian in-text references. APA style is described in the *APA Publication Manual*, 7th edition.[1]

Some seminaries use the APA style, especially for Doctor of Ministry projects or missiology papers, since they often report information from the social sciences. Even if your school uses APA, however, they may adapt some of the rules. For example, APA mandates double-spaced reference list entries. Some seminaries may require single-spaced entries. Please follow your school's rules.

The APA citation style consists of two parts: in-text citations and a reference list. Without the reference list, the citations would not be understandable. The citations must exactly represent the reference list so that a reader can easily find an item in the reference list.

APA does not deal with the preliminary pages of academic work. It is basically for publication. Schools that use APA for citation in academic papers have their own rules on the use of APA in their classes. Be sure to follow the rules of your own school.

The examples in this chapter, given here in APA style, correspond to those that appeared in chapters 21 and 22 in the two Turabian styles.

1. The reference list entry would be: American Psychological Association (2020). ***Publication Manual of the American Psychological Association***, 7th ed. Washington, DC: Author. See also—among others—the following websites: http://apastyle.org, http://owl.english.purdue.edu/handouts/research/, http://www.dianahacker.com/resdoc/p04_c09_s1.html.

Because of the difficulties of applying APA format to biblical/theological studies, this chapter has been an international effort. Thanks to Bonnie Proctor, retired Dissertation Secretary at Andrews University, Berrien Springs, Michigan, and Shawna Vyhmeister, Director of Research at Middle East University in Beirut, Lebanon. Your school may have a different take on some of these; follow their rules!

Headings

Since this book uses the Turabian heading style throughout, we are not using APA headings here. Some institutions may use the same heading style for both Turabian and APA. Others may insist on the traditional APA heading style for their APA papers. Make sure you follow specific instructions. The Turabian heading style can be found in appendix D. In APA, headings are as follows:

First-Level Heading: Centered, Bold, Uppercase and Lowercase

Second-Level Heading: Flush Left, Bold, Uppercase and Lowercase

Third-Level Heading: Flush Left, Bold, Italicized, Uppercase and Lowercase

Fourth-Level Heading: Indented, Bold, Uppercase and Lowercase, Ending With a Period, Followed by Text.

Fifth-Level Heading: Indented, Bold, Italicized, Uppercase and Lowercase, Ending With a Period, Followed by Text.

APA in the Text of the Paper

The most important difference between APA and the traditional Turabian in the main text is the in-text citation in place of a footnote or endnote. There are also some format differences.

In-text Citations

In-text citations provide the reader with a source for a quotation, reference, or allusion in the text. These are enclosed in parentheses within the text. The basic format for the citation is the surname of the author (or authors) and the date of publication. If you refer to a specific part of the source named, or quote text from the original source, you must also add the page(s) where you found the quotation or idea (Smith, 2012, p. 25). Even when APA may not require page numbers, giving them is a help to your reader, who will not have to look through a whole article or—heaven forbid!—a whole book to find what you were reading.

For sources with one or two authors, repeat the surnames in subsequent in-text reference entries (Smith, 2006; Smith & Peterson, 2009). If an item has three or more authors, use only the first author's name with "et al." (Smith et al., 1999). If the author is a corporate entity, the first citation will read (United Nations [UN], 1985); successive notes will say (UN, 1985). The entry in the reference list will have the name spelled out: United Nations. If your paper uses two authors with the same surname, add an initial to distinguish between them: (N. Smith, 1947) and (B. Smith, 1976). Use the initial every time you cite the source.

When there is no author, the title (or a shortened form of the title) appears in the author position: (*Education Handbook*, 1987, p. 35); in the reference list, this item will be alphabetized under "Education." In the rare case that you have an "anonymous" item (Anonymous, 1977), the reference list must put the item under "Anonymous." If you cite more than one title by the same author, make sure the different year shows a different source. If two or more items are from the same year, signal the difference between items by using a or b or c after the year of publication (Smith, 1949a; Smith, 1949b) as in the reference list.

In APA the capitalization of titles is different from Turabian. In the APA reference list, you will capitalize only the first letter of a book title and the first letter after a colon. The titles of books and journals are in italics. Journals do retain title-case capitalization. There are no quotation marks for titles of articles. Note that in APA in-text citations, the abbreviation "p." for "page" is mandatory. It is always followed by a dot and one space before the page number.

The date of publication follows the comma after the author's surname. This date is the year the book or article was published, not the year in which it was written. You will not need to invent the year Irenaeus wrote *Against Heresies*; put only the year in which it was published in the reference list.

Since APA does not use "ibid.," the author and date are repeated if there is more than one source by the same author or each time the same article is mentioned in the text. In this sense, there is no "second note" form. Anytime an author's surname is used, a date also appears.

Letters and other personal communications (such as email and interviews by the author) appear only in the text; they do not appear in the reference list, as they are considered irretrievable as sources for other scholars. The in-text reference, however, should have information that is as specific as possible, such as the complete name of the speaker and the specific date of the conversation.

When you have more than one item in an in-text citation, alphabetize the entries by author's surname. Then separate them with semi-colons (Anderson, 2010; Hendley, 1999; Smith, 1987).

If there is no page number (as in an online source), use the paragraph number, or count from the nearest subheading (Gleason, 2018, Conclusion section, para. 3).

General Format Issues

The way you introduce the quotation will determine whether author and date are in one set of parentheses and the page in another, or all three are together. For example:

> Speaking of the differences between Acts and Galatians, Johnson (1992) notes that "both sources are partial and tendentious" (p. 270).
>
> One opinion regarding the differences between Acts and Galatians is that "both sources are partial and tendentious" (Johnson, 1992, p. 270).

A quotation of more than forty words must be treated as a block quotation, which in APA is indented five spaces from the left margin and double spaced (unless your school mandates single spaces, as we have here). The page number in parentheses follows the final period of the quotation. For example:

> Ouro (2000) concludes his discussion of the state of the earth in Gen 1:2 by saying:
>
>> Our study of the OT and ANE literature has found that Gen 1:2 must be interpreted as the description of the earth as it was without vegetation and uninhabited by animals and humans. The concept that appears in Gen 1:2 is an abiotic concept of the earth, with vegetable, animal, and human life appearing in the following verses. (p. 66)

Reference Lists

Proper APA style for article submission requires the reference list to be double-spaced with all lines of each entry except the first line indented, which is called a "hanging indent." For theses and dissertations, many institutions prefer single spacing, as in a Turabian bibliography. The important difference between the two systems is that the date of publication appears in parentheses immediately after the author statement, which ends with a period.

The names of all authors are inverted. Initials are used instead of first names: Johnson, L. T. Use the ampersand (&) instead of "and" when there are multiple authors, following the style set forth in the in-text citations. The list is alphabetized by the (first) author's surname, the corporate author, or the title (if there is no author). These items should exactly match the information in parentheses in the in-text references.

The copyright date is placed in parentheses and followed by a period. When a particular author has more than one work, the items are ordered chronologically, from oldest to newest. Should there be two or more items published by the same author in one year, add a letter to the year: 1993a, 1993b, 1993c. Make sure the in-text citations have the same dates as the reference list.

In the facts of publication in the reference list, use the name of the city and the official two-letter abbreviations for states. Use the short form of the publisher's name.

Samples

The samples given below for in-text citation (C) show how to report an allusion or citation. A direct quotation requires a page number, either in the same parentheses with the date or at the end of the quotation. Sources that are not referenced in the text may not be included in the reference list. The sample reference list entries (R) are single spaced, in modified APA format.

General Books

Authorship

One or two authors

C (Lederleitner, 2018)

R Lederleitner, M. (2018). *Women in God's mission.* InterVarsity Press.

C (Neyrey & Stewart, 2008, p. 43)

R Neyrey, J., & Stewart, E. (2008). *The social world of the New Testament: Insights and models.* Hendrickson.

Three to five authors

C (VanGemeren et al., 1993)

R VanGemeren, W. A., Bahnsen, G. L., Kaiser, W. C., Jr., Strickland, W. G., & Moo, D. (1993). *The law, the gospel, and the modern Christian.* Zondervan.

Corporate author

C (Southern Baptist Convention, 2000, p. 53)

R Southern Baptist Convention. (2000). *Annual of the Southern Baptist Convention.*

In this example, the author of the item is also the publisher. Don't repeat "Southern Baptist Convention."

No author, edition other than first, with translator

C (*Bhagavad-Gita as It Is*, 1972)

R *Bhagavad-Gita as It Is* (Abridged ed.). (1972). (A. C. Bhaktivedanta Swami Prabhupada, Trans.). Bhaktivedanta Book Trust.

Editor instead of author; joint publication

C (VanderKam & Adler, 1996, p. 78)

R VanderKam, J. C., & Adler, W. (Eds.). (1996). *The Jewish apocalyptic heritage in early Christianity.* Van Gorcum.

Component part by one author in a work edited by another

C (Ruguri, 2015, p. 411)

R Ruguri, B. M. (2015). Biblical principles for tribal unity. In B. Bauer & W. Kuhn (Eds.), *Biblical Principles for Missiological Issues in Africa* (pp. 409-431). Department of World Mission, Andrews University.

Multivolume Works

One author

C (González, 1970-1975, vol. 1, p. 176)

R González, J. (1970-1975). *A history of Christian thought* (Vols. 1-3). Abingdon.

C (Latourette, 1970)

R Latourette, K. S. (1970). *Three centuries of advance: Vol. 3. A history of the expansion of Christianity.* Zondervan.

Series by several authors—independent titles for each volume

Without an example in the APA book, different schools have differing ideas on how these series are recorded. Listen to what your school says.

C (Rapske, 1994)

R Rapske, B. (1994). *The book of Acts and Paul in Roman custody.* In B. W. Winter (Gen. ed.), The book of Acts in its first century setting (Vol. 4). Paternoster.

Part of a Series

C (Booth, Colomb, & Williams, 1995)

R Booth, W. C., Colomb, G. G., & Williams, J. M. (1995). *The craft of research.* Chicago guides to writing, editing, and publishing. University of Chicago Press.

Reprint

C (Nevius, 1894/1968)

R Nevius, J. L. (1968). *Demon possession.* Kregel. (Original work published 1894)

C (Reynolds, 1913/1977)

R Reynolds, H. R. (1977). Introduction to the Gospel of St. John. In H. O. M. Spense & J. H. Excell (Eds.), *The pulpit commentary* (Vol. 17, pp. iv-clxi). Eerdmans. (Original work published 1913.)

Secondary Source

C In their *Critical Commentary on Romans,* Sanday and Headlam noted that Junia was a male (as cited in Epp, 2005, p. 71).

Give the author (and title, if you wish) of the primary source, as well as the page in the secondary source. If there is no mention of the title in the sentence, the in-text citation would look like this: (Sanday & Headlam, as cited in Epp, 2005, p. 71).

The reference list mentions only the secondary source.

R Epp, E. (2005). *Junia: The first woman apostle.* Fortress.

Periodicals

In periodicals, please note that the volume number is in italics, as well as the journal title. If volume and issue are present, there is no need for a date other than the year.

Magazines

C (Vanhoozer, 2018)

R Vanhoozer, K. J. (2018, November). Core exercises. *Christianity Today, 62*(9), 46-57.

Journals

C (Damsteegt, 2016)

R Damsteegt, P. G. (2016). Decoding ancient Waldensian names: New discoveries. *Andrews University Seminary Studies 54*(2), 237-258.

When a journal begins each issue from page 1 (rather than continued paging throughout the volume), specify which issue of the volume you have used. *Newsletter 4*(1), 9.

Specialized Books

Classical Authors and Church Fathers

C (Irenaeus, *Against heresies* 2.2.3) or (Irenaeus, *Against heresies* 2.2.3, ANF 1:421)

R Irenaeus. (1989-1990). *Against heresies.* In A. Roberts & J. Donaldson (Eds.), The Ante-Nicene Fathers (Vol. 1, pp. 315-567). Eerdmans.

C (Chrysostom, *The priesthood* 3.17)

R Chrysostom, J. (1862). *The priesthood.* In J. P. Migne (Ed.), *Patrologia graeca* (Vol. 48, cols. 623-692). Apud Garnier Fratres.

C (Josephus, *Jewish war* 2.14.5)

R Josephus, F. (1869). *Jewish war.* In W. Whiston (Ed.), *The works of Josephus* (Vol. 3, p. 317-Vol. 4, p. 352). Oakley, Mason & Co.

Rabbinical Works

C (Mishnah *Sanhedrin* 10:3)

R *The mishnah* (H. Danby, Trans.). (1933). Oxford University Press.

C (B. T. *Sanhedrin* 97a) or (B. Talmud *Sanhedrin* 97a)

R *The Babylonian talmud* (I. Epstein, Ed.). (1935). Soncino.

Bible Commentaries and Concordances

Commentaries—author given

C (Polhill, 1992)

R Polhill, J. B. (1992). *Acts*. New American Commentary. Broadman.

C (Campbell, 1975)

R Campbell, E. R. (1975). *Ruth*. Anchor Bible, 7. Doubleday.

C (Delitzsch, 1949)

R Delitzsch, F. (1949). *Biblical commentary on the book of Job* (Vols 1-2). Biblical commentary on the Old Testament. Eerdmans.

C (Craddock, 1998)

R Craddock, F. B. (1998). The letter to the Hebrews: Introduction, commentary, and reflections. In *New interpreter's Bible* (Vol. 12, pp. 3-173). Abingdon.

C (Wright, 1954)

R Wright, G. E. (1954). Exegesis of the book of Deuteronomy. In G. A. Buttrick (Ed.), *Interpreter's Bible* (Vol. 2, pp. 331-540). Abingdon.

Commentaries—no author given

C (Hastings, 1971, Vol. 17, p. 159)

R Hastings, E. (Ed.). (1971). *The speaker's Bible* (Vols. 1-18). Baker.

Concordances

C (Young, n.d., p. 785)

R Young, R. (n.d.). *Analytical concordance to the Bible* (22nd American ed.). Eerdmans.

Dictionaries and Encyclopedias

Dictionaries and encyclopedias with unsigned articles

C (*Webster*, 1976)

C (*Columbia Encyclopedia*, 1976)

Well-known dictionaries and encyclopedias do not appear in the reference list. Dictionaries and encyclopedias in the area of religion do.

C (Youngblood, 1995)

R Youngblood, R. F. (Ed.). (1995). *Nelson's new illustrated Bible dictionary* (Rev. ed.). Nelson.

C (*Seventh-day Adventist Encyclopedia*, 1996)

[Later references: (*SDA Encyclopedia*, 1996)]

R *Seventh-day Adventist Encyclopedia*. (1996). (Vols. 1-2). Review and Herald.

Dictionaries and encyclopedias with signed articles

C (Lapin, 1992)

R Lapin, H. (1992). Rabbi. In *Anchor Bible dictionary* (Vol. 5. pp. 600-602). Doubleday.

C (Bultmann, 1964-1976, *Aidōs*)

R Bultmann, R. (1964-1976). *Aidōs*. In *Theological dictionary of the New Testament* (Vol. 1, p. 169). Eerdmans.

C (Demsky, 1971-1972, Vol. 6, p. 384)

R Demsky, A. (1971-1972). Education: In the biblical period. In *Encyclopaedia Judaica* (Vol. 6, pp. 382-398).

Collected Works of Individual Authors

C (Barth, 1960, vol. III/3, p. 82)

R Barth, K. (1960). *Church dogmatics* (Vol. III/3). T&T Clark.

C (Luther, 1955-1976, Vol. 51, p. 259)

R Luther, M. (1955-1976). *Sermon on the sum of Christian life*. In *Luther's works* (American ed., Vol. 51, pp. 259-287). Concordia.

R Luther, M. (1955-1976). *Luther's works* (American ed., Vols. 1-55). Concordia.

Book Reviews

C (Bauer, 2018, p. 223)

R Bauer, Stephen. (2018). Review of the book *Christian Ethics: Four Views*, ed. Steve Wilkins. *Andrews University Seminary Studies 56*(2), 220-224.

Unpublished Materials

Theses and dissertations

C (Tsegaw, 2017)

R Tsegaw, Melak Alemayehu. (2017). *Whole-body gestures with the context of worship in the book of Psalms* [Unpublished doctoral dissertation]. Adventist International Institute of Advanced Studies.

APA distinguishes between unpublished dissertations (as given above) and dissertations accessed by means of Dissertation Abstracts International. The format for the second is:

R Choi, P. R. (1997). *Abraham our father: Paul's voice in the covenantal debate of the second temple period* [Doctoral dissertation]. Dissertation Abstracts International database. 58 (05A), 1759.

C (Magdy, 2015)

R Magdy, R. (2015). *The implications of Christ's method of ministry to women in a women-to-women ministry among Muslim women in rural villages of Upper Egypt* [Unpublished master's thesis]. Middle East University.

While APA makes no distinction among different kinds of doctoral dissertations or master's theses, your school may allow you to specify the type of dissertation (DMin, EdD, or PhD) or thesis (as in the above example).

Miscellaneous academic papers

Class papers

C (Reeve, 1997)

R Reeve, T. (1997). *The 'Just Man' in the writings of Philo* [Unpublished class paper]. THEO 611 Philo Seminar, University of Notre Dame.

C (Fanwar, 1999)

R Fanwar, W. M. (1999). *He who created the heavens and the earth: Contributions of Isaiah to Rev 14:7c* [Unpublished seminar paper]. GSEM 920 Religious Studies Seminar, Theological Seminary, Andrews University.

Syllabi

C (Vyhmeister, 2008)

R Vyhmeister, Nancy. (2008). *Course outline for GSEM 820 Thesis and Research Writing*, Middle East University.

Class notes

C (Saghbini, 2019)

R Saghbini, Paul. (2019). "An Introduction to Literary Theories" [Class notes]. Literary Criticism and Theory, Middle East University, January 24, 2019.

Miscellaneous Unpublished Sources

Reports

C (Seventh-day Adventist Theological Seminary, Far East [SDATSFE], 1985)

[In subsequent notes: (SDATSFE, 1985)]

R Seventh-day Adventist Theological Seminary, Far East. (1985). *Financial statement of graduate apartments, 31 August*. Silang, Cavite, Philippines.

C (Association of Theological Institutions in Eastern Africa, 1979)

R Association of Theological Institutions in Eastern Africa. (1979). *1978/79 Bachelor of Divinity degree syllabus*. Nairobi, Kenya.

Speeches and presentations

C (Maxwell, 1976)

R Maxwell, C. M. (1976). *Which sacrifice, Lord?* [Typescript]. Seminary Chapel sermon. Andrews University, Berrien Springs, MI, October 20, 1976.

C (Paulien, 2018)

R Paulien, J. (2018). *The 1260 Days in the Book of Revelation*. Paper presented at the *Fourth International Bible Conference*, Rome, Italy, June 11-21.

Manuscripts

C (Benoit, 1875)

R Benoit, P. L. (1875). Photocopy of typewritten transcript of Canon Benoit's diary of a trip to America, 6 January to 8 June 1875, including descriptions of Josephite missions among freed slaves. Archives, University of Notre Dame.

C (White, 1905)

R White, E. G. (1905). Letter to Dr. Patience Bourdeau, June 8, 1905. Letter 177, 1905. Ellen White Research Center, Newbold College, Bracknell, England.

Personal communications

In APA style, letters, interviews, and email are considered personal communications. The name of the source appears in the text; the phrase "personal communication" (or "interview") and the precise date are given in the in-text note. Since information from this communication is not available to the reader, nothing appears in the reference list.

C Bryan Ball, editor of *The Essential Jesus* (personal communication, March 13, 2000), stated that . . .

C George Knight, long-time writer and editor (interview, February 3, 2019), noted that . . .

Electronic Media

Video and Sound Recordings

C (Anderson, 1989)

R Anderson, K. (Producer). (1989). *Hudson Taylor* [Videocassette]. (Available from Ken Anderson Films, P.O. Box 618, Winona Lake, IN 46590.)

C (Landriscina, 1985)

R Landriscina, L. (1985). Judío en el Vaticano. In *mano a mano con el país* (Vol. 5) [Audiocassette No. 64232]. Phillips.

CD-ROMS

C (Bunyan, 1998)

R Bunyan, J. (1998). *Pilgrim's progress, stage 2* [CD-ROM]. Logos Library System 2.1 (Vol. 1). Logos Research Systems.

Websites

APA never puts a period after the URL. Runover lines begin with punctuation.

C (Whitman, 2006)

R Whitman, Shelly. "Women and peace-building in the Democratic Republic of Congo: An assessment of their role in the inter-Congolese dialogue." *African journal on conflict resolution* 6 (2006): 29-48. http://center.the parentscircle.org/images/ebf709980d3642e8af0ecca3df18a051.pdf

C (Gaikwad & Obaya 2018, 137)

R Gaikwad, P., & Obaya, B. (2018). Wish to WISHCRAFT: A peek into an environmentally friendly school. *International Forum 21*(1), 134-149. https://internationalforum.aiias.edu/images/vol21no01/8GaikwadObaya.pdf

C (UNICEF, 2013)

R UNICEF. (2013). *Female genital mutilation/cutting: A statistical overview and exploration of the dynamics of change.* United Nations Children's Fund. https://data.unicef.org/wp-content/uploads/2015/12/FGMC_Brochure_Lo_res_1613.pdf

C (Beecher, 1915, Vol. 1, p. 57)

R Beecher, W. J. 1915. "Adonijah," *International Standard Bible Encyclopedia*. Vol. 1, ed. James Orr. Howard Severance. https://www.christianresearcher.com /uploads/1/6/2/9/16298120 /isbevol1.pdf

C (Augustine, n.d.)

R Augustine (n.d.). Of the miracles wrought by the true God. In *Augustine, City of God and Christian doctrine*, chapter 12, Nicene and post-Nicene Fathers 1-02. http://www.ccel.org/ccel/schaff/npnf102.iv.X.12.html

C (Questions Muslims ask, n.d.)

R *Questions Muslims ask* (n.d.). http://jesustomuslims.org/equip/questions -muslims-ask-christians

C (Church Growth Institute, n.d.)

R Church Growth Institute. (n.d.). *Free spiritual gifts analysis*. http://www.church growth.org/analysis/intro.php

CONCLUSION

This book has described several different types of endings for papers and dissertations. There is the summary-conclusion ending or the summary-conclusion-recommendations finale. You have also read about the theological issue in ministry with an "application-to-ministry" ending. The conclusion ending for this book does not follow any of these patterns.

In fact, it is not for us to conclude this book. It is for you, the student, to do so. The work you produce following these guidelines summarizes, concludes, and applies any conclusion that we could have written. Your work will speak for us as well as for you.

May the skills you have honed and the abilities you have developed, to say nothing of the masterpiece you have produced, satisfy you and your professor. May this have been a battle well fought, a victory won with honor.

If you have written a good paper, we shall be content. Nancy Vyhmeister's motto has long been: ἐκ χαοῦ κόσμος (lit., "out of chaos, order"). To organize words and ideas—life in general—is a difficult task. To bring order out of chaos requires dedication and effort. It also implies a Master's touch. If your paper is well done, beauty and order have come out of chaos, and we are satisfied.

And as we all strive to bring order and beauty out of that which is unclear, confused, or unknown, may it be *soli Deo gloria*.

SELECTED BIBLIOGRAPHY

Badke, William. *Research Strategies: Finding Your Way through the Information Fog.* 4th ed. Bloomington, IN: iUniverse, 2011.

Belcher, Wanda Laura. *Writing Your Journal Article in 12 Weeks: A Guide to Academic Publishing Success.* Thousand Oaks, CA: SAGE, 2009.

Booth, Wayne C., Gregory G. Colomb, Joseph M. Williams, Joseph Bizup, and William T. FitzGerald. *The Craft of Research.* 4th ed. Chicago Guides to Writing, Editing, and Publishing. Chicago, IL: University of Chicago Press, 2016.

Bottery, Mike, and Nigel Wright. *Writing a Watertight Thesis: A Guide to Successful Structure and Defence.* New York, NY: Bloomsbury, 2019.

Brown, Scott G. *A Guide to Writing Academic Essays in Religious Studies.* New York, NY: Continuum, 2008.

Calabrese, Raymond L. *The Elements of an Effective Dissertation and Thesis: A Step-by-Step Guide to Getting It Right the First Time.* Lanham, MD: Rowman & Littlefield Education, 2006.

The Chicago Manual of Style. 17th ed. Chicago, IL: University of Chicago Press, 2017.

Core, Deborah. *The Seminary Student Writes.* St. Louis, MO: Chalice, 2000.

Cresswell, John W. *Qualitative Inquiry and Research Design: Choosing among Five Approaches.* 4th ed. Thousand Oaks, CA: Sage, 2016.

Davis, Gordon B., Clyde A. Parker, and Detmar W. Straub. *Writing the Doctoral Dissertation: A Systematic Approach.* 3rd ed. New York, NY: Barron's, 2012.

Denzin, Norman K., and Yvonna S. Lincoln. *The SAGE Handbook of Qualitative Research.* 5th ed. Thousand Oaks, CA: Sage, 2018.

Duce, Cameron, and Catherine Duce. *Researching Practice in Ministry and Mission: A Companion.* London: SCM, 2013.

Elliston, Edgar J. *Introduction to Missiological Research Design*. Pasadena, CA: William Carey Library, 2011.

Hacker, Diana, and Barbara Fister. *Research and Documentation in the Electronic Age*. 6th ed. Boston, MA: Bedford / St. Martin's, 2014.

Hancock, Dawson R., and Bob Algozzine. *Doing Case Study Research: A Practical Guide for Beginning Researchers*. 3rd ed. New York, NY: Teachers College Press, 2017.

Hopko, Joel, Gregory M. Scott, and Stephen M. Garrison. *The Religion and Theology Student Writer's Manual and Reader's Guide*. Lanham, MD: Rowman & Littlefield, 2018.

Hudson, Robert. *A Christian Writer's Manual of Style*. Grand Rapids, MI: Zondervan, 2016.

Joyner, Randy L., William A. Rouse, and Allan A. Glatthorn. *Writing the Winning Thesis or Dissertations: A Step-by-Step Guide*. 4th ed. Thousand Oaks, CA: Corwin, 2018.

Kepple, Robert. *Reference Works for Theological Research*. 3rd ed. Lanham, MD: University Press of America, 1992.

Kibbe, Michael. *From Topic to Thesis: A Guide to Theological Research*. Downers Grove, IL: IVP Academic, 2015.

Lester, James D. *Writing Research Papers: A Complete Guide*. 16th ed. New York, NY: Pearson, 2018.

Maggion, Rosalie. *The Nonsexist Word Finder: A Dictionary of Gender-free Usage*. Boston, MA: Beacon, 1987.

Moschella, Mary Clark. *Ethnography as a Pastoral Practice: Introduction*. Cleveland, OH: Pilgrim Press, 2008.

Northey, Margot, Bradford A. Anderson, and Joel N. Lohr. *Making Sense: A Student's Guide to Research and Writing: Religious Studies*. Don Mills, Ontario: Oxford University Press, 2012.

Pazmiño, Robert W. *Doing Theological Research: An Introductory Guide for Survival in Theological Education*. Eugene, OR: Wipf & Stock, 2009.

Proctor, Bonnie, ed. *Andrews University Standards for Written Work*. 13th ed. Berrien Springs, MI: School of Graduate Studies, 2015. Available online at https://www.andrews.edu/grad/documents/standards-for-written-work-2015.pdf.

Publication Manual for the American Psychological Association. 7th ed. Washington, DC: American Psychological Association, 2020.

Rallis, Sharon F., and Gretchen G. Rossman. *The Research Journey: Introduction to Inquiry*. New York, NY: Guilford, 2012.

The SBL Handbook of Style. 2nd ed. Atlanta, GA: SBL Press, 2014.

Smith, Kevin Gary. *Writing & Research: A Guide for Theological Students*. Langham, UK: Langham, 2016.

Strausberg, Michael, and Steven Engler, eds. *The Routledge Handbook of Research Methods in the Study of Religion*. Routledge Handbooks. London: Routledge, 2011.

Strunk, William, and E. B. White. *The Elements of Style*. 4th ed. New York, NY: Longman, 2012.

Turabian, Kate L. *A Manual for Writers of Research Papers, Theses, and Dissertations*. 9th ed. Revised by Wayne C. Booth, Gregory G. Colomb, Joseph M. Williams, Joseph Bizup, William T. FitzGerald, and the University of Chicago Press Editorial Staff. Chicago, IL: University of Chicago Press, 2018.

Vyhmeister, Shawna. *AIIAS Research Standards and Writing Manual*. 2nd ed. Silang, Cavite, Philippines: Adventist International Institute of Advanced Studies, 2013.

Walliman, Nicholas. *Your Research Project: Designing and Planning Your Work*. 3rd ed. London: Sage, 2011.

Yaghjian, Lucretia B. *Writing Theology Well: A Rhetoric for Theological and Biblical Writings*. 2nd ed. New York, NY: T&T Clark, 2015.

appendix a

TRANSLITERATION OF BIBLICAL LANGUAGES

The following is an acceptable academic scheme for transliterating biblical Hebrew and Greek. Students in advanced courses or who are writing dissertations may be required to use additional diacritical marks for the Hebrew. Students should consult their adviser on this matter. Transliteration is usually done in italics.

Hebrew

Consonants

א	=	ʾ	ט	=	*ṭ*	פ	=	*p*
ב	=	*b*	י	=	*y*	צ	=	*ṣ*
ג	=	*g*	כ	=	*k*	ק	=	*q*
ד	=	*d*	ל	=	*l*	ר	=	*r*
ה	=	*h*	מ	=	*m*	שׂ	=	*ś*
ו	=	*w*	נ	=	*n*	שׁ	=	*š*
ז	=	*z*	ס	=	*s*	ת	=	*t*
ח	=	*ḥ*	ע	=	ʿ			

Masoretic Vowel Pointing

ַ	=	*a*	ֱ	=	*ĕ*	ָ	=	*o*
ָ	=	*ā*	ֵי or ֶי	=	*ê*	ֳ	=	*ŏ*
ֲ	=	*ă*	ִ	=	*i*	וֹ	=	*ô*
ֶ	=	*e*	ִי	=	*î*	וּ	=	*û*
ֵ	=	*ē*	ֹ	=	*ō*	ֻ	=	*u*

No distinction is made between soft and hard *begadkepat* letters; *dāgēš forte* is indicated by doubling the consonant.

Koine Greek

Α α	=	*A a*	Κ κ	=	*K k*	Τ τ	=	*T t*
Β β	=	*B b*	Λ λ	=	*L l*	Υ υ	=	*Y y*
Γ γ	=	*G g*	Μ μ	=	*M m*	Φ φ	=	*Ph ph*
Δ δ	=	*D d*	Ν ν	=	*N n*	Χ χ	=	*Ch ch*
Ε ε	=	*E e*	Ξ ξ	=	*X x*	Ψ ψ	=	*Ps ps*
Ζ ζ	=	*Z z*	Ο ο	=	*O o*	Ω ω	=	*Ō ō*
Η η	=	*Ē ē*	Π π	=	*P p*			
Θ θ	=	*Th th*	Ρ ρ	=	*R r*			
Ι ι	=	*I i*	Σ σ ς	=	*S s*			

Breathing marks: ᾿ is smooth, no transliteration; ῾ is rough, transliterate with *h*.

Before *g*, *k*, *x*, or *c*, gamma is transliterated as *n*. In a diphthong, upsilon is transliterated as *u*.

For further details on transliteration of ancient languages, see *SBL Handbook of Style*, 5.1-9.

appendix b

ABBREVIATIONS FOR BIBLE BOOKS

In the text of your paper, the names of the books of the Bible are written out. In papers on biblical topics, you may place references to biblical texts in abbreviated form in parentheses, as in (Gen 1:1). There is a caveat: if you cite three or more texts, you must put them in a footnote.

Several schemes exist for abbreviating the names of Bible books. In the following list, the full name is in the left-hand column. The second column shows the traditional abbreviation system. If you take the periods away from these, you have an intermediate system, used by SBL (not shown). In the third column, you have Turabian's short form (9th ed., 24.6.1, 24.6.3).

So, these are your options. Make sure your choice matches the rules at your school.

FULL NAME	TRADITIONAL	SHORT FORM
Genesis	Gen.	Gn
Exodus	Exod.	Ex
Leviticus	Lev.	Lv
Numbers	Num.	Nm
Deuteronomy	Deut.	Dt
Joshua	Josh.	Jo
Judges	Judg.	Jgs
Ruth	Ruth	Ru
1 Samuel	1 Sam.	1 Sm
2 Samuel	2 Sam.	2 Sm
1 Kings	1 Kings	1 Kgs
2 Kings	2 Kings	2 Kgs
1 Chronicles	1 Chr.	1 Chr

FULL NAME	TRADITIONAL	SHORT FORM
2 Chronicles	2 Chr.	2 Chr
Ezra	Ezra	Ezr
Nehemiah	Neh.	Neh
Esther	Esth.	Est
Job	Job	Jb
Psalm (Psalms)	Ps. (Pss.)	Ps (Pss)
Proverbs	Prov.	Prv
Ecclesiastes	Eccl.	Eccl
Song of Solomon	Song of Sol.	Sg
Isaiah	Isa.	Is
Jeremiah	Jer.	Jer
Lamentations	Lam.	Lam
Ezekiel	Ezek.	Ez
Daniel	Dan.	Dn
Hosea	Hos.	Hos
Joel	Joel	Jl
Amos	Amos	Am
Obadiah	Obad.	Ob
Jonah	Jonah	Jon
Micah	Mic.	Mi
Nahum	Nah.	Na
Habakkuk	Hab.	Hb
Zephaniah	Zeph.	Zep
Haggai	Hag.	Hg
Zechariah	Zech.	Zec
Malachi	Mal.	Mal
Matthew	Matt.	Mt
Mark	Mark	Mk
Luke	Luke	Lk
John	John	Jn
Acts	Acts	Acts
Romans	Rom.	Rom
1 Corinthians	1 Cor.	1 Cor
2 Corinthians	2 Cor.	2 Cor
Galatians	Gal.	Gal
Ephesians	Eph.	Eph
Philippians	Phil.	Phil
Colossians	Col.	Col

FULL NAME	TRADITIONAL	SHORT FORM
1 Thessalonians	1 Thess.	1 Thes
2 Thessalonians	2 Thess.	2 Thes
1 Timothy	1 Tim.	1 Tm
2 Timothy	2 Tim.	2 Tm
Titus	Titus	Ti
Philemon	Philem.	Phlm
Hebrews	Heb.	Heb
James	James	Jas
1 Peter	1 Peter	1 Pt
2 Peter	2 Peter	2 Pt
1 John	1 John	1 Jn
2 John	2 John	2 Jn
3 John	3 John	3 Jn
Jude	Jude	Jude
Revelation	Rev.	Rv

appendix c

WEBSITES FOR ABBREVIATIONS IN THE AREA OF RELIGION

Perhaps the most complete list of abbreviations in the area of religion is found in *The SBL Handbook of Style*, 2nd ed. Atlanta, GA: SBL, 2014. Look for this title in your library to find interesting help for your paper.

An excellent list of abbreviations appears in http://ecumenism.net/docu/abbrev.htm.

For a British point of view on abbreviations, see Theology on the Web, at http://www.theologyontheweb.org.uk/abbreviations.html.

With this much information available, there is no need for a list of abbreviations here.

appendix d

TIPS ON FORMAT

Here you (and your typist) have a summary of format tips. Topics are listed in alphabetical order to simplify finding them. Don't overlook chapter 20 on format.

Corrections

No visible or hand-written corrections are allowed in a final draft of a paper, a thesis, or a dissertation. You may turn in a photocopied paper, but with no corrections visible.

Footnotes

Use the automatic footnote feature in your word-processing program. A 20-space line should appear one line below the last line of text and one line above the footnote. The footnote number is indented the same 0.5 inch as a paragraph and is usually—but not always—superscript. An empty line comes between footnotes. The student is responsible for footnote content and format. When footnotes are relatively short, they should be on the page on which the superscript number appears in the text. If they are long, they should begin on the page on which the superscript number appears in the text, but they may spill over onto the next page. Word and Open Office do these well.

Headings

Chapter numbers and titles are typed in uppercase letters, on lines 13 and 15 (2 inches from the top of the page and double space below). Other headings in Turabian are as follows:

First-Level Heading: Centered, Bold

Second-Level Heading: Centered, Not Bold

Third-level Heading: Flush left, Bold

Fourth-level heading: flush left, not bold, only first word capitalized

Fifth-level heading: indented same as paragraph, bold. Only the first word is capitalized. The paragraph follows immediately.

Leave two lines blank before a set-apart heading; one line blank after. More information in chapter 20.

Headings for APA papers are as follows:

First-Level Heading: Centered, Bold, Uppercase and Lowercase

Second-Level Heading: Flush Left, Bold, Uppercase and Lowercase

Third-Level Heading: Flush Left, Bold, Italicized, Uppercase and Lowercase

Fourth-Level Heading: Indented, Bold, Uppercase and Lowercase, Ending With a Period, Followed by Text.

Fifth-Level Heading: Indented, Bold, Italicized, Uppercase and Lowercase, Ending With a Period, Followed by Text.

Indentation

Indentation is 0.5 inch from the left for the first line of paragraph, block quotations, and footnotes. If a block quotation starts at the beginning of a paragraph in the original source, indent another 0.5 inch. Bibliographical entries are set as a hanging indent, with the first line not indented and every runover line is indented by 0.5 inch.

Margins

The left margin should be 1.5 inches. The other three margins should be 1 inch. In 12-point Times New Roman type, there will be room for 60 characters per line. Margins must be observed meticulously.

Page Length

Letter-size paper of good quality must be used. In order to fit within the margins indicated above, there must be no more than 54 single spaces or 27 double spaces of text on a normal letter-size page. In areas where A4 paper is the norm, this size paper can be used. The margins should remain the same, giving a slightly narrower and longer area for the text.

Pagination

Page 1 is the first page of the introduction. Page numbers (in Arabic numbers) are centered at the bottom of the page. Program the footer through the computer to do this automatically.

Pagination of preliminary front matter begins on the title page and appears, centered, at the bottom of the page in small Roman numerals. However, no number is printed on the title page.

Punctuation

The spacing required after punctuation marks is one space after a period, comma, colon, and semicolon. For page references for books, there is no space after a colon, 5:66. For pages of journals, there is a space after the colon (1998): 66.

In American usage, commas and periods go inside quotation marks, unless these enclose a single letter or number: He said, “Good-bye.” This is Phase “A”.

In typing, a dash is represented by two hyphens or an em dash, with no space on either side of them. For example: He said--or wrote, I’m not sure which--that he was coming next week; or, He said—or wrote, I’m not sure which—that he was coming next week.

While an en dash between numbers may be ideal, for students the simplest character to use is a hyphen: 34-36.

In an enumeration, a comma follows each item: He asked for a pen, some paper, an envelope, and a stamp.

Quotations

All materials quoted from another source must be enclosed in double quotation marks. Single quotation marks are used only for a quotation within a quotation. The comma and the period (full stop) go within the quotation marks; the colon and the semicolon go outside. If a quotation is a question, the question mark goes inside the quotation marks. If the quotation is only part of the question, the question mark goes outside the quotation marks.

Block quotations are used for quotations longer than two sentences and five lines in Turabian style and with two sentences in APA style. A block quote is single spaced and indented 0.5 inch (same as the paragraph) from the left margin. But if the quotation was the beginning of a paragraph in the source, the first line of the block quote is indented more (a total of 1 inch) to show that it was the start of a paragraph.

Spacing

Research papers, theses, and dissertations are double spaced. Block quotations are typed single space with a blank line space before and after the quote. Footnotes and bibliography entries are single spaced, but have a blank line between them. Three lines are left blank above and below a table or figure. Two blank lines precede a heading; one follows it.

Spelling

In the United States, or for an American institution, use American spelling. For places where the Queen's English reigns, use British spelling. However, do not mix spellings—except in quotations that appear in a different spelling. The student is responsible for the spelling. The typist is responsible for correct word division at the end of a line, if that is used.

Table of Contents

Follow the model on page 260 in chapter 20.

Title Page

Follow the model on page 259. For theses and dissertations, add the approval page as given on page 258. However, be sure to check with your school.

appendix e

ABBREVIATIONS FOR U.S. STATES

This information is primarily for those who do not live in the United States.

Choose one of the three forms and use it consistently throughout your paper. Following this book, as well as in APA, always use the postal code.

STATE	STANDARD ABBR.	POSTAL CODE
Alabama	Ala.	AL
Alaska	Alaska	AK
Arizona	Ariz.	AZ
Arkansas	Ark.	AR
California	Calif.	CA
Colorado	Colo.	CO
Connecticut	Conn.	CT
Delaware	Del.	DE
Florida	Fla.	FL
Georgia	Ga.	GA
Hawaii	Hawaii	HI
Idaho	Idaho	ID
Illinois	Ill.	IL
Indiana	Ind.	IN
Iowa	Iowa	IA
Kansas	Kans.	KS
Kentucky	Ky.	KY
Louisiana	La.	LA
Maine	Maine	ME
Maryland	Md.	MD
Massachusetts	Mass.	MA

STATE	STANDARD ABBR.	POSTAL CODE
Michigan	Mich.	MI
Minnesota	Minn.	MN
Mississippi	Miss.	MS
Missouri	Mo.	MO
Montana	Mont.	MT
Nebraska	Nebr.	NE
Nevada	Nev.	NV
New Hampshire	N.H.	NH
New Jersey	N.J.	NJ
New Mexico	N.M.	NM
New York	N.Y.	NY
North Carolina	N.C.	NC
North Dakota	N.D.	ND
Ohio	Ohio	OH
Oklahoma	Okla.	OK
Oregon	Ore.	OR
Pennsylvania	Pa.	PA
Rhode Island	R.I.	RI
South Carolina	S.C.	SC
South Dakota	S.Dak.	SD
Tennessee	Tenn.	TN
Texas	Tex.	TX
Utah	Utah	UT
Vermont	Vt.	VT
Virginia	Va.	VA
Washington	Wash.	WA
West Virginia	W.Va.	WV
Wisconsin	Wis.	WI
Wyoming	Wyo.	WY

INDEX